1999

Also by Matt Dickinson

Bobby Moore: The Man in Full

1999

MANCHESTER UNITED, THE TREBLE AND ALL THAT

Matt Dickinson

SIMON &
SCHUSTER

London · New York · Sydney · Toronto · New Delhi

First published in Great Britain by Simon & Schuster UK Ltd, 2022

Copyright © Matt Dickinson, 2022

The right of Matt Dickinson to be identified as the author of this work has
been asserted in accordance with the Copyright, Designs and Patents Act, 1988.

1 3 5 7 9 10 8 6 4 2

Simon & Schuster UK Ltd
1st Floor
222 Gray's Inn Road
London WC1X 8HB

www.simonandschuster.co.uk
www.simonandschuster.com.au
www.simonandschuster.co.in

Simon & Schuster Australia, Sydney
Simon & Schuster India, New Delhi

The author and publishers have made all reasonable efforts to contact
copyright-holders for permission, and apologise for any omissions or errors in the form
of credits given. Corrections may be made to future printings.

A CIP catalogue record for this book is available from the British Library

Hardback ISBN: 978-1-3985-0377-9
eBook ISBN: 978-1-3985-0379-3

Typeset in Bembo by M Rules
Printed in the UK by CPI Group (UK) Ltd, Croydon, CR0 4YY

For Helen, Joe and Fin

For Roy, who was among the ecstatic throng in the Nou Camp

*And for all the endless joys, thrills — and
agonies — of the game. Football, Bloody Hell!*

The first draft of history

On the evening of 26 May 1999, the stadium clock showed that we were in the 90th minute of the Champions League final. Up in the press box of the Nou Camp, the first draft of history had been written and dispatched.

Tyrannical deadlines required that we send our copy for the newspapers' first editions shortly before the match ended and, in any case, the contest was over. With Manchester United trailing 1-0 and Bayern Munich's ribbons on the trophy, our stories of defeat were already on their way back to England (at least we assumed so – this was the 20th century and, on these newish laptop devices sending down analogue phone lines, you never could be sure).

Down beneath us, standing alone near the side of the pitch in a slate-grey Versace suit, Alex Ferguson was also composing words in his head. He was imagining how to tell his players, and the world, about his pride in this team and all they had accomplished.

They had reclaimed the Premier League title and won the FA Cup; a third Double in six seasons. They had come the closest of any Manchester United team since 1968 to recapturing the European prize that was the club's obsession. Defeat hurt when they were so damn close, especially when it meant missing out on an unprecedented Treble, but they would be back. 'Keep your dignity in defeat,' the United manager told himself.

And then, as the fourth official held up a board signalling three minutes of added time, United won a corner to our left and David Beckham ran over to take it. The most astonishing story in my lifetime of covering sport was about to unfold in front of our disbelieving eyes.

Ferguson would never deliver that speech and we would have to perform the fastest rewrite in the history of Fleet Street. Covering sport is not brain surgery, but the intensity of those few minutes is still talked about, with wonder and battle scars, as an unparalleled frenzy in football writing.

Sometimes we go back in time and find our memories have tricked us. Was it really as amazing as we like to remember? To relive that evening in Barcelona, and the tumultuous year that led up to it, was to be struck by the joyous realisation that the characters were even more fascinating and complex, the feats even more astonishing, the drama even more jaw-dropping than the stories we have told ourselves, and anyone else willing to listen, zillions of times since 1999.

If there is one year in the history of English football that deserves to be retold, it is this one. 'The greatest season English football has ever known,' Ferguson said. You do not have to be a Manchester United fan to know he was right.

It was a privilege to be on the journey as a sportswriter; close enough to feel Ferguson's hot breath on the days when he would blow his top; close enough to have David Beckham's mobile number, at least for the 24 hours before he became the dictionary definition of famous; close enough to be intimidated by the furious intensity of Roy Keane, to marvel at the thrilling genius of Ryan Giggs, the relentless drive of Gary Neville – to know, in short, we were watching a very rare and special group of footballers. It is no coincidence that, long after they finished playing, these men remain some of the most compelling figures in British sport.

You would struggle to find a dressing room containing more

interesting personalities than the Manchester United squad of 1998-99 led by Alex Ferguson, the greatest of British football managers. We have come to know many of them in different guises – as outspoken pundits, human billboards or for personal peccadilloes – but I wanted to go back and capture them in their athletic prime. I wanted to rewind and celebrate an unprecedented achievement before life and reputations grew (how shall we put it?) more complicated.

There is nothing more fascinating for a sportswriter than watching and studying greatness; trying to comprehend what distinguishes the very best; examining not just the talent but the character of champions; seeing what can be accomplished by competitors who never accept that a cause is lost.

This is a story about the most successful football team, and season, in the history of English football. It is about the most magical sporting drama I have witnessed, and the people who made it possible. But it is also, I hope, about much more.

I wanted to celebrate a time when life had never seemed more thrilling; certainly not for me, who had come to love Manchester. Covering United was a prized job, not just for reporting on the biggest club in the world but experiencing a city so alive with music and nightlife, and much cooler people than me. Was there anywhere better to live in the '90s? It was a joy to relive those exuberant times when, as Jaap Stam remarked after watching some old footage, it seemed like we were all wearing XXL clothes. Manchester made baggy more fashionable than anywhere on earth.

They were formative years for a young reporter, for Manchester and for English football, too. The '90s explosion shaped the game we see today. It was in 1998-99 that United became the richest and most recognisable sports entity in the world. The global acclaim English football enjoys today owes more to this United team, and the glory of 1999, than any side.

It made the reputations of many players, too, and they loved retelling their stories. I lost count of the number of times a member of this United squad said, 'It's bringing goosebumps just talking about it.' They gave their time freely and willingly – from Beckham to Peter Schmeichel, Dwight Yorke to Gary Neville, Denis Irwin to Paul Scholes and many more – to recall the dressing-room forces that shaped this campaign. Success was built on a rare camaraderie, but there were also rifts and rows and furious bust-ups among the complex dynamics.

The more sport I have watched, the more clear it becomes that the thrilling ride of 1999 was the distillation of everything you could hope for from football, or from any sport. Days you never forget, and so many of them. And that was even before the tumultuous denouement in Barcelona.

'I've seen your first editions,' Ferguson told us when we had recovered some time later from the drama. He knew those early pieces from the Nou Camp were a scrambled mess. Mine certainly was. United had turned the world upside down in 102 seconds and we had even less time to make sense of it.

For that reason, and many more, I wanted to go back and relive it all. I wanted to revel again in the wonder, excitement, chaos and disbelief. I wanted to write another draft and try to do justice to a season, and to a sporting story, that still seems unsurpassable.

1

Reunited

Twenty years after they passed into legend, they gather in the dressing room at Old Trafford. The Manchester United squad of 1998-99 have come together to take to the pitch one last time against their old Bayern Munich foes in aid of charity, and nostalgia, and to evoke all the glorious memories of when they were kings.

Exactly two decades on from the 1999 Champions League final, some of the players have barely seen each other since, but the years slip away and the dressing-room wisecracks quickly resume – though, now, the jokes are mostly about weight gain and hair loss.

Nicky Butt is taking the mickey, as usual. Jaap Stam, who never had much hair to lose in the first place, renews friendships with Ronny Johnsen, Ole Gunnar Solskjær and the Scandinavian bunch. David Beckham and Gary Neville are catching up about family. Dwight Yorke is making everyone laugh. Roy Keane is fuming somewhere, refusing to come at all.

For some, the years have not been kind. Andy Cole has battled a terrible kidney condition, which almost killed him and required a transplant. This lithe quicksilver striker is desperate to take to the pitch but has suffered so much that he says that he will have to walk off as soon as the match begins. Peter Schmeichel warns that he will not last long because of the bad back which is a legacy of those years throwing himself around in goal.

And then Sir Alex Ferguson walks in. It is as if royalty has entered the room. The conversation hushes as the revered manager prepares to give one final talk to the most successful team of all.

Ferguson has to pull up a chair to speak. He is physically fragile, though it is a minor miracle that he is alive. It is little more than a year since he needed emergency surgery for a brain haemorrhage. Aged 76, Ferguson collapsed at home in May 2018. Even after he pulled through, defying the doctors' worst fears, he had lost his voice for a while. He was terrified at losing his memory. To help him recover, the doctors gave him a pen and notepad and asked him to write down names of friends and family, and football teams, to stimulate his mind. He would scrawl one word repeatedly – remember – as if it was a prayer, a mantra.

In the dressing room, Ferguson starts talking and it is immediately clear that he still retains his familiar command. His words transport the players back 20 years. It is deeply moving seeing their old indomitable boss after all he has been through, and now the emotions are making some of them well up with tears. Ferguson tells them how proud he is of them all, not just as footballers but people. They should be proud of themselves, he says, not just for what they accomplished together but for the ethos of a team which will forever be remembered for fighting to the death, for never giving in.

There are more than 61,000 fans waiting outside but there is a pin-drop silence in the dressing room. A few of the players will come to say they wish they had caught the speech on film, but maybe it is best that it is a private moment of bonding. Some of them have heard Ferguson give a pre-match address hundreds of times, but this feels like the perfect encapsulation of every word they ever heard from this man who shaped their lives.

Ferguson tells the players how lucky they were to have had the opportunity to play for the mighty Manchester United. But they had seized that chance. They had made history. Everyone would be talking about the team of 1999 as long as they talk about football. The manager looks around the room. He could alight on any but he turns to Henning Berg. 'Bloody hell, Henning, that block you made here against Inter Milan,' he says. The point is made: this was a squad effort. Another point is made: Ferguson remembers it all.

He tells them that this might be a friendly, an anniversary fixture, but they are wearing the United shirt. The fans have come to see them perform. They must show what made them great 20 years ago. They must attack, and they must win.

Suddenly, from the laughs when they first walked in, the United players start to feel the competitive fires stoked once more. The blood is pumping. They could be back in their prime, ready to march out, inspired by their leader who has transformed his own fragility into fighting spirit. In Ferguson's presence alone, there could hardly be a more apposite symbol of the resolve of this team to bounce back against any odds. It is as if they are back in the 1998-99 campaign, with the sense that anything is possible. Ferguson's greatest gift was to fill them with the ambition and belief that they could conquer new worlds.

'Some people want to go to Blackpool for their holidays,' he had told them as they chased the Treble. 'You boys have a chance to fly to the moon. Not many people can do it, not many people are ever in a position to do it. Some don't even want to do it. I can't understand that. You can fly to the moon . . .'

They have goosebumps now. They slap and exhort each other, as if they are back at the start of the greatest campaign ever waged by an English football club. Fly to the moon, Ferguson told them.

Build a rocket, boys . . .

2

Hitting the bottom

It begins with a flick. Just one silly flick of a leg at around 9 p.m. on a Tuesday night in June 1998. At that moment the pubs are packed, rammed not just with people but hope and dangerously fragile expectation. England are playing in a World Cup and while nothing brings the country together like it, nothing sets it more on edge.

The audience for England v Argentina will peak at 26 million, the highest for an ITV programme since the channel went on air in 1955. This is not just a match but the sort of occasion that makes reputations – occasionally for better, though, in England's case, generally for worse. It seems mad that lives can be shaped on the bounce of a ball, the haphazardness of a single game, but David Beckham is about to write one of the great chapters of notoriety.

In the 47th minute, the score at 2-2, Beckham will cause the country to convulse emotionally – not by breaking the law, hurting anyone, or causing malicious offence, but with one silly waggle of his right leg.

When he is barged to the ground by Diego Simeone and retaliates by tripping his Argentine provocateur with an instinctive, irritated flick, it is not immediately clear what has happened. No one at home sees it live. The TV producer has been drawn to a close-up of Beckham prone on the ground, missing the crucial moment. Camera lenses will be torn between his right foot and his face for years to come.

It takes a replay to show the impetuously raised limb, and Simeone tumbling theatrically backwards over it. 'That's all it was,' Brian Moore says in commentary. But it is enough. Enough to merit the red card that Beckham gazes up at, numb with shock. Enough to set off a zillion words of condemnation that begin to flow in a furious torrent as Beckham shakes loose his billowing white shirt and walks off into infamy.

Watching the incident back, it seems so footling, but the pettiness is part of the problem. What offends so many, as Beckham fatefully tips the balance against England, is not that his offence is so bad, but that it is so trivial. Petulant is the word used most often. Childish. Unmanly. And in English football, far more in 1998 than now, to be lacking manliness might be the gravest offence of the lot. Daft as it sounds (but when did football ever encourage rationality?), Beckham might have been better off punching someone; perhaps careering into them with a kung-fu kick à la Cantona or maybe a Zidane-esque headbutt. At least it would reveal a tough, uncompromising character; a menacing air.

What did a sneaky trip say about Beckham? If it is a newspaper's job to capture the public mood, the *Mirror* does it most pointedly with the headline across the front page '10 HEROIC LIONS, ONE STUPID BOY'. As the story spills across every section of the papers, even art critics pile in. 'It was a girlish act,' Brian Appleyard writes in the *Sunday Times* Culture section in a critique of blondes. 'A man would have punched the Argentinian, a real man would have done nothing. But Beckham the blond simply executed a furtive foot-slap.'

What more did we expect from a man who wears a sarong? Beckham is easy to characterise as a poseur; a pretty boy engaged to a pop star who does not just present his fiancée with a £65,000 diamond solitaire ring, but receives a diamond-encrusted one worth £50,000 in return. This is a man who cares every bit as much about fashion and hair highlights as his bride-to-be. 'Suicide Blond,' says the *Mirror.* An editorial in the *Daily Telegraph* denounces Beckham as, among other things, 'a Gaultier-saronged, Posh-Spiced, Cooled Britannia, look-at-me, what-a-lad, loadsamoney, sex-and-shopping, fame-schooled, daytime-TV, over-coiffed twerp'.

When a scaffolder comes to hang the notorious Beckham effigy outside the Pleasant Pheasant pub in south London in the coming days, he makes sure to include that sarong. Perhaps, in all that followed, this was football's first case of metrosexual abuse.

Even for those of us with an understanding of English football's need for a scapegoat – and, indeed, playing a part in that demonising – the scale of vilification is hard to comprehend. But, in the familiar madness of England's departure from another World Cup, we are too caught up in the stampede to wonder if the condemnation will escalate out of control.

After another England campaign has finished in tears, with Glenn Hoddle's team eventually losing to Argentina in a penalty shoot-out – an agonisingly narrow defeat that only serves to exacerbate Beckham's crime – we start the pursuit of him in St Etienne. We want a quote, an apology to the nation, but Beckham charges straight past us, baseball cap pulled down over his face, like a guilty man trying to evade the mob outside Crown Court. He wants to slip past unnoticed. No chance of that in the Stade Geoffroy-Guichard; or anywhere else, for years to come.

Beckham only stops when he sees his parents and bursts into heaving sobs in the arms of his father, Ted, who has taken him to the local park all those countless times, developing the skills that have made Beckham one of the most exciting young players in Europe. Here is a man capable of scoring a goal from the halfway line or curling an unstoppable free-kick as he had against Colombia only four days earlier to be a national hero – but also putting that right foot to self-destructive use. For what feels like an age, Beckham is a child again in his father's embrace. As he clambers on to the team bus, he can have only a vague idea of the fury he has unleashed from the English public that will escalate over the coming days.

It is certainly too soon to understand what he has stirred within himself. He cannot know, sitting desolate on that bus, Gary Neville imploring him to wipe away the tears – 'don't let anyone see you like this,' his friend and teammate says – that 12 months later he will be at the peak of life, personally and professionally. Perhaps to reach those heights, Beckham first has to go to the bottom. Maybe he needs that moment of disgrace to discover his depths of resilience and fortitude. 'Whatever else happens to me, those sixty seconds will always be with me,' he notes. He will come to say it was a defining moment that helped make him a better footballer and a better man.

That is going to take one hell of a comeback. As it turns out – for Beckham, for Manchester United and for English football – 1999 will be a year of them like none we have ever seen before, or since.

3

New Labour, New Football

On the night of the General Election in May 1997 that would mark a transformation in British life, a mobile phone* rang in Tony Blair's constituency home in Sedgefield, County Durham. The manager of Manchester United was on the line.

Alex Ferguson was watching the news coverage of this historic evening on television and called to warn Blair and Alastair Campbell, Labour's spin-doctor-in-chief, that cameras were prying outside. 'Be careful,' Ferguson advised. 'They can see through your curtains.' After the view had been blocked, they chatted briefly and then returned to the unfolding drama. The following morning, Blair, Campbell, Ferguson – all of us – would wake up in a very different country.

Amid scenes of rock-star euphoria, following a dawn flight to London, Blair stood beaming on the South Bank of the Thames with crowds lined along Waterloo Bridge and the Embankment to hail the new prime minister. Labour had won 418 parliamentary seats to the Conservatives' 165; a record post-war majority and a crushing repudiation of the Tories after 18 years in office. As Blair spoke at the Festival Hall, the sun broke through as if he had even choreographed the weather. 'A new dawn has broken, has it not?' Blair said. And a lot of us felt it, too. Ah, happy days.

These were good times to be alive, were they not? Nostalgia can beguile us, but I was in my 20s, upwardly mobile and,

I fear, had all the cocky swagger of the age. Cool Britannia, Britpop, the Spice Girls, *TFI Friday*, lads' mags, ladettes, Chris Evans, Gail Porter, Zoe Ball, coke and Es, Red Stripe and Grolsch, Oasis v Blur; to scan back through some of the UK's cultural reference points is to plunge, a little wasted, back into '90s revelry.

'Most of the Western world was still locked into the decade-long spell of carefree optimism that had begun with the fall of the Berlin Wall and would end with the events of 11 September 2001. A kind of giddy optimism was in the air,' John Harris, journalist and author of *The Last Party: Britpop, Blair and the Demise of English Rock*, observed in the *New Statesman* of Britain in the '90s. We inhaled deeply.

As we counted down to the Millennium, serious people discussed whether planes would fall from the sky, among other potential catastrophes, because of a Y2K bug that might disable computer software, but I don't recall any fretfulness. We were, as Prince instructed us, partying like it was (almost) 1999.

Even the Union Jack was cool; stuck on Noel Gallagher's guitar in the world's biggest rock band. Blair was so eager to become part of the Britpop chorus – to make Labour the 'political wing of Cool Britannia,' as Harris noted – that he invited Oasis inside Number 10 for drinks. When Gallagher asked Blair how he had kept going all night as the election results came in, the prime minister leant over and said, 'Probably not by the same means as you did.' 'At that point I knew he was a geezer,' Gallagher said. The youngest prime minister since 1812 was determined to join the laddish entertainment, which also meant parading football credentials.

As that call from Ferguson on election night demonstrated – a football manager ringing to advise the next prime minister at a moment of history – Blair's Labour tapped into the national game as part of their cultural appropriation. It made sense.

Football was now firmly in the mainstream of an expanding middle class. To embrace the sport was also a means to strike further distance from a Conservative Party which, especially under Margaret Thatcher, had treated football, and its supporters, with open disdain.

New Labour, New Football. The '90s were transformative for the English game, more than any decade before or since. The game sneered at by Thatcher in the '80s, despised for its hooligans, had enjoyed a spectacular boom. Out of the horror of Hillsborough in 1989 came shiny new all-seater stadiums. The rebranding of the Premier League from 1992 and the surge of money from Sky Television paid for a new wave of foreign stars; Cantona, Klinsmann, Gullit, Zola, Bergkamp and Vialli. Euro 96 fuelled the Cool Britannia mood. 'Football's Coming Home', we sang merrily, even if, ultimately, it wasn't.

As Campbell remembers it from his time as Blair's head of communications, he was at the heart of a government pushing the football agenda. No political campaign was complete without a bit of keepy-uppy in front of the cameras. 'The whole Cool Britannia thing, we didn't coin that,' Campbell explains. 'That was *Newsweek*, a front cover with a bit of Tony, a bit of music, the Queen, the Spice Girls. There was that famous party at Number 10 with Noel Gallagher. It became a mood. It wasn't strategised as such but it just kind of emerged from that mood. I do think football was an important part of that.

'Whether I was slightly pushing my own agenda I don't know, but both Tony and Gordon [Brown] were big fans – not as obsessed as I am – but they watch a lot of football. Football was booming and in that period, Manchester United became the club that defined the time. And then you had Alex Ferguson, a big Labour supporter who did stuff with us. So it all kind-of knitted.'

Never before had a football manager had a direct line into

Downing Street, but then never had a prime minister felt it so advantageous to attach himself to a man who ran a football team. As Blair noted, 'I can meet ministers and monarchs and my children are not much impressed. But when we meet Alex Ferguson they realised there was some point.'

---

* We did have mobile phones in the late '90s, but they were smart as a brick. The must-have device of 1998 was the Nokia 5110, one of the first to feature the game 'Snake'. Sophisticated, it was not. We would have to wait several more years for cameras in phones.

Wifi? Never heard of it. We had a working internet but Google was only just being born and searching on Yahoo! required a dial-up connection, with the chance to make a cup of tea while a page loaded. It could be quicker to find the news on Teletext.

There was email but the nearest thing to social media was the graffiti on the walls of a public toilet. Maybe that was a blessing, certainly for David Beckham. 'If social media was around when I was going through that time in '98, it would have been a whole different story,' he said in 2020 when backing a mental health campaign.

4

Mad fer it

The centre of the cultural universe is endlessly – and excitingly – shifting, but on Sunday 28 April 1996 I came as close as I ever will to standing at the very epicentre. It was a glorious place to be. All that Manchester could offer – its vibrancy and swagger and the global allure of its music and football and nightlife – came together under the heading 'If Carlsberg did perfect weekends with your mates . . .'

We began with a Saturday night out in the city and, most likely, ended up in the sweaty cavern of the joyfully uncool 'Conti' club, with its sticky floor, no-frills DJ ('If you want to fight, fuck off outside and do it') and pissed crowd of twentysomethings on the pull. There were friends, booze and, this being Manchester in the '90s, almost certainly quite a few drugs. The memories are hazy, but the glow endures.

Sunday. Well, how could you improve on it? We began at Old Trafford watching a majestic Manchester United put five goals past Nottingham Forest; Ryan Giggs dancing down the wing, David Beckham and Paul Scholes chipping in goals, Eric Cantona conducting this magnificent orchestra before thumping home the last of a 5-0 rout and falling to the floor for a celebratory embrace. United were irresistible. They were a force of beautiful power, striding towards a second Premier League and FA Cup Double in three seasons. Their unprecedented dominance carried an air of permanence. United had become English football's royalty, Dieu Et Mon Droit.

Adventure and swagger. Belligerence along with the brilliance. They were captivating for Cantona's strut; for Giggs running as if his feet barely touched the grass; for Fergie's Fledglings reprising the Busby Babes, and all the romance of home-grown youth. For Alex Ferguson, furiously chewing his gum on the sidelines, and for the siege mentality he created. United against the world! For wingers and attacking and chasing a game, building an irresistible momentum. For being England's super-club. Many loved them even if they had never been to Old Trafford.

More than 53,000 of us were treated that day to United in their pomp and we moved on, via Dry Bar where the cool people hung out in Manchester's Northern Quarter, to Maine Road where Oasis were performing at their spiritual home. There was no hotter ticket in the musical universe. The footage on YouTube still gives me the thrills; Noel walking on to the stage with his cagoule and Union Jack guitar followed by Liam in an Umbro sweatshirt asking, 'Manchester, are you mad fer it?' Oh yes.

'I don't know what it is / That makes me feel alive.' They ripped into 'Acquiesce' and we sang every word of that, and 'Supersonic' and 'Live Forever' and 'Wonderwall', and bounced around like deliriously happy fools. You did not have to like United or Oasis to be swept along in the euphoria (though life must have been a whole lot duller if you didn't).

They were the best of times. Manchester did not get any better than that. *Life* did not get any better than that. Except in 1998-99, it could.

It is history now – the stuff of museums and tourists. The 'Rock and Goal Tour' led by Joe takes you back to a boarded-up Dry Bar to see brass etchings in the paving slabs outside – one signifying 'Madchester', another of the Union Jack motif from Noel's guitar. Mosaics on the wall outside Afflecks Palace indoor market display the legends of Cantona and the Gallaghers, Bet Lynch and Emmeline Pankhurst, Vimto and Alan Turing to represent the best of the city. A mural of Ian Curtis of Joy Division is on the side of a house in Ancoats.

I dragged along a teenage son to hear how Manchester was the heart of a cultural boom through the '80s and '90s; indie music and the rave revolution; the Hacienda on Whitworth Street and Sankeys Soap in industrial Ancoats as old warehouse buildings were reclaimed as nightclubs. We recalled the vibrant gay scene, around Manto on Canal Street, which was another reason Manchester felt on the cutting edge.

Some of it was history even by 1999 when Dave Haslam, a former Hacienda DJ, published *Manchester, England – The Story of the Pop Cult City* to trace how this industrial metropolis became such a musical powerhouse from Northern Soul through all the glories of Madchester and the Smiths, Stone Roses, Happy Mondays, New Order and Factory Records, and on to Oasis. Or Simply Red, if that was more your thing.

'It is the city with the most highly developed music consciousness in the world, and sometimes you imagine you can reach out and touch it, a palpable buzz of a night-life culture that's evolving, absorbing,' Haslam wrote.

Manchester never stood still. The Hacienda closed for the final time in 1997, after becoming a place where people went looking for cool people only to find the cool people had moved elsewhere. The building was converted into loft apartments which was the sign of a different boom. Urban regeneration was changing, and improving, the face of Manchester, boosted by preparations for the Commonwealth Games in 2002. A new stadium was being built which would become the modern home of Manchester City. New bars were springing up, and they still do. Manchester had a vibrancy that won me over – a love for the place that endures.

Haslam's book could not have been written about Birmingham, Leeds, Newcastle, Sheffield, or even Liverpool. Or anywhere else in the world, for that matter. Manchester was more 'Cool Britannia' than London could ever be. I tell myself I saw the very best of it in the '90s, and I think that might even be true.

5

Or you hated them

ABU. Anyone But United. The more United won, the more crushing was their '90s dominance, the more fans of other clubs found a rallying cause in opposition, taking raucously against their success. 'Stand up if you hate Man U' was such a ubiquitous chant that it seemed to be the official anthem of half the clubs in the Premier League.

By 1997, Robert Crampton was writing in *The Times* that 'the ABU (Anyone But United) supporters' club is probably the largest informal grouping in English football'. It met in grounds and pubs and around water-coolers whenever fans gathered. 'The accepted etiquette of your average English fan, the vindaloo and later children of the late Seventies and Eighties, unashamedly decrees that, irrespective of United's feats, they must be derided and despised at all times; it's almost a mantra for the Millennium,' Ian Ross noted in the *Guardian* during the 1998-99 season.

'Hated. Adored. Never Ignored', a banner held up at Old Trafford would later read. You could love to hate them. Anyone But United.

Des Cahill was not responsible for the antipathy – that had more to do with the psychology of envy – but the Irish broadcaster does have the considerable claim to fame of being the original ABU. 'Yes, I was the founding father for better or worse,' he explains over the phone from Dublin. 'I'd like to have done something greater with my life, but still.'

The story he tells cheerily is of creating a popular movement out of a single joke. Cahill was a West Ham United fan ('long story') and radio presenter who became fed up with the proliferation of United shirts in the Republic of Ireland through the '90s, everyone jumping on the red bandwagon. It was not just in Ireland. As Roger Nouveau said in a sketch on *The Fast Show*, representing the new '90s breed of middle-class supporter with his hamper on his lap, 'I used to support Manchester United, but then you had to where I came from ... in Hampstead.'

Cahill presented the sports bulletins on one of Ireland's most popular breakfast shows, on 2FM. For a bit of mischief, he started openly supporting United's main title rivals – Liverpool, Aston Villa, Newcastle United, Blackburn Rovers – as the original ABU, and playing 'Zip-a-dee-do-dah' on the morning after any United defeat as the rallying song.

Zip-a-dee-doo-dah, zip-a-dee-ay
My, oh my, what a wonderful day
Plenty of sunshine headin' my way
Zip-a-dee-doo-dah, zip-a-dee-ay!

'And it became a huge thing,' he says. 'People would wait in their cars for the sport on the morning after United lost just for the zip-a-dee-doo-dah. Manchester United permeated every level. Mothers who didn't follow football would say to me, "There was murder in my house this morning with your ABU."'

ABU appeared on T-shirts. Badges were made. Cahill even drew up a crest, with a Latin inscription which read 'Uppus Cantonis Aris'. 'Juvenile, I know,' he laughs. 'Up his arse. It grew to a ridiculous level. There was a big telethon over there at the time, a bit like your *Children In Need*, and a couple of hundred grand was raised just by me dressing in United gear and singing "Glory, Glory Man Utd".

'When Beckham came on the scene in a sarong I sang a song about it. People used to send in poems. Any event where I was speaking I'd be greeted by a mixture of hissing and applause. That's how divisive United's success was. It was a bit of fun but United fans took it so seriously. Once or twice, it really did get hairy with fellas held back from hitting me in bars in Dublin.'

The ABU phenomenon spread across the Irish Sea, taken on by fans of United's rivals up and down the country. ABU passed into common football parlance. You loved or you hated them. But you could not ignore them. And that was even before the season when the United phenomenon reached its zenith.

'It probably culminated in the European Cup final in 1999,' Cahill says. 'There was a jumbo jet going from Dublin so I boarded with one of my friends, Kieran. We were seated at the back of the plane and as I walked down the aisle the whole plane was singing "Dessie is a wanker", which was amusing for my friends.' Personally, Cahill could enjoy the dramas of the 1998–99 season. 'It was only ever meant to be fun, you can't take sport too seriously,' he says. 'But, of course, what happened that year made ABU people even more demented.'

6

Fucking smart arse

It was not only David Beckham enduring a turbulent summer in 1998. As the World Cup was playing out in France, Alex Ferguson was unwinding at Oaks Day, Epsom at the end of his 12th season in charge of Manchester United. He had developed a passion for horse racing as a way to relax from the strains of running the growing empire at Old Trafford. Ferguson loved to hob-nob with trainers and fellow owners – there was a little champagne in his socialism – and on this June day Sky Sports TV reporter Olly Foster spotted the United manager by the winning post, where he was nursing the disappointment that his horse, Queensland Star, had faded to fourth in the 2.10.

Foster saw a chance to ask for a quick interview. Ferguson agreed. Thinking on his feet, Foster suggested that Queensland Star went much like United in the Premier League campaign just concluded, looking to have it won only to falter unexpectedly. So much for the soft opening gambit. 'Fergie took it badly,' Foster recalls, with understatement.

'FUCK OFF! FUCK OFF NOW, YOU FUCKING SMART ARSE!' Ferguson shouted in Foster's face, incandescent with rage. The reporter had prodded a deep wound.

In the 1997–98 season not long finished, United's usual domestic invincibility had cracked. Ferguson and his players had known the deflation of a trophyless season before, but not like this, beaten by such an impressive opponent as Arsène Wenger's Arsenal.

In February 1998, some bookmakers had paid out on bets for United to win the title when they were 11 points clear at the top. But, to the delight of the ABUs, Arsenal had put together a run of ten consecutive victories, including a 1-0 win at Old Trafford, to snatch the championship by a solitary point. They made it a Double by beating Newcastle United in the FA Cup final. United had been knocked out of the FA Cup by Barnsley, and the Champions League quarter-finals by Monaco – not exactly Real Madrid or Juventus – in a season when they had lost Roy Keane to a knee operation and Ryan Giggs to a succession of injuries. Eric Cantona had retired abruptly in May 1997, with Teddy Sheringham struggling to fill his large chaussures.

No wonder Ferguson was soul-searching when he sat down with Oliver Holt from *The Times* as the title slipped away in the spring. Sitting behind his desk at United's training ground the Cliff, munching toast, Ferguson sounded like a man struggling to digest failure. 'You have to say that the team of two years ago or the team of '94 would not have lost any of the games we have lost this season,' he said. He talked of a lack of hunger, the ultimate crime in the relentlessly driven world of Ferguson. There would be changes, he warned.

'People like myself and the staff and the supporters do not deserve to have it thrown away by the players like this. Not after all the work that has been done here. But the club is like a moving bus. We are not waiting at the stop for anyone who is late.'

If that was a direct challenge to his players, there was one for the board too. Ferguson had long felt that United had failed to use their muscle in the transfer market – a club that aspired to be the greatest in Europe, and the world, but never spent like it. They would look at A-list targets – Ronaldo, Gabriel Batistuta, Marcelo Salas – but back off because of a self-imposed salary cap. Chelsea, Liverpool and Arsenal had players on higher wages than United's ceiling of £23,000 per week (how quaint!), but success had been achieved without lavish outlays. That is how the directors wanted it to remain, with little more than 30 per cent of turnover spent on salaries.

Ferguson was increasingly bolshie that he had allowed himself to be knocked back by 'all the Cityspeak about institutions and dividends and the harsh realities of the business world'. Told by the board that he would have around £14 million available for transfers that summer to put United back on top, he had committed a club record £10.6 million for Jaap Stam, the big Dutch defender from PSV Eindhoven, and recruited Jesper Blomqvist from Palma for £4.5 million as a back-up for Giggs, but he was not satisfied. His biggest deals were still dwarfed by others at home and abroad, like the world record £15 million fee that took Alan Shearer to Newcastle United (1996), Ronaldo to Inter Milan for £20 million (1997), and Denílson to Real Betis for £21 million in 1998.

'The club has got to get to grips with what actually makes a winning club in Europe,' Ferguson told Holt. 'It has not approached that. It is not even anywhere near that. It is not a Barcelona, it is not an AC Milan, it is not a Juventus, it's not a Real Madrid. In terms of the quality of the club, it is. In terms of the people working in it and the effort the players put in, it is. But other clubs have a mentality that is different from our mentality.

'What may happen after I leave is that it will dawn on them that, when a new manager comes in, he may ask for £60 million to build a team to win in Europe. But they may not get the best manager to replace me. And then the dawning part comes in and they will say, "I wish we had done that five years back down the road." There are big strides this club has got to take, but when they will do it, I don't know.'

It was a blunt challenge to his employers: a warning that United could be left behind, and not just by a resurgent Arsenal. But what Ferguson had not anticipated was that some of the directors felt that it was the manager who was slipping.

7

Fergie: I quit!

'We are worried about your focus.' Alex Ferguson could hardly believe his ears. The most successful manager at work in the game had been summoned back from a family holiday in the south of France expecting to discuss transfer targets. Instead he was being accused of being a cause of United's slump.

Across a table in offices in central London, Martin Edwards, United's chairman, flanked by Sir Roland Smith, chairman of the club's PLC board, looked down at his pages of printed notes which set out a list of concerns, even grievances, with the manager. This was not carping from the terraces or the media; it was the most senior directors questioning whether Ferguson was committed to his job.

As Edwards told me, and he still has the paperwork to refresh his memory, there was talk of Ferguson revelling in 'celebrity status'. Was his growing passion as a racehorse owner impinging on his work? Edwards told Ferguson that the board feared he had taken his eye off the ball, leading to a disappointing season.

Brian Kidd, the manager's assistant, had been taking the vast majority of training sessions. Was Ferguson leaving a vacuum? A comparison was made by Edwards with how the manager's job grew too much for Sir Matt Busby after the European Cup triumph of 1968, as success and profile led to heightened interest and heavier demands. Had United's run of trophies meant that Ferguson was being pulled in too many directions?

There was mention of the manager's previous six signings – Solskjær, Johnsen, Poborsky, Berg, Cruyff and Sheringham – and the fact that none of them had looked like taking United to the next level. Could the board back Ferguson now with the unprecedented budget he was demanding given his recent record in transfers was not exactly reassuring?

At the headquarters of HSBC, next to Southwark Bridge, Ferguson felt he had returned from his rented villa on a clifftop in Cap Ferrat, spending time in the sun with his kids and grandkids, into an ambush. He would later reflect that if he had been younger and more headstrong, 'my pride and my temper wouldn't have allowed me to tolerate such a farce'. As it was, he kept his cool, just about. Ferguson's first instinct was to wonder if there was a deeper motive to the criticism. 'Do you want to call it a day?' he asked. Edwards assured him that this was not about forcing a change of manager but making sure they were getting the best out of the one they had. The previous season had left doubts about Ferguson's dedication.

Gathering his thoughts, and returning fire, Ferguson explained that he needed release from football. It was a huge stress running United, keeping the team dominant. Horse racing was a healthy outlet. As for transfers, Ferguson demanded to know who was better equipped to decide. Edwards could have his list but Ferguson rattled through his own – Schmeichel, Ince, Irwin, Keane, Cantona on top of all the home-grown players he had brought through. 'If you don't recognise that I am the best person to judge which players should be bought by the club, I may as well leave now,' he said bluntly.

Perhaps Ferguson should have seen this confrontation coming. He and Edwards had already shared a difficult telephone conversation in which Ferguson had continued to push for the signing of Dwight Yorke from Aston Villa, as well as Patrick Kluivert, who was available after a difficult year at AC Milan. Ferguson wanted to overhaul his strikers, on top of the purchases of Stam and Blomqvist.

When Edwards had told Ferguson over the phone that there were doubts about Yorke – 'we are not sure he is the right man' – the manager had exploded, especially when informed that one of the sceptics was Kidd. 'Brian Kidd? Who's the bloody manager?' he asked. Ferguson was even less impressed when Edwards informed him that Kidd preferred John Hartson, the bruising West Ham United and Wales striker. 'Hartson?' Ferguson spluttered. 'Are you serious?'

It was not the only strain in Ferguson's relationship with Kidd, the man he had elevated from coaching the youth teams, and who had been by his side in the dugout for the past seven years. Kidd had been approached about the vacant manager's position at Everton, who were offering to triple his salary. Edwards advised Ferguson to talk to Kidd to clear the air. Hardly ideal preparations for a new campaign.

As Ferguson departed back to France to rejoin his family, Smith instructed Edwards that he should put the points raised in writing. A letter to that effect was delivered to Ferguson internally at Old Trafford on the morning of 7 July, when the manager was back for pre-season training. Edwards had softened the tone a little by commending Ferguson over his youth policy, and eradicating deadwood among the players. Inevitably, Ferguson's eye was drawn to the criticisms, including the reiteration of concerns at the lack of a trophy, the warning over outside interests impairing his focus, and an instruction to be cautious when speaking to the media so as not to fuel criticism of the PLC board being stingy over transfers.

The letter had a predictable effect, like prodding a hornets' nest. Within a few hours of delivery, Edwards took a call that Ferguson wanted to see him. The manager came in raging, saying that he had no option but to resign. 'The language Alex used was a little bit more fruity, but that was the basic gist of it,' Edwards says.

'Well, if that's the way you feel, Alex, we'll have to accept it,' Edwards replied. He was confident he could call the manager's bluff and, later that day, Ferguson came on the phone to withdraw his resignation. 'I think what he'd done is spoken to his solicitor who'd probably said, "Well, you won't get a penny on the two years left on your contract,"' Edwards explains. 'So, he withdrew his resignation which I was happy to do.

'All I wanted to do was shake it up a bit and make sure we got back on course. He'd done the Double in '94 and '96, won the league in '97, so it wasn't as if he was a bad manager. It was just purely a case of "let's get back on track". In '98 we had a huge lead of 11 points clear just after Christmas and we blew it. When it came to it, we still supported him with signings. But if we were going to spend that sort of money, we had to be absolutely certain that he was 100 per cent on board. And I think the combination of that letter plus the transfer buys, we did what was needed.'

Edwards believes he deserves a bit of credit for having the balls to challenge Ferguson. He had certainly succeeded in stoking the manager's competitive fires. As Gordon Strachan, one of the more shrewd observers of Ferguson from his playing days at Aberdeen and United, once said, 'Fergie is driven by anger. It's like petrol to him.' Heading into the new season, he had a tank full of the stuff.

8

Beckham flees

David Beckham needed sanctuary, some peace and quiet as the country fulminated over his red card. So, obviously, he went on tour with one of the most popular bands in the world.

Chased by paparazzi after he landed at Heathrow with the England team; pursued through airport corridors as he headed straight on to another Concorde flight bound for New York City; greeted by more photographers as he landed at JFK airport; Beckham fought through the throng to climb into a car to be driven straight to Madison Square Garden where the Spice Girls were performing that evening. In walked Madonna. 'Oh, you're the soccer player, aren't you?' asked the biggest pop star on the planet. Perhaps she had watched the game, or maybe there really was no one in the world who now did not recognise the Manchester United and England No.7.

If New Football had a face – to swoon over, to admire, to envy and, now, for many to scapegoat – it was the Hollywood-handsome looks of David Beckham. The peak of his fame was still some way off (perhaps that was when he told me in an interview in 2000, chatting in his Mercedes in a lay-by as the only way to avoid being mobbed, that fans had been going through the bins at his hairdressers seeking out remnants of his locks), but he was in determined pursuit of celebrity, even if he had to go via infamy to get there.

He had shown a knack for stardom ever since scoring from the halfway line against Wimbledon on the opening day of the season in August 1996, standing with arms outstretched and nodding his head as if to say, 'What else did you expect?' On and off the pitch, Beckham wanted it all: to be one of the world's supreme footballers but also to develop a profile, riches, fame.

When he saw a pop star on television in a black PVC catsuit, like a rather mild-mannered dominatrix, and said, 'Ohhhh I like that one,' he was sure that Posh Spice was the woman for him. They would soon be an item. David and Victoria announced their engagement in January 1998. 'I'd be lying if I didn't admit that her being a pop star was part of the attraction,' he said. The Spice Girl was more famous than the rising young footballer when they started dating.

Together, they straddled sport and celebrity, which some loved, and many derided. There was a backlash to the rapid inflation of footballers' wages and prominence through the '90s, and Beckham's profile put him on the receiving end. With that red card, the pretty, petulant boy with a squeaky Essex voice had given all those critics a free hit.

It was to embrace his fiancée that Beckham headed over to the United States as soon as he could following that ignominious exit from the World Cup. Alex Ferguson had called to say that there would be a supportive reception waiting for him back in Manchester – 'Don't worry about what anyone says. Get yourself back here, where people love you and support you,' Ferguson told him, offering a paternal arm around the shoulder – but there was an added reason to join Victoria as fast as possible.

She had rung him on the eve of that fateful Argentina match to say that she was pregnant. Arriving in New York, dashing across the city, Beckham hugged her in the band's dressing room and then the two of them disappeared into a toilet cubicle where she could show him the first scan of their baby, still only pea-sized.

New York was where Victoria discovered she was pregnant, which would come to be uppermost in the parents' minds when it came to naming their baby.

Beckham spent his summer break travelling on the Spiceworld tour bus for 11 days, watching from the side of the stage, hanging around the back of the room at promotional events. It was as well that he was out of the country. At home in Chingford, Essex, Beckham's parents Ted and Sandra needed a private security firm for protection. A swarm of media were constantly outside and they were convinced their phone was being tapped, given that his mum would turn up at places to find photographers already there. The home number was easily obtainable – Ted was a gas fitter – but instead of job orders the line was filled with abusive calls.

When Ferguson got through, Beckham's father was too upset to speak. Ted eventually spoke to *The Sun* to say that he had been in contact with a very apprehensive son. 'I'm just glad David's been out of the country. He hasn't seen half of what's gone on and I won't let him. I'm no longer proud to be British after what they've done to my son, and all through a game of football. He's made a mistake. We all know he made a mistake but he's certainly paying for it now. I'm disgusted with what has gone on. I've had enough.' He questioned whether Beckham might be forced to play his football abroad.

'Take Your Fury Out On Our David Beckham Dartboard', urged the *Mirror*, making Beckham the bullseye. Piers Morgan was editor at the time and, while never shy of a strong opinion, retreats a little when reflecting on the excesses.

'I would certainly say on the night, we completely and perfectly encapsulated what everyone was thinking when I ran the headline "10 HEROIC LIONS, ONE STUPID BOY". But I certainly don't absolve myself from the responsibility of rattling the cage a little too hard. I would regret the dartboard. Funny though it may have seemed at the time, I don't look back at that now and think that was acceptable to be honest. It was a stupid thing with hindsight which may have encouraged the more Neanderthal element out there to take things too far.'

'God forgives even David Beckham,' declared a sign outside one church in Nottingham. But would the British public? As Beckham was flying back into England from the United States, he was approached in his first-class seat by the chief steward. 'When we disembark, there'll be police waiting for you at the gate,' he explained. Beckham could wonder if they were there to arrest or protect him.

9

Effigy

SOCCER FANS' SICK STUNT

POLICE have removed an effigy of David Beckham left hanging from a scaffold by angry soccer fans. Officers ordered the dummy – dressed in Beckham's No.7 England shirt – to be cut down from outside the Pleasant Pheasant pub in South Norwood following complaints.

Steve Snadden, 26, who runs the Pleasant Pheasant, noticed the dummy this morning. He said: 'It was my proudest World Cup moment. I laughed out loud when I saw it. The punters are just doing what everyone in Britain feels.'

Scaffolder Lee Tickner, 32, who was behind the stunt, added: 'Everyone in the pub has been fuming about Beckham's behaviour. He needs teaching a lesson.'

Lee Tickner is still in scaffolding, but it has been a very long time – more than 23 years, in fact – since he was asked about Beckham. 'You're having a wind-up, aren't you?' he says when I explain that I have tracked him down to talk about the effigy that remains a lasting symbol of fan hatred, before the days when you could simply type all the bile and abuse into Twitter.

'I dunno how you got my name,' Tickner says. From the papers, I explain. You were said to be part of the hate mob that was going to ruin Beckham's life. He sighs. 'We was all just pissed up in the pub. It was a load of us done it. Next thing, it comes up on the front page of *The Sun*. It was many years ago. I'm 55 now. It wasn't how it was written in the paper, hate mobs and all that. Ridiculous. It was done as a total wind-up and it got taken the wrong way. Listen, it was only done as a laugh.'

So what does he think of Beckham now? 'I don't even like football, mate, to be honest with you,' he replies. But that didn't stop him having an opinion. Everyone did. Football was — is — the most popular soap opera of our age. And every soap needs a villain.

In 1998, Beckham was that sinner. He had let down the whole country. He epitomised all that was wrong with the national character. Whereas, of course, putting an effigy in a noose and Beckham's face on a dartboard, screaming abuse, sending hate mail and singing that 'Posh Spice takes it up the arse' were fair game.

10

A big Dutch man

Jaap Stam looked like he came straight out of prison, according to his new teammates, but the hulking frame and shaven head did not protect him from the insecurities of proving himself at a club where they seemed almost insanely competitive from the first kick in training.

Even as the world's most expensive defender at £10.6 million, with a mission to elevate the Manchester United defence to one capable of winning the Champions League, it was daunting to arrive at a football club of such stature. Stam was the new boy on his first day at school, facing a cast of big personalities who both welcomed him and tested him in those early weeks.

How was it to walk into the United camp in 1998? Stam still grimaces at how his autobiography, *Head To Head*, published in 2001, brought him far more trouble than it was worth when he tried to answer that question. His comments were sensationalised and he became a more wary figure, which is a shame because he had only been honest. The description of his new teammates still rings true. There was Peter Schmeichel, the huge angry goal-keeper. 'A terrific goalie but, at times, he could be a real pain in the arse as well,' Stam noted. They would soon be screaming at each other whenever there was defensive chaos.

Among the Class of 92 cabal of home-grown talent, the Neville brothers, Gary and Phil, were the 'busy c***s'. Gary, in particular, seemed to have a view on anything and everything – nothing changes – though Stam was also struck by the analytical football brain that would serve the elder Neville so well. Ryan Giggs and Nicky Butt were the 'terrible twins', constantly winding him up with pranks, like hiding his car keys or making his socks disappear. In training, Giggs would glide over the grass. Butt would tackle anything.

David Beckham was easily misjudged. Yes, he was a pretty boy putting gel in his hair when the rest of the players were preparing for action, but he was also a top-class footballer and the last man standing when the rest were gasping for breath in the bleep tests of fitness. Paul Scholes? Like almost every teammate that ever played alongside the little ginger midfielder, Stam would instantly be taken aback by the vision and ball-striking of a 'world-class player'. The quiet ones were Denis Irwin, going about his job with maximum efficiency and minimum fuss, while Andy Cole kept himself to himself even down to stretching on his own before games while the rest of the players were warming up together.

Socially, Stam was drawn to the crowd of Scandinavians – Henning Berg, Ole Gunnar Solskjær, Ronny Johnsen and fellow new arrival Jesper Blomqvist – and greatly helped by the presence of a fellow Dutchman in Jordi Cruyff to help him settle. It was Cruyff who could translate some of the manager's barely comprehensible Glaswegian.

For Stam, there was no escaping the pressure to impress these new colleagues. He had felt it even as he reached the semi-final of the World Cup with the Netherlands in the summer of 1998, sensing that English eyes were staring at every move and wondering if he was worth the money.

Talking from home in Holland, Stam is a serious figure, not without charm or lighter moments, but you sense the pride and the drive. Stam did not just want to succeed; he needed to. Just the type of intense character that Ferguson liked.

*

For Stam, it was a bumpy start to joining United. He returned home from the World Cup, and a bruising semi-final defeat to Brazil, to a wife, Ellis, who was heavily pregnant. He was so eager to impress his new employers that the couple agreed to have their first child, Lisa, induced a couple of weeks early so that Stam could go on the pre-season tour to Norway. That was the sort of dedication his manager appreciated.

Ferguson had been pursuing Stam since 1997, struck by a defender who combined pace with his obvious physical power. The United manager felt that he needed defenders who could cope one-on-one in Europe given that his way of setting up the team, with 4-4-2 and two wingers, was never likely to afford much protection. Stam's speed for a big man was an insurance policy.

Ferguson had tapped up Stam when he was at PSV Eindhoven, arranging a meeting through the player's agent in a flat near Amsterdam airport. 'Jaap, I want you to command our backline and help us take that extra step and win the European Cup,' Ferguson told him. Stam was instantly seduced. 'Ferguson's passion was overwhelming,' he says. He was so eager to make the move that he had even waived £1.65 million due to him from PSV as a cut of the record transfer fee.

At 26, the peak of his physical powers, he was a man to build a defence around following the departure of 33-year-old Gary Pallister, but the weight of expectation was not easy to bear, even on the broadest shoulders. Rattling around a Cheshire hotel waiting for his wife and baby to receive medical approval to fly over to join him, Stam had to adjust to an elevated profile and an extraordinary intensity. The tackling in training at United seemed as feisty as on matchday. There was a bluntness and a hard edge about the exchanges between teammates that startled him, too. Any mistake could lead to a harsh word, or a confrontation. Stam could speak excellent English but he had to adjust to the constant piss-taking and the slang. What did 'mingin'' mean?

He had stepped out of his comfort zone, and no one made that more plain in the early weeks than Roy Keane. The captain had an initiation rite for any new signing; a test not so much of skill but of mettle. He would put in a thunderous challenge or whack the ball at the new boy and see how they responded. Would they shrink away from confrontation? Would they stand up for themselves? Most of the new arrivals had experienced it. Sheringham told me how Keane had blasted a ball at him on his debut, in the 1997 Charity Shield, as a test. 'Fucking hell, what's that about?!' he thought. Raimond van der Gouw, the reserve goalkeeper, dived to collect the ball in one of his first training sessions at United and felt a painful stamp. He knew who had inflicted it without looking.

In one of Stam's early training sessions, the Irishman fizzed the ball at him with deliberate force and scoffed when he could not control it. Stam was sure that Keane had a problem with him. As he soon learnt, this was nothing unusual. It was simply Keane's way.

11

Roy is back, and with a bang

The Charity Shield, 9 August 1998, a hot day at Wembley. It is particularly stifling for Manchester United, beaten 3–0 by Arsenal in what seems an emphatic continuation of last season's narrative. But one man is furiously determined to make a statement about the campaign to come, even in defeat. Roy Keane has returned with his skull closely shaven: a hard, murderous look, and an approach to match.

Early on, David Beckham (booed by Arsenal fans with every touch) passes loosely to Patrick Vieira in midfield. The ball is not there to be won, but Keane dives in anyway, scything down Vieira's standing leg with ferocious intent, like he has razor blades on his boots. In the commentary gantry, Andy Gray senses the wider significance in that challenge. 'That was bordering on the reckless from Roy Keane, I have to say. He launched at that tackle as if to say, "You might have ruled the roost last year, but there's going to be a bit more of a contest this year."'

One of the great, and still not fully appreciated, individual seasons in Premier League football has just started with Keane announcing that he has returned from serious injury with his competitive fires more intense than ever. Roy is back, and with a bang.

Keane had been at Old Trafford for five years (winning three titles, two Doubles), but it was a different figure, Roy 2.0, who came out into the sunlight that day at Wembley. It had been more than ten months since he had played a competitive game. That is a lot of time to brood – and no one broods like Keane.

The United captain had not been seen in competitive action since he crumpled to the ground at Elland Road in September 1997 as he ran into the Leeds United penalty area. It looked like a freak injury as Keane collapsed in pain, his anterior cruciate knee ligament ruptured, but he knew that it had been self-inflicted.

A few nights earlier, he had gone out with adrenalin still pumping following a 2-2 draw against Chelsea. A few drinks then – ah, why not? – another one. One too many. In the early hours, some fans from Dublin wound him up, which, as Keane would admit, is as difficult as lighting a bonfire with a match and a can of paraffin.

There were fisticuffs and as Keane crawled home past the milk-men starting their rounds he was already envisioning headlines like 'Roy Keane in 4 a.m. bar punch-up!' Rightly, as it turns out. He was still annoyed about the episode as he took to the field at Leeds, and then Alf-Inge Haaland decided to wind him up, too. It was in trying to trip his marker, out of sheer irritation, that Keane injured himself, and very badly.

Dave Fevre, United's physio, had the task of handling Keane as they travelled back across the Pennines to a private hospital in Whalley Range. He recalls watching *Celebrity Squares* during the wait for the specialist and Keane suddenly grabbing the remote control to turn down the volume. 'What the fuck is wrong with me knee?' he demanded to know. Fevre told him his worst fears. 'Well, let's get on with it,' Keane replied.

'And from that minute he was unbelievably compliant,' Fevre explains. 'I could have asked him to jump off a cliff and he'd have been "fine".'

Fevre knew the uncompromising figure he was dealing with – perhaps the least compromising sportsman in history – so he devised a six-day programme of recuperation with one day off for blow-outs. 'I knew Roy would rebel if it was too rigid,' Fevre says. 'I thought there's a fair chance that on the Sunday he might have been out, a bit worse for wear, so on Monday I'd leave an exercise sheet for him at the top of the stairs at the Cliff and let him get on with it. Then we'd pick it up later and work hard through the week. And when Roy commits to something ...'

They would go cycling on mountain bikes around Salford, and swimming at a local David Lloyd gym where Keane would see Manchester City players sitting in the jacuzzi for two hours while he, flippers on, was smashing out lengths in the pool. Keane asked Fevre why the City boys got to relax instead of working out, but he, better than anyone, knew the answer: the difference between winners and also-rans.

For Keane, the recovery after surgery (involving a strip from the patellar tendon used to rebuild the anterior cruciate ligament) was not just physical. Missing almost an entire season brought the scary realisation, as he turned 27, that a football career is a fragile thing. In the endless, lonely days in the gym rebuilding the strength in his leg, Keane set himself a vow never again to take his fitness for granted.

Those heavy binges – 'been on an Irish weekend?' Ferguson would ask pointedly if he saw Keane looking rough and unshaven on a Monday morning – would now be rationed. Reflecting in his first autobiography, Keane said that he returned 'a different person from the lunatic who'd hunted Alfie Haaland'. 'I decided to bury Roy the Playboy,' he noted. 'He might get the odd outing, but the carousing days were – more or less – over.'

That time to look around and think about what mattered in his life and career prompted the famous passage in his memoir in which Keane ranted about wasters in the game, and resolved to crank up his intensity to Spinal Tap's 11.

'Seen from a windowless gym on a winter afternoon, the

game looked like a bad movie, full of spivs, bluffers, bullshitters, hangers-on, media whores and bad actors. If you played your hand correctly you could be a big man without achieving anything ... I had always instinctively hated bullshit – a lot of it associated with my own club. Now my tolerance level was zero. Only one thing counted in football: winning, actually achieving. For that I was hungrier than I'd ever been.'

Fevre saw the application first-hand, not just in Keane returning with his leg as strong as it could be, but with a different, leaner physique. Keane had stripped down his body fat until the veins showed. Even that new haircut, a convict's buzz cut, seemed to show that this was a man down to the bare, necessary essentials.

'I'd worked with a lot of serious injuries and I said to Roy, "I guarantee this will change you as a person, one way or the other,"' Fevre says. 'You look at the way his physique changed. He could be quite podgy at times before that, but he suddenly realised that if he carried five per cent body fat then he was going to be helping himself not just with knee recovery. So that was his whole attitude.'

By way of further proof, Fevre sends over footage of Keane on a Cybex isokinetic dynamometer gym machine at the Cliff, bought by United on the physio's instruction to test the strength in each leg. In the film Keane straightens his leg with manic intensity, as if trying to find the breaking point – not of his knee but the machine.

Keane had worked incredibly hard to get himself ready to launch into the new season, and into Vieira, the opponent he now regarded as his ultimate midfield foe. Fevre was so struck by that tackle, capable of smashing concrete, that he still uses it as a teaching tool more than two decades later. 'When I'm lecturing I show that clip,' he says. 'I was so chuffed because it told me that the knee was as good as it's ever going to be. If it will hold that it will hold anything.'

That season would be Fevre's last at United, before moving to Blackburn Rovers in the summer of 1999. Like everyone who worked closely with Keane, he saw the ferocious, scary side but also tells of another, more hidden, part of this very complex man.

'I was intimidated by Roy when I first started at United, a bit nervous, but you learn as a physio how to deal with different characters. I got very close to Roy during the recovery and you see a different side. The first day I arrived at Blackburn I was told there was a parcel for me. It was from Roy and his wife Theresa, a big box of Waterford crystal and a note to say "thanks for everything you've done for me in the last couple of years". That's the sort of thing that Roy and his missus would do, and people don't see that side of him.'

What they did see was Keane hurling himself at Vieira, ranting and arm-waving at Graham Poll when the referee (rightly) went to admonish him for a dangerous tackle, and refusing to accept that United were going to have another season like the last one even as they lost 3-0 at Wembley on a nightmare day for Jaap Stam, who was pulled all over the place.

Armband back on his bicep – taken from a reluctant Peter Schmeichel, who had to be ordered to surrender it by Alex Ferguson – Keane was back. 'As the season progressed I began to play the best football of my life,' he said. No one could – or would would dare to – disagree.

12

A Roy night out

Teddy Sheringham sits in a kitchen in Essex so big and airy it could house a five-a-side game – in a home called 'Camp Nou', which makes it unique in Chingford – and mentions in passing the awkwardness of his relationship with Roy Keane in their time at United. Pushed to explain, he looks reluctant at first. It is not a story he has told before and there is something in his head that is mindful of picking a public argument with the Irishman. As Alex Ferguson once said, 'The hardest part of Roy's body is his tongue.'

Just when I think Sheringham is about to change the subject, he smiles with a look of 'ah, why not' and starts relating an incident from almost 25 years ago. He remembers it with perfect clarity, as he would given the extraordinary consequences.

As Sheringham tells it, United's first-team squad were on a night out in 1998 to mark the retirement of Eric Harrison, the club's revered youth coach. Keane was still on his year out through injury and liable to those occasional binges. After a solid night of drinking, the players were on the way back to be dropped off in Cheshire's wealthy footballer belt. 'All pretty pissed, not overly, but had a few drinks, not smashed pissed,' Sheringham says. 'All in a minibus coming back to where we got picked up from. I'm sitting behind the driver, Keany was next to the driver. Steve Bruce is next to me [the former United defender still lived in the area], Pallister, Denis [Irwin], a couple of others in there. Bit of banter flying about in the car.'

And then, out of nowhere, the mood darkened. 'All of a sudden, Keany said, "Why don't you fuck off back to London in your fucking red Ferrari and your penthouse?"' Sheringham recalls. 'I went "Eh?" And he says, "Yeah, fuck off back to London."'

The row quickly escalated. 'I'm like, "Are you coming for me, Keany? Why are you coming for me, you Paddy? Fucking what?" And he went "fuck off", and he goes on: "Fucking red Ferrari, penthouse ..." And then he jumped round, still with his bad leg, got me by the tie, pulled me towards him, grappling with him. Suddenly everyone's going "what's going on?" and pulling us apart.'

The rest of the players had to stop a brawl erupting in the minibus. Separating the two men, they told Sheringham to leave it. They said that Keane was drunk and would forget about it by the morning. It was not the first time they had seen the Irishman erupt without warning, especially in drink. 'And I'm saying, "No, what's going on, Keany? Let's have it out. Why are you snapping at me for? I haven't said anything to you."'

Sheringham and Keane were meant to be dropped off at the same place, but suddenly that did not seem such a smart idea in case it all kicked off in the street. When the minibus door slid open, Keane stomped away. Sheringham headed home, adrenalin pumping. He knew what he was dealing with. The pair had been awkward teammates at Nottingham Forest. Sheringham has vague memories of a niggly exchange once when he was visiting his mate Tony Cascarino at the Republic of Ireland camp and Keane had taken offence. He knew Keane was not the type to back down. He also knew Keane could hit people.

'I couldn't sleep that night thinking, "It's going to go off as soon as I get into training, it's going to go off." I've seen Roy in the gym so I know it can go off. So I go in thinking, "Get yourself ready." I actually go in to change thinking, "I'm ready for him." You have your own cubicle so I was either next to Keany, or maybe the one after, and as I walked in, he's there doing his shoes up. I walked in past him and I'm thinking he's going to get up and boot me in the face. I'm thinking "here we go".'

Sheringham braced himself for the fight that he thought was inevitable. No soft touch himself – he did once play for Millwall, after all – he knew that, at the very least, he was going to have to stand up for himself in the dressing room. Gunfight at the O.K. Corral, but with studs on.

'And Keany gets up and walks out. He didn't say a word to me. He didn't say a word to me for the next three-and-a-half years.'

Sorry, what? You were teammates until 2001. Keane must have said something in all that time?

'Nothing.'

Sheringham sees my incredulity but insists that 'nothing' really did mean nada, zilch, zero from the captain. Not a word in meetings, in the dressing room, or out on the pitch.

'I was always a good talker on the pitch whoever I was around up front, Coley or anyone. "Man on," watching the centre-back. With Keany, I've got good eyes for whatever he's planning in midfield. "Watch yourself. Get up early, protect yourself." I'd always give him good information. But after that, not a word. On the pitch he didn't say anything to me. Nothing socially for the next four years, not even in the dressing room.'

As he tells this story, and I express my bemusement, Sheringham is quick to add that he thinks Keane was the key figure of the 1998-99 season. No one was more vital. Just by his presence, Keane could change the mood and, in this season after his injury, that meant bringing a unique intensity around the training ground. The captain was talismanic.

'There were so many great players at United but if Keany didn't play we weren't the same team,' Sheringham says. 'If he wasn't in training, it wasn't the same training session. If you put him in, he'd be snarling and snapping at you on your team. And if you put him in the opposition, he'd be having a go at you. There's competitive people and ultra-competitive people and he was just on it. If it was the time when he'd come off the drink, at a time when he was a bit more hyped up, it made it intense in every moment that you were in and around the ground. Players knew if he had the hump with you, even just in the canteen. He might say something to them like "I see you're the first to get your fucking lunch, eh." It could be anyone, Jesper, Yorkie, he didn't care. It made it a very intense place to be.'

Sheringham did not feel uniquely singled out by Keane. As he and other players acknowledge, tension between the captain and Peter Schmeichel was never far from the surface. The goalkeeper was a big presence, in every respect, and another dressing-room alpha. 'Peter would put himself up there to test the situation but Keany still ruled the roost,' Sheringham says. 'Two big personalities who don't want to back down. It would be nice if everyone gets on but that was obvious from an early stage that that wasn't going to happen.'

Even all these years later, Sheringham is perplexed by Keane's silent treatment. Long after they had finished playing, the two men bumped into each other at a charity match. Keane shook hands as if nothing had happened, which only made it even more baffling.

'I'd always loved Keany. Loved him as a man, what he stands for. He's very outspoken at the moment and everyone loves that, but I know him as a person. I love his drive, his leadership, funny lad as well, comically. So, I was disappointed that that had happened because I'd never slagged him off. I didn't want to be upset and fall out but that was the way he was going to be.

He's obviously got a real problem with me. Everyone else at the time was saying, "Don't worry, he's a fucking idiot." I couldn't understand it.'

Team spirit? As we will discover, it is – like Keane himself – a very complex thing.

13

Character is fate #1

Manchester United 2 Leicester City 2, 15 August 1998

It is deep into injury time on the opening day of the 1998-99 Premier League season, and the story of the campaign – of this book – is being given its first trial run. Here you go, world, see how you like this for a plot ...

The essentials are all there. United are trailing, 2-1 down to Martin O'Neill's feisty Leicester City. On the sidelines Ferguson is pointing at his watch as if he – and only he – has the definite take on time. 'My watch is never wrong,' he growls afterwards. He demands control of everything at Old Trafford, even the clock.

A tepid United have had to claw back from 2-0 down, to goals scored by Emile Heskey and Tony Cottee. Teddy Sheringham has grabbed a lifeline, coming off the bench to divert a David Beckham shot in the 79th minute, but it is all getting a little desperate. Can United somehow rescue a point?

In the third minute of added time, when all hope seems gone, Muzzy Izzet fouls Paul Scholes 10 yards outside the box, just left of centre. It is Beckham's range. You might want to guess what happens next.

In the season that will define whether he can endure playing in England, on an afternoon where he had felt riddled with nerves before kick-off not knowing the reaction he will face (incessant cheers and jeers depending on allegiance), he places the ball down and sizes up the opportunity, demanding the wall is fully 10 yards back.

Beckham talks of an eerie silence before he takes that kick, which only heightens the roar that follows the arcing flight of the ball over the wall and into the bottom corner. As Old Trafford erupts, Beckham runs to the corner flag, arms outstretched, and then spins around with a pirouette of pure delight. His teammates run over to mob him, knowing the significance of the moment given all that he has been enduring.

In the broader scheme of things, it is a home point from a malfunctioning United team that requires plenty of improvement if it is to challenge for the top honours. And, yet, Ferguson is looking not at performance but character. 'I believe the identity of the new team was revealed today,' he explains. 'People at the match watched unfolding before them the kind of resilience and refusal to accept defeat that we will need.'

There is work to be done on the details of the narrative, but it is already showing promise.

14

The Cliff

A Monday morning at the Cliff late in 2021. Two groundsmen are sitting on lawnmowers, cutting the lush grass. They are the only people here inside the old training ground in Salford, but to look across the pitch is to sense the ghosts. This is where Duncan Edwards trained and Bobby Charlton honed his cannonball shots; where Lou Macari and Martin Buchan sought to revive a grand club in the '70s and '80s; and where the Treble team came together, the last United squad to tackle and pass and to prepare themselves for greatness on this turf.

It is strange to drive through the open gates one quiet morning to a place where so much history was shaped and to see it so small and empty, almost derelict; to think that this quiet corner of Salford is where I once ogled Ryan Giggs's new Aston Martin DB7 and Teddy Sheringham's bright red Ferrari 355 in the tight car park; chased Eric Cantona in vain for a word; hid among the autograph hunters in the hope that Alex Ferguson could not see me while I tried to snatch a few minutes with a friendly player (thank you, Steve Bruce).

United's homely base since 1938 never could sustain a modern giant of a club, but something was lost in 2000 when they moved to a vast new complex – not just that tangible sense of history, the link with the past, but a precious intimacy too.

In Ferguson's time, a sign on the main building warned that there was 'absolutely no admission without the manager's permission', but the Cliff was a world away from the modern Fort Knox complex with checkpoints preventing fans, and journalists, from getting within half a mile – and all the better for it. Throughout the '90s, the big red metal gates would open at the end of training and fans would loiter around the car park, or we would come in for the media briefings/diatribes with Ferguson in the lobby area of a building which was more like a municipal gym than the heartbeat of one of the great sporting institutions on the planet. It was basic, but there was a sense of proximity, of human interaction. We were allowed to breathe in the same air.

In 1998, a visitor would arrive to find Ferguson upstairs in his office soon after 7 a.m., rifling through the newspapers, eating his cereal and toast while the smell of bacon wafted out of the canteen. His lair had a huge glass window overlooking the training pitch from which he could observe everything, banging on the glass and using a crooked finger occasionally to summon a miscreant player.

This was the office where Paul Ince once pulled a gun on him after a bust-up (surely the bravest prank ever played on the United manager), and where a teenage Ryan Giggs was sent packing after asking if he could have a club car. 'Fucking car?! You don't deserve a club bike!' Ferguson shouted, as Giggs's teammates erupted with laughter outside.

The manager had a TV and video player for going through tapes of games; bookshelves crammed with yearbooks and United programmes; framed photos, posing with Jack Charlton and with Bob Paisley. A sign was pinned on the wall, where it could not be missed, to celebrate his Glaswegian heritage: 'HACUMFIGOVAN.' There was even a bath where Matt Busby had once soaked after training, although Ron Atkinson had preferred to find room for a sun-bed.

In Ferguson's time, that office was pure football. The Cliff was a place for work and the building oozed ambition and competition. Upstairs was a school-style canteen, gym, coach's room and physio area with three treatment beds. Downstairs, the players were on top of each other in three dressing rooms for first team, reserves and youth team. In 1998, the main dressing room still had a big communal bath. 'You wouldn't want to be last into that,' Nicky Butt recalls with a laugh.

It was a primitive base. Stam was startled that such an elite team was working in facilities which were, at best, 'archaic'. Jesper Blomqvist had trained at AC Milan's Milanello HQ and could not believe what he found. Yet there is something magical about the place which still makes players nostalgic. Butt was not alone in talking wistfully about this training ground located at the smart end of Lower Broughton Road, surrounded by plush detached houses.

'Me and Scholesy would get off a bus aged 16 to walk up to the Cliff and we'd have the England captain, Bryan Robson, driving past and picking us up in his big Mercedes,' Butt says. 'We were right on top of each other and that could only help how we developed. You're seeing the first-team players, how they behave, how they train.'

As someone who coached the United youth teams at their 21st-century base, Butt has mixed feelings about the way that clubs have built ever-bigger training HQs, like industrial complexes. 'You see these academy centres now built miles from the main training ground, or the youth players put in a different building out of the way. They might have the best facilities but what about learning the ethos? The Cliff was old-fashioned but it was a great place for us to learn how to be United players. It's like one team is passing the baton to the next. We'd seen the '94 team, what it took for them to win. We'd see them in the corridors or cleaning the training ground, just to be sitting on the nearest table in the canteen.'

Butt and his contemporaries had learnt the ropes here the hard way, enduring initiation rites from Hughes, Ince and Robson but also absorbing the ferociously competitive edge of Ferguson's first great United team. They would see Ferguson in the corridors, and learn the ways of this domineering leader. 'Then it was our turn to show what it means to be a United player and pass it on to the Rooneys and the rest,' Butt adds.

Ferguson knew the history, and savoured it, but felt the club had outgrown the Cliff. He wanted more privacy too, which he certainly found in more than 100 acres of secluded land in Carrington, less than ten miles from Old Trafford, heading out of the city into green fields, which United began developing in 1999. For the start of the new century, United would move to that new base – eventually to become the Aon Training Complex – built with an initial budget of £14 million, which became more like £60 million over more than a decade of development.

The Cliff was more recently used by United's women's side and for community football. It still has an indoor pitch and the grass where the greats trained, though the main building is empty, almost ghostly. To return there is to appreciate what Peter Schmeichel meant when he said, 'What's amazing is that possibly the biggest result ever in English football history was achieved from those facilities.'

They seem very outmoded, but Schmeichel, too, felt the magnetic, magical pull of the old place when he went back for a meeting post-retirement. By then, he had no wish to play again at Old Trafford, the glory days long gone, but he did have a hankering to pull on the tracksuit and gloves one more time and throw himself around in the mud at the Cliff. Old Trafford brought clamour and crowds but also pressure and expectation; training was where they spent their happiest days, competing among themselves, winding each other up, spurring each other on.

15

The chairman

European football leads to some glamorous locations. You can also end up in Lodz – or 'Woodge' as we are tickled to discover that Poland's third-largest city is pronounced. It is an insalubrious venue for United's Champions League qualifier (punishment for finishing second to Arsenal) with little drama expected – until a few of us go for a drink with Martin Edwards, the club chairman, in one of the city's basement bars.

Some of us have established a decent relationship with Edwards because he is, generally, accessible and helpful. He takes a phone call, not always to give you the inside track but certainly to tell a reporter when he is about to write something that will be embarrassingly wrong. Socially, he can be lively company and says he will meet us for a drink when, perhaps, we will glean a few titbits of information about the manager's contract talks or the summer's transfer business.

I cannot remember if Edwards did divulge any secrets that evening and, in any case, what was more notable was what happened after he departed. A couple of lubricated fans wandered over, demanding to know why we had been mixing with 'that c*** Edwards'. One called him 'a fucking traitor'. As journalists we occasionally get it in the neck from punters – 'you're press and you know you're scum,' fans of Leeds United once serenaded a group of us outside the San Siro – but, this time, it is not our presence but that of Edwards that has caused grave offence. We explain we just want a quiet drink. The fans are not appeased. We make our excuses and scarper.

This is how it is for Edwards. United are in the midst of the most successful period in the club's history, yet among a hefty number of supporters (arguably the most devoted hardcore if they have paid to come to Lodz), the chairman is hated. Just to be seen with Edwards can be a dangerous business.

'No man in English football has probably had more abuse heaped on him than Martin Edwards,' Mihir Bose wrote in *Manchester Unlimited*, published in 1999. Bose, a former sports writer and broadcaster, is a defender of Edwards, which distinguishes him from most historians of United. Jim White, then a sportswriter for the *Guardian* and a prominent United supporter, scathingly described Edwards as 'the Ringo Starr of football' – the one without the talent who got to be rich and famous thanks to the brilliance of others. 'Martin Edwards is the luckiest man. This thing has happened despite him not because of him,' White wrote. 'He is only interested in making money.'

Sitting at a dining table in his beautifully situated Cheshire home, Edwards seems as unperturbed by the debate as ever. He always was remarkably unruffled by any amount of scorn from the media or terraces, and he never sought PR advice to change perceptions. 'Can you imagine Winston Churchill appointing numerous people to write his speeches?' he asks, despairing of dissembling modern politicians.

Edwards did it his way, untroubled by what was being said or written about him, and avoiding the media manipulations of many in his position. 'Once you lie your credibility has gone. I think that's upbringing, that is,' he says.

The vast wealth helped to insulate him, but so does a record of success. As Edwards talks, behind him on the wall is a framed photo of the celebratory bus parade in 1968, with the European Cup on the top deck. Edwards' father Louis, United chairman before him, stands there proudly with Matt Busby and the players. Next to it is the 1999 version signed by Alex Ferguson at the conclusion of a spectacularly triumphant decade. Yet still Edwards knows the question that is coming. 'I wasn't popular, was I?' he asks rhetorically.

If football was any ordinary business, it would not make sense. During Edwards' time in charge, United's annual profits grew from £210,000 in 1980 to almost £40 million in 2003. The club's value increased 400-fold from £2 million to £800 million. That is huge success by any normal measure; given football's history of profligacy and mismanagement, those numbers were miraculous. But football is not a regular business and Edwards grew fantastically rich through his ownership, which some fans saw as a crime. He tried to sell the club on several occasions, which was also an offence (the same fans who wanted him out would also object to him selling up).

He is not about to say sorry for any of it – not that an apology would have made any difference – and he can keep coming back to his stewardship of the era which made United a modern super-club. There was serendipity in that, but also a need for someone to make hard decisions, and Edwards never ducked those.

When it came to chasing popularity, he was not bothered about chumminess with managers – certainly not with Ferguson. Edwards backed him through difficult times in the 1980s, but he was never a pushover even in the face of an angry Glaswegian. Edwards felt his father had grown too close to Tommy Docherty, which inevitably made life uncomfortable when he had to sack him. 'I don't think it necessarily works, a chairman and manager being too close. It's short term because as soon as somebody gets the sack, they fall out. We were never bosom pals, Alec and I, but I always respected his ability and his achievements.

'I supported him on buys if I thought they made sense. If it's not right you've got to step and make your point and that's all I ever did. So, the strength was there, and I don't care what people say, whether it was a good or bad relationship – it doesn't matter. What matters is are we winning, are we losing, are we winning trophies? Are we satisfying the public? That's what counts.'

No amount of trophies on his watch seemed to buy goodwill for Edwards. As Andy Mitten, editor of the popular *United We Stand* fanzine, put it, Edwards' cross to bear was being 'the former rugby-playing rich Cheshire kid into whose lap fell the greatest football club in the world'. Almost selling the club to Michael Knighton for £10 million in 1989, a fraction of what it would be worth just a few years later, became a stick to beat Edwards, though it is not as if others formed a queue to grab a bargain. Even when United followed Tottenham Hotspur's lead with a flotation in 1991 – the club valued at £47 million – and Edwards became a seriously rich man, the public offer did not sell out.

The unprecedented growth of the '90s changed everything, and it was Edwards who ensured that United rode that wave better than any club in England. By February 1999, a survey by Deloitte Touche ranked it the richest club in the world, with a turnover of £87.9 million, which dwarfed all of their European rivals, including Real Madrid and Barcelona. 'We were voted the number one club in the world and also voted the number one franchise in the world, so the richest sporting club in the world. That took in all the American football teams and basketball teams so that was quite an achievement in itself as well,' Edwards says.

But no one was going to thank him for that – especially not after they found out that he was in secret talks to sell United in a deal that could transform not just the club but the entire English game.

16

Sold!

Once upon a time in 1878, it began as Newton Heath Lancashire and Yorkshire Railway Football Club, established by the workers to escape the drudgery of their daily toil. Playing on the mud of North Road, next to the new railway line that served steel and chemical works during Manchester's Victorian industrial expansion, the football club started as a way to relieve a hard week's labour. As competitive fun.

In 1892, Newton Heath joined the Football League which had been founded in Manchester four years earlier (walk through Piccadilly Gardens in the city centre to the corner of Mosley Street and Market Street, crane your neck and you can see a plaque high on the wall of what was then the Royal Hotel, now a Santander Bank, to mark the historic gathering. Bustling along, few notice).

As interest in football grew, there was kudos in being on the team. Crowds gathered, bringing social elevation to a player. A job would be found for those with talent and, soon, extra income. From its earliest days, this was professional, a business – sometimes well run, in other periods rather less so – but also an institution that served a community and bound it together. What was Manchester United for by the end of the 20th century? To win football matches? To entertain? To make profits as a public listed company?

Perhaps the point demonstrated one Sunday morning in

September 1998, when a sensational story broke about United being sold to a media tycoon, was that you could make the club whatever you wanted it to be if you were rich enough.

No one knows who leaked the story on 6 September that Rupert Murdoch's BSkyB were in talks to buy United, only that it represented a hell of a scoop for the *Sunday Telegraph*. The front page revealed that the United board had been in talks for more than two months and were ready to hand the club over to the Australian media mogul. It was a deal that threatened to change not just the path of Manchester United but the entire trajectory of English football.

Clandestine negotiations had been going on in the background since late June when Mark Booth, the American chief executive of BSkyB, invited Martin Edwards to his offices in London on the pretext of talking about broadcasting, specifically a proposal for matches on pay-per-view. When Edwards and Maurice Watkins, a lawyer and United director, turned up at BSkyB's Isleworth headquarters on 1 July, they almost choked on their smoked salmon when Booth admitted he had invited them in under false pretences. BSkyB wanted to buy United.

'We were in the middle of lunch,' Edwards says. 'It was a shock, and you think, "bloody hell".' As soon as Edwards left BSkyB, he made contact with Roland Smith, chairman of United's PLC board, and said that they needed to meet immediately.

'Roland thought positively about it,' Edwards says. 'If these people from Sky come in, our financial worries are probably over. We're doing all right now but we'd be doing even better if we can afford some of the best players in the world. I just thought that this was a way that would have made Manchester United much stronger. And I still to this day wonder, if Sky had taken over, where would we be? Would we have been competing more with Abu Dhabi and Abramovich?'

Others would soon start deliberating the downsides, like whether the country's most successful club would become uncatchable with Murdoch's backing, and the breakdown of competitive balance in the league and collective bargaining. This deal had the potential to blow a hole in the unity of the Premier League. But Edwards could only see the benefits, including £80 million for his 14 per cent stake and the chance to stay on as chairman. Booth was happy to keep the current directors. BSkyB were not planning to transform the club but to use it, as Murdoch put it, as a 'battering ram' in the burgeoning satellite TV world and to cover all bases by not just having the main broadcast rights to the Premier League but control of its biggest club.

If pay-TV matches were going to take off, and they were being discussed, United would be the biggest draw. If there was going to be a European Super League – and, in July, it had emerged that the Milan-based Media Partners had been talking to the leading 16 clubs – this was an insurance policy. The move was strategic, rather than financial. Even if United were that very rare beast, a profitable football club, £27 million annual profit on a business valued at £575 million by the initial Murdoch offer was relatively small-fry when BSkyB alone had recently announced its own pre-tax profits for the year to June of £314 million, up 22 per cent.

The deal mirrored Murdoch's strategy in the United States, where he owned the Los Angeles Dodgers baseball team as well as the television rights to the sport through his Fox network. He also had stakes in the Los Angeles Lakers and New York Knicks basketball teams. The story was both a colossal shock and the logical extension of a business plan.

'You have to be interested in the price because you're not just talking on behalf of yourself, you're talking on behalf of the other shareholders and directors. I would have been a beneficiary but I honestly wasn't bothered about it. I had enough money even if it was half that. So, it wasn't the money. It was more what I thought Sky could do for us and I honestly thought that with Sky behind us we would have been stronger and independent.'

Edwards' claims about his motivation will not wash with many United fans, given the personal riches he would make from the deal, which was as much as anyone had ever made from the sale of an English football club. But he was right that the price on offer required that he take it to the board and shareholders.

United shares were trading around 157p when Booth expressed interest. By the time Edwards and Watkins sat down with a startled board of directors shortly before the 1998 Charity Shield, they had haggled the offer up to 217.5p per share, which was almost a 40 per cent premium. There was no way the institutional shareholders were turning that down.

On 6 August, Roland Smith told the board that a formal offer had been sent via fax, though it remained so secret that even Alex Ferguson had no inkling. There had been discussions about whether to include him, and to get him on side, but Edwards blocked that idea, fearing that Ferguson might not keep the secret and, worse still, be hostile. Edwards was going to inform the manager when they were ready to go public, and then the news broke. It was a story that dominated bulletins for the coming days – vying for the lead item on the front pages with Kenneth Starr reporting on President Clinton's shenanigans with Monica Lewinsky in the Oval Office.

The coverage was about more than the fate of the biggest club in the country, but the direction of football; whether it was all about big business, and too in thrall to television. A twist on the same debate that had begun in the '60s, when many predicted that putting matches on television would destroy attendances, and still rages now about whether paying punters are less important than armchair viewers on the other side of the world.

As Simon Barnes wrote in *The Times* (cover price of 30p), the Murdoch offer was one of those crystallising moments when the game was forced to face up to modernisation, to change, which was always unsettling in a sport which was deeply nostalgic and conservative. Football has always wanted the best of all worlds – the benefits of modern life (e.g., grounds that are not death traps) but also to remain rooted in comforting traditions.

As Barnes noted, 'Time passes, shock. Things change, horror. The fact is that the proposed Murdoch deal rubs in this difficult aspect of life to an altogether unacceptable degree. But it has been coming since the first papapa POM papapa pompom of the *Match of the Day* theme tune was poured into the porches of our ears.'

English football enjoyed the riches from TV, which attracted stars from around the world, and television had made football more wealthy, glamorous, fashionable and popular than ever. But there were limits, and Murdoch's offer was severely testing them.

To read most of the coverage back now is to be struck by how there was an expectation that the deal would probably happen, whatever the objections. The Office for Fair Trading was obliged to inspect the paperwork, but lawyers for BSkyB and United were bullish, albeit as lawyers would be in the circumstances.

In the *Sunday Times*, Hugh McIlvanney wrote about the inevitability of such a deal as soon as the club had floated eight years earlier. Even in a Murdoch-owned title, he was given the freedom to call it a 'regrettable' move, but it was also just another step in the 'money-driven revolution that has been transforming the national game throughout the Nineties'.

'Football has long been ripe for a commercial explosion, since it is one of the few areas of business that give scope for the legal exploitation of addiction. Fans, by definition, are largely captive customers. That is why talk of a Manchester United supporters' protest solid enough to make a significant dent in the club's revenue was always fanciful. Addicts don't boycott the stuff that feeds their habit.'

But Edwards was not about to have an easy ride. When he stepped off a train at Euston on the morning of 7 September for a fraught board meeting to push through the deal, he walked into a scrum of photographers and news crews and a few fans shouting 'Judas'. Speaking to Edwards that week, he knew that this was a hell of a storm that he would have to endure, though, typically, he was not about to be knocked off course.

As he told me then, 'I know I will be vilified but there are business aspects to consider. If I had rejected it, they could simply have come in with a hostile bid. If I had turned down the offer and the company had not reached the share price within two years, we could have been sued. If I woke up suddenly one morning and found out Sky had bought Liverpool or Arsenal, as a Manchester United fan that would have worried me. It would have given them that extra competitive edge.

'All I say to people now is before you string me up, give things a chance. People wanted to string me up at the time of the flotation and it went well. Now, I am being castigated for this. I believe it is in the best interests. I have been a director for 28 years, my family have been involved for more than 40. I am not about to do anything that destroys the health and tradition of this club. If I do then I deserve to be strung up. But give me a chance first. Let it run and then judge me.'

17

Who plays left-back for Manchester United?

Judging by his mischievous grin, Greg Dyke takes very obvious pride in his role in the resistance against Rupert Murdoch's takeover. 'They said, "it's effing Dyke that's blocking it,"' he says, beaming.

He is in his 70s now, but Dyke still loves to be disobedient and disruptive. He relishes life in the thick of the news. He enjoys a reputation for telling it straight, like the day he became director general of the BBC in 2000 and, in his first address, instructed the staff to 'cut the crap and make it happen'.

Murdoch's bid for United was exactly the type of situation in which Dyke revelled. 'You're right there in the middle when this ridiculous drama was taking place,' he says. From his seat around United's boardroom table as a director, his mission was to make sure that Murdoch's takeover failed. He was the opposition on the inside.

As chief executive of Pearson Television, and formerly in that role at ITV, Dyke had been brought on to the United board because of his extensive experience in broadcasting. Any smart football club needed to be attuned to how the TV market was shifting, and Dyke had been in the negotiations at the launch of the Premier League. 'They brought me on to the board because

I knew about television and TV rights and then they took no notice,' Dyke says.

When it came to the Murdoch offer, Dyke decided from the start that he was against it. He was not quite a lone voice on the United board. David Gill, then finance director, shared his reservations but could resist only for as long as was pragmatic given that he was a paid employee. Dyke's version of events does not paint Roland Smith, Edwards or the rest of the board in the best light, saying they could not wait to push through the deal.

'Roland said we'd had a great run, but this could be coming to an end. They should take it. Martin was determined to sell from the beginning. He quite clearly wanted to get some money out and he had tried to sell it to Michael Knighton and a couple of other times before. It was funny watching Maurice Watkins, who was much more concerned about keeping his seats whether he voted for or against it. It was weird how the rest of the board were quite happy to go along with it.'

Dyke's antipathy to Murdoch was not yet full-blown – he would later go on to talk of the media mogul undermining democracy and the British political system – but he says there were so many reasons to be highly sceptical, including a wider, existential threat for the English game if Murdoch owned the richest and most successful club as well as the broadcast rights to the league through BSkyB. 'I thought it would break up the Premier League,' he says.

He felt it was terrible for United, too, if the club became the subsidiary of a media corporation. 'When I talked to Booth, I said, "You're not doing this because you want to own Manchester United, it's because you want to own their TV rights." I went out for dinner in the middle of it all with [Howard Davies] who ran the LSE, used to be deputy governor of the Bank of England, a massive Manchester City fan. He said, "I hope it goes through because United was created as a brand because of Munich and it will be destroyed by Murdoch. There will be hatred."'

Taking separate legal advice, Dyke was told that his sole responsibility as a director was to the shareholders. His best means of resistance was to insist that Murdoch's offer massively undervalued the club and especially its future TV income. His argument was that collective broadcast rights had already shown significant growth – around £60 million a year from BSkyB in the first five-year deal with the Premier League in 1992 to almost £170 million per season by 1998 – and that the value would keep increasing. He was certainly correct on that call.

BSkyB had rung before the board meeting on Monday 7 September to increase the offer to 230p per share (a premium of more than 45 per cent on the trading price when the news had leaked). Dyke insisted on more. 'Greg, if we lose this deal because of you then I shall sue you,' Edwards told him as tempers became strained. Dyke laughed it off, then and now. 'Martin didn't know anything about company law. I said to Roland, "You've got the majority of the board so why not go with that?" But he wanted it to be unanimous.'

When Murdoch's offer increased to 240p per share, valuing United at £623 million, the United board agreed that it was as far as they could hope to push the price. A fax was sent to BSkyB accepting it, signed by all, including a reluctant Dyke. To maintain a sense of resistance, he suggested giving away all directors' profits to charity, to the homeless, or a children's cause. Dyke had a lot fewer shares than Edwards and so, on that issue too, he ended up a solitary voice.

'I didn't want to make a profit out of it at all as I didn't like it, so any gain I was going to make on the shares I was going to give to a children's hospital. I couldn't see any advantage to [Murdoch's takeover]. I knew the fans would hate it. They've ended up with the Glazers and they hate that.'

*

In the offices of the *Mirror*, editor Piers Morgan was working out how to block the deal. He had two reasons, personal and professional. As an Arsenal fan, he feared United becoming stronger than ever with Murdoch's backing. As a newspaper editor, there was the risk that all the scoops about the biggest club in the world would end up in his main rival, *The Sun*, owned by Murdoch.

The front pages revealed just how polarising this deal could be, as *The Sun* declared 'Gold Trafford' with a promise of riches to improve the team. Its readers were told that the deal would lead to 'an amazing spending revolution. It will give manager Alex Ferguson a fortune to splash out on the world's best players and make the Reds the most valuable team on Earth.' By contrast, the *Mirror* ran a 'Red Devil' headline above a picture of Murdoch with horns superimposed.

Morgan hatched plans to embarrass those involved, and detected the weak spot in the involvement of Booth, as an American. With smart news instincts, Morgan sent a reporter, Graham Brough, with one specific question to ask Booth in front of the TV cameras at the press conference to announce the deal, 'Who plays left-back for Manchester United?' Kansas-born Booth did not have a clue. He floundered, saying that 'football is not my area of expertise' before someone dived in to try to spare his embarrassment. Too late.

'Our apparent madness was a highly effective counter campaign, which basically revolved around one question at a press conference,' Morgan says. 'It was a very deliberate question aimed at what was going on here culturally which was an American–run company, run by an American chief executive trying to get his hands on our big football team.'

One day, that Americanisation in English football would become perfectly normal. But as Booth stumbled over that question, Morgan was watching gleefully in the office. 'We'd ruined their whole day,' he says.

*

'It was a hot potato. Murdoch is Murdoch, football is football. Biggest broadcaster, main club.' Inside 10 Downing Street, Alastair Campbell was busy trying to work out what this all meant, not just for English football but for Tony Blair's government. Would a Blair administration block the deal when Murdoch had thrown his considerable clout behind New Labour; when Peter Mandelson, the Trade and Industry Secretary with oversight on the takeover, was friends with Rupert's daughter Elizabeth; when even the spin doctors were close contacts, given that Tim Allan, director of corporate communications at BSkyB, had recently been a Downing Street press officer?

Caught unawares when the news broke, Campbell's first call was to Alex Ferguson. 'I was getting calls but I knew nothing about it and so I called Alex but he'd gone to play golf. He'd been kept out of the loop.' Campbell insists that there was never a sense of expectation of automatically approving the deal. 'We were very clear from the very start that there are organisations, and processes in law. I don't remember feeling any pressure and Tony was clear to stay out of it and let the Monopolies and Mergers deal with it.'

By 17 September, the Office of Fair Trading (OFT) had launched an inquiry, inviting submissions as to whether the deal should be referred to the Monopolies and Mergers Commission. The OFT would report to Mandelson by the following month. In the *Guardian*, Hugo Young questioned whether the government could be trusted to rule on the deal given 'the social and professional entwinements between the Labour high command and the Murdoch minions'. Campbell insists that he was sceptical from the start whether the deal would go through given that it could undermine the collective bargaining on which the Premier League depended. But Murdoch had a habit of getting his way.

'Dear Mr Murdoch you come down from on high, you even bought up the air waves, you control all our sky.

Dear Mr Murdoch you do it with zing, at lowering standards you're really the king.'

They are, we can safely conclude, not the finest lyrics ever uttered by a member of the rock group Queen, though, in defence of Roger Taylor, they made more sense than 'Scaramouch, Scaramouch, will you do the Fandango!'

Count this among the more unusual protests against Murdoch's takeover of United as Taylor, the Queen drummer, adapted a version of his latest solo single 'Pressure On' for a special edition in support of the Independent Manchester United Supporters Association (IMUSA). It was not Taylor's only contribution to the campaign. When an anonymous music star donated £10,000 for the hire of Bridgewater Hall in Manchester for a rally of anti-Murdoch supporters within days of the takeover attempt becoming public, the assumption was that it was Mick Hucknall of Simply Red, a renowned United fan. But it was Taylor's money.

The drummer was not a United supporter but had been persuaded to chip in by his son, Rufus, who was. 'He doesn't feel that the commercialisation of sport is a healthy thing at all,' a spokesman for Taylor explained. 'He is trying to protect the sport in the interests of the fans.'

Among those fans, it was a curious mixture of forces that set up against Murdoch, confirming that United's appeal reached every corner of cultural life. A rock multimillionaire mixed with a Mancunian hardcore while opposition would also come from lawyers, journalists, accountants and from within City institutions. 'It was as much Oxbridge as Stalybridge,' Jim White, the sportswriter, noted.

White was an outspoken campaigner himself along with Michael Crick, the broadcast journalist. Both took to the dais for that Bridgewater Hall gathering and spoke passionately against Murdoch and his deal-makers. 'Mark Booth probably believes that Best, Law and Charlton are a firm of Manhattan attorneys and that the Neville brothers are a blues band,' Crick told the assembly. Nice line.

Crick set up Shareholders United Against Murdoch (SUAM) with Richard Hytner, boss of an advertising agency, to try to stop Murdoch seizing overall control. They mailed every one of the 28,000 shareholders. While they had little hope with the City institutions, around 23 per cent of the club was in the hands of individuals.

Then there was IMUSA, which had been founded in 1995 as a reaction to the club's growing commercialism, and the demand that fans sit down during matches. It was as if the group had been formed for a day like this. 'Rupert Murdoch will rape and pillage the club,' Andy Walsh, its spokesman, told the media. Fans Against Rupert's Takeover (FART, obviously) was also formed, while Holders of Season Tickets Against Gross Exploitation (HOSTAGE) had been around for a while campaigning against increases in ticket prices.

If it all sounds a little like Monty Python's 'The People's Front of Judea' and 'The Judean People's Front', there was no doubting the passion, but the scale of outrage was questionable. Fewer than 1,000 turned out at Bridgewater Hall for IMUSA's big meeting, with blocks of empty seats. The *Manchester Evening News* reported that it was a fervent meeting, but 'a tiny fraction of United's regular 55,000 home attendance and a drop in the ocean of the club's reputed four million supporters worldwide'. The speakers were preaching to the converted and some were not optimistic, fearing that the battle had been lost in 1991 when United was floated on the Stock Exchange.

Which group represented the 'average' United fan, or a majority view? If the home game against Charlton Athletic on the day that the deal was announced was anything to go by, apathy was the overriding sentiment. There were a few placards, and IMUSA leaflets handed out, but no mass demonstration. This was not like the anti-Glazer protests which flared up in 2010, and not even close to anti-Super League demonstrations in 2021.

The most notable protest I recall from the night came from a male streaker who ran onto the pitch, with 'Takeover My Arse' scrawled on his back with an arrow pointing helpfully down to where the sun does not shine. A crack in the empire? There was a devoted core of Murdoch opponents but, as far as many fans were concerned, one of the world's richest men could have the club provided he used his wealth to buy the biggest superstars.

18

What if . . .

Patrick Kluivert last night signed for Manchester United as the spearhead of a new strike force.

The Dutch forward joined in a £9 million deal that looks certain to lead to Andy Cole being sold in a major shake-up. Already a Champions League winner with Ajax, Kluivert will be expected to score the goals that finally end United's 31-year quest for European glory. Last night a thrilled Alex Ferguson predicted great things for his new signing. 'I'm delighted because we are talking about one of the best young centre-forwards in the world,' the United manager said. 'Patrick has already won in Europe and he is just the striker we need to go all the way.'

Ferguson believes United's attack has become lightweight, and he has previously chased after Alan Shearer, Gabriel Batistuta and Ronaldo. At 6ft 2ins, Kluivert will bring a physical presence as well as goals. His arrival leaves a major question mark over Cole after three-and-a-half seasons at Old Trafford which have included two titles but also spells of injury and low confidence.

Meanwhile, Tottenham Hotspur have made a bid for Ole Gunnar Solskjær, with the United board happy to sell the Norwegian for £5.5 million to recoup funds. The signing of Kluivert also puts in doubt the pursuit of Dwight Yorke, the Aston Villa striker. Ferguson is keen on Yorke but it is hard to see the United board sanctioning a move unless Cole and Solskjær leave . . .

Napoleon would have admired Alex Ferguson. As it turned out, he was not only a good general but a lucky one, too.

19

Dwight

'Making love and scoring goals, is there a better way of spending your time on this planet?' Dwight Yorke chuckles as I read out the quote. 'Did I really say that?' he asks. He did, and Yorke is not about to withdraw the sentiment as he chats from his home in Dubai.

That line captures the essence of Yorke; certainly the 26-year-old incarnation who arrived at Manchester United on transfer deadline day in August 1998 with a smile of pure sunshine. It was as if Ferguson had just introduced a Hawaiian shirt and a cocktail bar into Salford.

There have been many players, strikers in particular, who had found the transition to United daunting. They have been overawed, inhibited by carrying the goalscoring expectations. To talk to Yorke of pressure is like trying to communicate in a foreign language. He looks bemused. Trepidation? Anxiety? 'I see the miserable faces of some of these guys,' he says. 'I don't know how people use that word of pressure in such an environment.' He was, he says, living the dream.

Yorke came dancing and laughing into the United dressing room, smiling even as Roy Keane gave him the familiar acerbic welcome, belting a ball at him in his first warm-up session. 'Cantona would get those,' Keane said deadpan as the ball bounced off the new record signing. Some players would be intimidated. Yorke smiled. 'Ah, so that's how it is,' he thought. He would take everything in his stride, even Keane's snarl. To Yorke, the chance to play on the grandest stage in English football alongside great players, revelling in the service of Ryan Giggs, David Beckham and Paul Scholes from midfield, was an opportunity to embrace and enjoy after eight seasons at Aston Villa.

Ferguson had liked the look of him for a couple of years. Others at Old Trafford were unconvinced. Brian Kidd was not sure, Keane uncertain that Yorke was a top-class striker, and some of the directors had reservations. The fans were not exactly blown away. They saw a decent Premier League forward, but not one who was prolific or sought after by the world's elite.

The idea of Patrick Kluivert, Ferguson's main target, carried much more glamour. He was already a European champion. United had a £9 million bid accepted by AC Milan and Ferguson had high hopes that he would come to lead the attacking line, but the Dutch forward decided to join Louis van Gaal at Barcelona without even entering talks. 'Maybe he doesn't know how big Manchester United is,' Ferguson fumed.

Rejection from Kluivert brought one notable consolation; the directors felt obliged to complete the deal for Yorke, at a club record £12.6 million, just as the transfer window closed in August. With Ferguson also going behind the board's back to tell Ole Gunnar Solskjær to reject a proposed move to Spurs, it meant that United had an unprecedented four senior strikers. Among this quartet, there was no disputing who was the lead violin.

To be there on the night of Yorke's home debut against Charlton Athletic on 9 September was to see a man totally at ease with his surroundings. Earlier in the day came the confirmation of the deal to sell United to Rupert Murdoch, but soon everyone was talking about the new recruit. 'Dwight Yorke swept into Old Trafford like he owned the place,' I typed in the press box. 'Perhaps he had not heard the news.'

Yorke had arrived three hours before kick-off in his club suit and tie to find fans already clamouring for autographs. He felt like a movie star as he walked into the ground. The attention made him feel a million dollars – or £12.6 million.

The great roar of support as the players ran out was bigger than anything he had ever experienced. 'Electrifying,' he says. After a 0-0 draw away at West Ham on his debut in which Ferguson had said that he was disappointed with the lack of chemistry between Yorke and Cole, he had been paired with Solskjær and was soon off and running.

After Charlton took an early lead, Yorke helped Solskjær grab an equaliser with a one-two and then bagged his first United goal shortly before half-time when he met a perfectly delivered Beckham free-kick with a powerful header into the bottom corner, leaping joyously into the arms of fans in the East Stand. Sweeping another Beckham cross into the net shortly after the interval, Yorke was chasing a hat-trick on his home debut, having also assisted Solskjær's second, so he could not believe it when one of his new teammates said that he was being taken off with more than 20 minutes left. 'That was a bit bizarre. I didn't get substituted when I was playing for Villa unless I got injured.'

He hid his dismay with that beaming smile, especially as the fans rose to give him a standing ovation. It had been a superb early riposte to those who doubted his ability to improve United's attack but also an introduction to one of Ferguson's management methods. 'I think the manager was trying to hold me back, to say "don't get above your station" when he took me off. He wanted me to understand that this is only the beginning. But I was gutted at the time.'

Yorke did not show his deflation. 'I love life,' he says. Ask him where this approach comes from and he cannot help wondering if it is something to do with the accident that almost killed him as a young boy.

He was almost three when he ran in front of a passing car near the family home near Canaan, Tobago. 'I have no recollection of the accident but I do have a huge scar on my back that reminds me each day that I probably shouldn't be here,' he says. 'I think I've taken that on board and lived each day for what it is. I embrace what I do.'

As he talks, it is all too easy to slip into stereotypes. You know, Caribbean equals laid-back. And Yorke sometimes *was* horizontal. But his upbringing was also hard. Tobago looks idyllic, a paradise island, but rather less so when you are one of nine children in a two-bedroom house lugging water from the standpipe at the end of the road. Beguiling as it is to think of Yorke strolling off a beach into professional football, he talks of the many challenges of hauling himself from a far-away village to a cold and distant English city as a teenager, and proving himself in this foreign country.

'Coming to England I was always told you had to be three or four times better than the players here. So, I always knew from the very beginning that I had to work my butt off. That whole stereotype thing really gets under my skin a little because people don't know you or the challenges you have to go through to get to where you are.'

Yorke liked a party but, to him, it was not incompatible with hard work. 'Gary Neville is tucked up in bed at nine o'clock. I'm different but that doesn't mean I'm not giving my all. Because Keano is wearing the armband, and being Keano and making much more noise, that doesn't mean I'm less committed than Roy Keane.'

Arriving at United, Yorke was already one of the fittest, behind only Beckham when it came to the bleep tests, but quickly realised that he would need to prove his commitment day after day in this intense environment.

'No strolling through sessions still being the top man like at

Villa. There I could be bang average and still be the best player without a doubt. At United it's a whole different ball game. The competition within the squad was so intense. I thought I was a damn good player until I saw these players and knew I had to up my game or I'd get left behind or be on the substitutes bench. It was relentless that way but I loved it.'

Ferguson had his quartet of strikers but there is no doubting the sun around whom the rest would orbit. Yorke could adapt his game to fit with any of them; a roaming No.10 with an ability to link play, dribble (his early years at Villa were on the right wing) or arrive in the box as a muscular No.9. Ferguson had backed his own judgement about a player at his peak, one with transformative calibre. There could only be one Eric Cantona, but Yorke had his own galvanising effect, not just through his talents but his effervescent character.

It was the way he seemed able to lighten the mood, juggling a ball in the dressing room, using a dustbin for target practice, playing keepy-uppy with rolled-up socks. 'The other players would say, "Can you not sit down for a minute?"' He would say to them, 'I'm smokin', baby' and then wander out to entertain – a United player even the ABUs found unusually hard to dislike given there was nothing belligerent about him.

Yorke was on his way to one of the great debut seasons, and to the time of his life. 'Playing for United, dating all these beautiful women, going out, playing football, getting vast sums of money doing it, enjoying it, that's just the dream of the kid growing up and to accomplish it, well it's wow, amazing. I did embrace it. I hear people say they are struggling with the challenge of playing football, the expectation, the stress and all that kind of stuff. You hear it often. They say they can't deal with the pressure. Pressure, in my opinion, is when you can't afford your bills and your mortgage and do the thing you want to do for your kids and family. I've lived the ultimate dream of being a footballer. So when I hear people say about regrets, that gets me disappointed. It's supposed to be the most magical time and yet you're missing out with regrets. That was meant to be your time.'

---

* Kluivert joined Barcelona for £8.75 million in August 1998 after rejecting the chance to join United. In six years at the Nou Camp, he won one La Liga title.

20

Yorke scores!

If there was one challenge for Dwight Yorke, it was the scrutiny that came with being a Manchester United star. A busy private life was suddenly precious tabloid currency. He had only been at Old Trafford for a month when *The Sun* ran a front-page story of a sex tape involving some clothes-swapping, light spanking and, no doubt, much more besides with a group of women and Aston Villa teammate Mark Bosnich. Yorke claimed that he had left the tape in his collection of football and porn videos – somewhere, presumably, between *Deep Throat* and 'Aston Villa's Coca-Cola Cup Final Glory 1996!' – and it had been pilfered. 'My theory is the world would never have known about them had it not been for my move to United,' he said.

At United, Yorke found that newspapers seemed to know everything about his love life. Breathless details of various flings – with a married brunette, a cable TV presenter, a lapdancer and 'two beauties at two hotels within the space of six hours …' – would provide endless tittle-tattle as well as amusing gossip for his teammates, while some like Ryan Giggs delighted that the attention had been diverted away from them. Yorke had a fling with Tracy Shaw, the *Coronation Street* actress, and escaped from her home through the back garden, jumping over fences to avoid paparazzi. They still found out. He wondered if his phone was bugged. His suspicions would later make sense, receiving damages from Mirror Group Newspapers for hacking.

'[I was] the only determinedly single guy in the group. And I was determinedly single,' Yorke insisted. Ferguson wanted his players to settle down to married life – 'I know where you were last night,' he would growl at Yorke in a veiled warning – but the striker could not see any upsides in commitment. 'Pretty much all I have seen from this culture is misery. Painful, bitter divorces. Or players cheating on the side,' he wrote in a reflective passage in a memoir that was knowingly titled *Born To Score*.

The irony of all those tabloid 'scandals' was that Yorke was the player with the least to hide. Where was the shame if Yorke merrily recounted the details in his own book, including the 24 hours when he slept with four different women while also squeezing in a training session? As Mrs Merton might have said, no wonder he kept so fit.

21

Everest

Towards the end of the 1997-98 season, the United manager agreed to allow cameras to follow him for a two-part documentary to be shown on ITV. *The Alex Ferguson Story* declared its ambition early on to show that the Scot was not just a walking bad mood. The programme opened with Ferguson in his office at Old Trafford filling in a form about his health. 'High blood pressure, heart attack, angina or any disorder of the heart or blood vessels?' he reads, before turning to smile at the camera. 'No, but that's coming the way my team is playing the noo.'

'Contagious disease?' he reads. 'Not other than losing.'

There are repeated shots of Ferguson crooning to himself as he jauntily goes about his business. He even allows access into the family kitchen. There is a rare interview with his wife Cathy who is wonderfully no-nonsense as she talks about bringing her husband back down to earth – 'we cannae all be superstars' – and reminding him there is more to life than football. Ferguson acknowledges the point but you could never say he accepts it. He is a man obsessed with winning – and winning in Europe most of all.

That is the other aim of the fly-on-the-wall programme; to capture United finally conquering Europe after all their domestic success. There is always a touch of vanity – and a risk of hubris – in such a venture and so it proves as the cameras show another failure, with Ferguson left to explain how it all went wrong. In this instance, to be fair, United had to cope with a terrible run of injuries. After a goalless draw away to Monaco in the quarter-finals, United went into the return leg in March 1998 without Peter Schmeichel, Gary Pallister, Ryan Giggs or long-term absentee Roy Keane; all of them badly missed.

On the documentary, Ferguson's desperation leads him to order Keith Kent, the United groundsman, to turn the Old Trafford pitch into a bog to slow down David Trezeguet and Thierry Henry – 'I don't care how much water you put on the fucking thing, get it fucking flooded,' he says – which is hardly the height of continental sophistication. A 1-1 draw put United out of the competition on away goals.

Another disappointment. For Ferguson that was his seventh attempt at the European Cup – three with Aberdeen, four with United – and still success was proving maddeningly elusive. No English club had made it to the final since 1985, when the Heysel Stadium disaster brought a five-year exclusion from European competition, but it was becoming a particular stain on United's record given all their domestic domination.

'I think everyone in life has an apprehension about success,' Ferguson says on the documentary. 'But I say to myself, "What's going to trip me up?" Because people can say, "He never won the European Cup." And you can start looking for the demons again, you know what I mean? I keep reminding myself, "Just let your players get on with it. They are good enough. They know the guidelines and they don't let me down."' But would they?

The first part of the ITV show was broadcast in September 1998, the night before United set out once again on the European challenge that Ferguson would often compare to climbing Everest – the ultimate measure of achievement but also the ruination of many.

There had been painful retreats, and some good men lost

along the way. Eric Cantona had been the catalyst for domestic success but by the time United had lost to Borussia Dortmund in the semi-finals in 1997, Ferguson admitted that his French talisman had developed 'a mental block' in Europe. Cantona felt he could not overcome it and disappeared weeks later in a puff of smoke. The 1994 side had problems with team selection in Europe because of limits on overseas players; and there had been episodes of tactical naivety with Ferguson's gung-ho 4-4-2 picked apart by great teams like Juventus and less-than-great ones like Dortmund. In *Managing My Life*, Ferguson reflected on 'our own lack of the absolute conviction needed to finish off the highest calibre of opponents when we had them at our mercy'.

He was painfully aware that European competition was an acid test of his stature. It was Matt Busby who made it a benchmark for managers in English football, and especially his successors at United, by determining that conquering Europe mattered. The Football League tried to intimidate United out of continental adventures; Busby was not easily deterred.

The visionary Busby saw that the world was contracting with air travel, and that football would become an international game. There was grandeur and adventure to the European stage. As Eamon Dunphy noted in his superb biography of Busby, *A Strange Kind of Glory*, there were practical benefits, too, with the extra games helping to pay for floodlights and an expanding wage bill. 'He saw the future, and he would not be deflected from it,' Jim Ryan says, linking past and present as one of Ferguson's coaches who also played under Busby. It was in striving to conquer Europe that the great Busby Babes had perished in the Munich air disaster in 1958; and in reaching the summit in 1968 that the great manager had achieved immortality. In Europe lay all the tragedy and glory of United.

There was something different about midweek European nights; the lights, the expectancy, the stakes and the sense of yearning, of striving. There was something exotic about the competition but it could feel as much an affliction as an ambition. Ferguson would admit that it became a personal crusade as he sought to stand shoulder to shoulder with Busby and Jock Stein, his mentor who had led Celtic to their famous triumph in 1967, the first British team to be crowned European champions. 'I knew I would never be judged a great manager until I won the European Cup,' he acknowledged.

The stakes were that simple. Win the Champions League or a life's work would always carry that significant blemish. If United were going to reach the mountaintop being drawn into a group of death in 1998-99 with Barcelona and Bayern Munich meant it was going to be the hard way. But, for Ferguson's United, was there ever an easy way?

22

Character is fate #2

Manchester United 3 Barcelona 3, 16 September 1998

If conquering Europe was like climbing Everest, United seemed intent on sprinting madly to the summit. They began not by warily picking a path, avoiding perils, but by charging into Louis van Gaal's Barcelona in an extraordinary, breathless 90 minutes that set the tone for a campaign of incessant drama. Under lights at Old Trafford, in front of a full house who came to see how United's best could compare to Rivaldo and Luís Figo, Luis Enrique and Sonny Anderson, the referee's whistle to start the game could have been a bugle call. Charge!

'Ninety minutes of inspirational football which defy simple explanation,' said the *Daily Mail*. 'A beguiling state of anarchy,' said *The Times*. Like film reviews for a 90-minute action flick, the reports all spoke of thrilling mayhem but, then, did Ferguson's United know differently? They were a team set up in the character of one of life's gamblers; bold, aggressive, daring. 'For me this was the perfect football match,' Ferguson said when he could catch his breath after the final whistle. 'Both teams trying to win with scant regard for the consequences.'

United set the tone, sticking with a full-throttle 4-4-2. Ole Gunnar Solskjær, starting up front alongside Dwight Yorke, had already hit the crossbar by the time that United went ahead in the 17th minute when David Beckham wrapped his right foot around the ball to hit a sensational cross on the run. Ryan Giggs pulled out a superb impression of Joe Jordan to leap for a far-post header, perhaps soaring on the exhilaration of the occasion.

By the 25th minute it was 2-0. This time Beckham crossed with his left foot, a floating ball which Yorke met with a spectacular bicycle kick. Ruud Hesp in goal parried it but only as far as Paul Scholes, who finished off the rebound with typical predatory instincts. 'Kluivert, Kluivert, what's the score?' they sang gleefully on the Stretford End. 'You should have signed for a big club,' they taunted him. The cup-tied striker was stuck in his seat in the stands, watching Beckham produce the game's outstanding performance, dominating Sergi on one flank, while Giggs had the better of Luis Enrique down the other side.

'We are no good at stifling teams anyway and we have players who like to attack and score, especially in big games,' Ferguson told us afterwards. 'So we went for the throat and the first half was absolutely fantastic for us. I just didn't want the first half to finish.' His only worry in the interval was that his team might have expended too much energy. And with Barcelona reorganising by pushing the full-backs forward, deciding to fight fire with a blowtorch, the momentum shifted straight from the restart.

Anderson took advantage of some indecisive defending to pull one back almost immediately. When Rivaldo went down under a naive challenge from Jaap Stam, Stefano Braschi, the Italian referee, pointed to the spot. 'A disgrace,' Ferguson said. Rivaldo was prone to theatrics, but Stam was guilty of being sucked into the tackle. That made it 2-2 after Giovanni's penalty.

United needed some inspiration and it was Beckham who rose to the occasion once more when Yorke was fouled fully 30 yards from goal – not too far from the spot where Beckham would line up a free-kick so memorably for England against Greece some years later. His curling shot into the top corner was one of his very best free-kicks, especially in the circumstances.

If only it had been the winner – but this breathless evening was not over. The fourth goal of the second half came in the 71st minute when Nicky Butt, who had replaced Solskjær as Ferguson sought to reassert some control (it was like pulling out an umbrella in a hurricane), blocked Figo's goalbound shot with his arm. A Luis Enrique penalty made it 3-3, and United were left to fight for a draw with ten men following Butt's dismissal.

Gary Neville said it felt 'like the Blitz' in those final 20 minutes, trying to fend off Figo (who before long would become the world's most expensive player) and Rivaldo (who would soon be voted the world's best footballer). The way Figo managed to be big and strong but also quick, beautifully balanced and two-footed, capable of going either way, marked him out as the toughest opponent of Neville's career.

It had been pell-mell football; United looking unstoppable for one half and then incapable of resisting Barcelona. Ferguson felt his team had stopped finding Beckham and Giggs, leaving the ball with the full-backs and allowing Barcelona to seize the initiative, but he refused to be disheartened. He said it had been a 'significant display' in going toe to toe with a team regarded as one of the best in Europe. This was not just about the point but the psychological confidence of feeling as if they were on a level with a team of Barcelona's superstars and supposed sophistication. To have overwhelmed them, if only for one half, had special significance to anyone at United with memories of losing 4-0 in the Nou Camp in 1994 in what had been a painful humiliation. This performance represented progress but, above all, a fearlessness in the latest European expedition.

23

Jesper

Jesper Blomqvist can predict the reaction, especially in football's world of conformity, when anyone finds out that he is running a pizzeria in Stockholm. 'They look down a bit on me,' he says. 'They think I've fallen on hard times.' Admittedly, he did make some bad investments after retiring from football but, for Blomqvist, the smart 450 Gradi restaurant, with its Neapolitan wood-fired oven, is a passion-project as much as a living. He exudes a love for the culinary world as he sits in his open-plan kitchen at home on the small island of Lidingo, a short drive from the centre of Stockholm, to reflect on life at Manchester United.

Still with a thick head of hair and a slightly shy smile, Blomqvist is engaging and warm; chatting one minute about expansion plans in the restaurant business while studying as a sommelier, and happily switching to memories as a willowy left-winger who came as Ryan Giggs's understudy in the summer of 1998.

He arrived from two years in Serie A, at AC Milan and Parma, where he started to develop the love of food that would be his future career. He talks of the smart Milanello base, with its backdrop of the Alps; a bucolic scene where fresh pasta and risotto were served to the players with a sprinkling of the finest Parmigiano. What did he find at the Cliff? 'Bacon butty with HP sauce,' he laughs.

There would be a few cultural challenges for this reflective Swede; the son of university academics from a quiet town in northern Sweden who started a maths degree at Gothenburg before dedicating himself to football. 'Noisier, old-school,' he says of his first impressions of walking into the United training ground. Like his fellow new recruits, Yorke and Stam, he talks of an overtly macho environment where the early test was not so much of ability but standing up for yourself.

Blomqvist had a taste of the merciless banter on his first day when Giggs grabbed him, turned him round so his back was pointing straight at David May and said, 'Maysie, you'd recognise this guy now, wouldn't you?' The lads loved that one. In November 1994, playing for IFK Gothenburg, Blomqvist had run rings around May in the Champions League. May only ever saw Blomqvist's back to chase after him.

Ferguson had kept an eye ever since on the slight, elusive winger who had followed up that European run, helping his Swedish club reach a Champions League quarter-final, with a celebrated goal against Helsingborgs in which he copied Pelé's 'runaround' move from the 1970 World Cup. 'You haven't seen it?' Blomqvist says, with mock indignation. 'Look it up on YouTube. The ball comes behind me, I jump over it and the ball runs on the other side of the goalkeeper who doesn't know which way to turn. I run around him and score. It's one of the moments I'm most proud of when I look back.'

Blomqvist admits he was short of his creative best when he arrived at Manchester airport to be picked up by Ferguson, who helped carry his luggage and gave him a lift to the Mottram Hall hotel in Cheshire. The personal touch was appreciated. As they sat down for lunch, the United manager explained that with injuries and rotation Blomqvist would have plenty of opportunities despite Giggs's extraordinary talents. 'Ferguson made you feel important,' he says. 'It was a clever trick!'

Blomqvist needed reassurance. He arrived with an injury, a problem with the fascia running under the foot, so had to train separately in his first weeks, which added to an early sense of isolation. He worked out with Dave Fevre, the physio, who remembers a timid figure. 'I saw Jesper at a tournament in Indonesia a couple of years ago and I said, "Back then you were a nervous little kid, coming to Manchester." He went, "I know, I hated it." The lads remembered how he had created mayhem, torturing David May, and they weren't sure at first if he was the same player. He was fragile, a bit nervous. Jesper realised that he needed that nursing-in period. He wanted reassurance. He was that type of character. He's a lovely guy.'

Fevre recalls an early training session and the familiar initiation. Yes, Keane smashing it at Blomqvist and watching the ball bounce off his shin. 'And Roy said, "Five fucking million for that shit,"' Fevre recalls. 'And I said to Jesper, "That's Roy, just the way he is." You've got to toughen up and accept the way he is.'

The way Blomqvist remembers it, Schmeichel gave him a tough time early on. They were warming up in the boxes – a daily ritual, with players in a circle firing a ball around as one in the middle tries to intercept – and the goalkeeper gave him a 'shitty pass'. Blomqvist was not happy and pinged the ball back at the goalkeeper. Suddenly, a huge angry Dane was coming at him. 'He ended up almost over me. He could have almost punched me. "What the fuck are you doing, Jesper?" I got so upset and wouldn't speak to him for two weeks, though I'm not sure he even noticed. That was the kind of time when they tested you. I like Peter but I had to stand up to him.

'It was different to what I was used to. In Sweden it was about lifting people and trying to encourage them. At United, they tested you to see if you can handle the pressure, to be their team-mate in the middle of the heat of a game. It took me a year to understand their mentality, particularly with Roy Keane. At the beginning, I was like, "Why all this shouting? It destroys you." For me, being Swedish, it was really hard to understand this constant pressure on players.' Blomqvist came to see how Keane was indispensable, and not just a raging ego. 'But in the beginning, it was tough,' he says. 'It affects your confidence.'

Adapting to his new surroundings also meant spending a lot of money, rather reluctantly, on a new car. Blomqvist arrived with a modest runaround, but that would never do among the fleet of Aston Martins and Ferraris at the Cliff. 'At the beginning I kept driving my Vauxhall Opel. Not even the security guards at Old Trafford wanted one of those,' he laughs. 'I wasn't really into cars but in the end I had to buy a decent one, a classic English Jaguar. I just bought one to fit in.'

Blomqvist had played with superstars in Italy – Maldini, Desailly, Weah and Baggio at Milan; Buffon, Cannavaro and Thuram at Parma – but he never had any reservations about the quality of his new teammates. Whose talent jumped out when he started training?

'I have to say David Beckham was underrated. One of the best players in the world at that stage. A right foot that no one could compare, and a vision to use it. Forget the celebrity. In that time he was one of the best footballers in the world, skills any team would have wanted. People were jealous of him and his lifestyle but look at what he does on the pitch and he trained so hard and his ability in the speed tests. He was fantastic.' He mentions Paul Scholes too, and being struck by his natural talent.

Blomqvist made his debut against Charlton Athletic, in the victory dominated by Yorke, and he would go on to start 20 Premier League games out of his 38 appearances that season. He would make as many league starts as Giggs. A run of games in November included his only goal of the campaign in a 4-1 victory at Everton, running on to Beckham's through ball, but Blomqvist always felt that it was a season of bedding in. He was performing at around 70 per cent of his true capacity. 'My confidence was going up and down. I had one or two great games then I might have an injury and my confidence would drop if I was injured. I needed more time to adapt, not like Dwight who found his feet very quickly.'

His closest friends were the Scandinavian crew of Solskjær, Johnsen and Berg, though he says that he did not really open up to any of them about his self-doubts. 'I wasn't sharing my thoughts with anybody. I kept those to myself.' He tried to help himself, using visualisation exercises he learnt in Sweden.

He had to work at it, a sensitive soul who later tried coaching but did not last long because he lacked ruthlessness, and knew it. He was happier in his restaurant, where fans still ask him to reminisce either about his involvement, aged just 20, in the Sweden squad which reached the 1994 World Cup semi-finals, or his victory on the Swedish version of *Strictly Come Dancing*. He performed an Abba medley for his final, triumphant dance.

A divorcee, Blomqvist helps to bring up his son Caspar, a United fanatic who regularly asks his dad to tell stories about the Old Trafford glory days. What does he talk about? Blomqvist says that he reflects less on medals won and more on the joy of being among a team that had a conviction they could score in any match, at any time. 'That's down to Ferguson. That's the belief he gave us.'

24

Old Vinegar Face

It is hard to overstate just how deeply Arsène Wenger dug under the skin of Alex Ferguson to shape the greatest managerial rivalry of the Premier League era. The enmity was about more than trophies, or two great sides clashing in epic battles, or the belligerence of many of the players. It was personal.

'Old Vinegar Face,' Ferguson called Wenger one day as we asked him about the Frenchman. 'That's off the record,' he added, with a growl. We could not write it but we could recognise that the insult came with feeling. Everything that Wenger was being lauded for by the media (once we had overcome the initial hurdle of not knowing anything about him when he arrived from Japan in 1996) would irritate Ferguson. Foreign managers were still quite a novelty and, to English eyes, the bookish-looking Wenger was urbane, and sophisticated. He was a football manager who was multilingual and had a master's degree in economics and sociology from Strasbourg University.

Ferguson was less impressed. 'They say he's an intelligent man, right? Speaks five languages. I've got a 15-year-old boy from the Ivory Coast who speaks five languages.'

As well as quickly proving himself a serious force as a coach by winning the Double in only his second season with Arsenal, Wenger was soon lauded for revolutionising the English game; educating and modernising it with the latest thinking on sports science. Ageing players were revitalised by the use of osteopaths and yoga and a strict diet. From the gushing write-ups, it was as though Wenger grew his own vegetables and invented pasta.

Who ate all the broccoli? Ferguson hated all that discussion about Wenger dragging the English game into a new, smarter era. Hadn't he recruited a dietician, Trevor Lea, a sports science lecturer from Sheffield University, as far back as 1991 to wean the United players off steak and heavy carbs? Lea, who also worked with British Athletics, had brought healthy options into the Cliff and installed a microwave on the team bus for rice-based meals after matches. Ferguson had been trying to drive alcohol out of his dressing room for years and the generations coming through, like the Class of '92, were almost puritanical in their off-field habits. But it was Wenger who took all the plaudits. 'The media in England are trying to turn him into some sort of guru,' Ferguson chuntered, with irritation. 'Just because he's French and different . . .'

Wenger was also different in that he declined to treat Ferguson as the fearsome Don Corleone of English football. Most managers would pay their respects, going to Ferguson's office for a post-match drink, to keep in with him. The few who didn't, including Kevin Keegan, would usually end up paying for it.

Wenger refused to play that game. He would not socialise over a glass of wine, which the United manager regarded as haughty arrogance. As Arsenal quickly proved a force, and Wenger kept plucking brilliant French recruits like Patrick Vieira, Emmanuel Petit and Nicolas Anelka out of his contacts book, Ferguson tried to find any means to attack his new rivals. Wenger may be studious but his team could be highly aggressive. 'The number of fights involving Arsenal is more than Wimbledon had in their heyday,' Ferguson told us.

The two managers would eventually come close to fisticuffs themselves as their feuding escalated, with Ferguson motivated by the rivalry but also rattled in 1998 by the unavoidable reality that Arsenal were such redoubtable opponents. When, on 20 September, United slumped to a 3-0 defeat at Highbury, repeating the scoreline of the Charity Shield, it was the fourth game in a row when his side had been beaten by Arsenal. 'Depressing,' Ferguson said afterwards.

He had tried to spring a surprise by playing Ryan Giggs up front with Dwight Yorke but Arsenal took the lead after 14 minutes when Tony Adams rose above Jaap Stam to score. The champions never looked like surrendering their advantage. Vieira was magnificent in midfield, and Nicky Butt was sent off for the second time in a week when he tripped the French midfielder. Of the United team, only David Beckham came close to playing well. The choice of funereal black kit matched Ferguson's mood afterwards.

Here was all the evidence of why this Arsenal side were rated by Gary Neville as the best domestic opponents he faced in two decades in English football; better than Mourinho's Chelsea or Arsenal's Invincibles. There was no Thierry Henry but, in his eyes, not yet that touch of haughty 'you can't touch us, we're French and we're brilliant' arrogance. Only Juventus could match them physically. Giggs agreed that this Arsenal side were harder to play against than the Invincibles because they were more robust. They combined speed, power and finesse. They could beat you with skill and go to war, too.

It was a shell-shocked Ferguson who admitted that he had not seen such a heavy defeat coming. There was alarm in seeing opponents who were more determined; hungrier to win a big match. Casting around for an explanation, he wondered, 'When did you last see my team play as badly as this?' Five games into the league season, United had eight points and were not only trailing Arsenal but John Gregory's unbeaten Aston Villa, the surprise league-leaders.

25

No dopes

Shortly after that 3-0 defeat and still smarting from it, Alex Ferguson sat down with journalists from the Sunday newspapers and delved into what footballers were ingesting – and he was not talking about broccoli.

'We're No Dopes,' was the headline in the *News of the World* as Ferguson discussed revelations that some of the England players at the 1998 World Cup, including United's, had been given injections by Yann Rougier, a French doctor. Glenn Hoddle, the England manager, knew Rougier from his days as a player under Arsène Wenger at Monaco and had recruited him to work with the national team. Rougier was also involved at Arsenal.

It was Gary Neville who had brought a delicate subject to the fore when he revealed that he and other England players felt that Rougier's pre-match injections at the World Cup had given them extra zip. In a diary, Neville spoke of preparations to face Argentina and how injections of magnesium, vitamins and minerals had revitalised him. He would later expand that they were taking so many pills 'that it felt like a meal in itself. There were all sorts of different-coloured smarties. I know that creatine, the muscle-building protein, was included, along with antioxidants.' With the injections, he said 'it was different from anything we'd done at United, but all above board, I'm sure'.

That reassurance was not going to stop Ferguson casting aspersions on Rougier's methods, and he was never one to miss an opportunity to stir up trouble. He demanded a written explanation from the FA about exactly what was in the pills and injections, and went public with his concerns, and insinuations. He talked of chemicals potentially becoming addictive, and insisted that United were not using anything other than 'the natural things; food, drink, water, fluids, rest and good training. I don't agree with the other methods.'

Quite who introduced erythropoietin (EPO) into the conversation was not clear, but at least one paper speculated about that notorious medication which was prevalent at the time, particularly among elite cyclists, to stimulate red blood cell production. Cycling had introduced checks in 1997 on haematocrit levels but there was still no test for EPO. It was being widely used, and abused, in many sports.

David Davies, the FA's director of public affairs, was quick to insist that Rougier's injections were entirely legal. 'We can't say specifically what was in them because their records are with Dr Rougier in France. But our doctors here are adamant that whatever they were given was NOT to increase the red blood cell count,' he said. Whether Ferguson had the right target or not – and there was no evidence of anything illegal involving England, or Arsenal – he was certainly asking the right questions.

To worry about doping in football was fully justified. Ferguson had previously wondered about the physical power of the Juventus team which had reached three successive European Cup finals – and he was not alone.

On the back of a scandal-plagued Tour de France in the summer of 1998, Zdeněk Zeman, coach of AS Roma, claimed that doping was rife in Serie A and that football needed 'to come out of the pharmacy'. He cited Juventus and, despite denials from the club, a criminal investigation was launched into medical practices from 1994 to 1998.

A raid on the training ground found 281 different medications, including prescription-only drugs which were not banned but had no therapeutic justification for use by healthy footballers. The place was stocked 'like a small hospital' according to one investigator. A case against club doctor Riccardo Agricola heard that drugs regularly taken by many players included Samyr, an antidepressant, and Neoton, for heart conditions. But it was the evidence around EPO which proved most controversial.

A leading haematologist, Giuseppe d'Onofrio, studied blood test results and testified that it was 'practically certain' that a couple of players had taken EPO to overcome brief bouts of anaemia, and 'very probable' that seven others had taken small doses. Agricola was convicted and handed a suspended prison sentence of 22 months for providing performance-enhancing drugs to the players, but acquitted on appeal in December 2005 with the court saying that use of EPO was not proven.

A Dutch television documentary in 2013 looked afresh at the evidence and D'Onofrio repeated his assertion that blood results from the Juventus players could only be explained by blood transfusions or by the use of EPO. But with the court verdict absolving Agricola and denials from all involved, football could all too conveniently look the other way. When it comes to doping, it still does.

26

Munich

'Before Munich it was Manchester's club. Afterwards everyone felt they owned a little bit of it.'

— Bobby Charlton

To understand modern Manchester United – the unique magnitude of its popularity, its heritage, its place in so many sporting hearts – you had to know the past, and there was nowhere more fitting to acknowledge it than Munich. On 30 September 1998, the players of United and Bayern Munich bowed their heads for a minute's silence in the city's Olympic Stadium. They were commemorating the team that died 40 years earlier – and the legend that was born.

It was hard to believe that this meeting in the Champions League group stage was the first time these clubs had faced each other in a competitive match given the two places felt so entwined: a deep historic and emotional connection.

Munich is where the Busby Babes perished in February 1958; cut down in their prime. This superlative side of home-grown stars had an average age of just 22 when they claimed their first league title in 1955-56, and they were aiming for a third successive championship. They were on course, they could dare to believe, for a first European Cup final – perhaps even an unprecedented Treble.

It was on the way back from knocking out Red Star Belgrade,

drawing 3–3 to reach the last four in the new European competition for the second year running, that they stopped to refuel in Munich. On a third attempt to take off, amid snow and ice and slush, the plane hurtled off the end of the runway and plunged the club into a mourning that has never really stopped.

A great team had been destroyed. Among the 23 casualties were eight players, including the towering figure of Duncan Edwards, who many felt would go on to captain England to glory. Tragedy on such a terrible magnitude gave United a place in the hearts of millions. There was global sympathy that such brilliant young men had been killed when they had so much to live for.

The regeneration that followed enveloped a whole new audience of fans. When Busby, whose injuries were so bad that he had been read the last rites in hospital in Munich, led Charlton and George Best and a new team to European Cup glory in 1968 – the trophy that would surely have belonged to Edwards and his young teammates had they not perished – it felt not just a sporting triumph but a spiritual journey.

It was impossible to play for United and not have some understanding of the history. Peter Schmeichel arrived from Denmark to sign for the club and was first led by Martin Edwards on a tour of the stadium and the museum. The chairman explained the honour and responsibility of playing for United as he pointed out the Munich clock.

Very little may have linked the modern-day players to those who died in Munich – just Beckham's Brylcreem, perhaps – but the youth team graduates like Beckham and the Nevilles, Butt and Scholes knew the heritage. They had encountered Busby when they were apprentices – 'in the presence of greatness, a United god,' Neville recalled – and they had heard all the stories of the era from coaches like Brian Kidd and Nobby Stiles who were on the Wembley pitch in 1968.

Ferguson had never shied away from the Busby legacy. Indeed, he had embraced the expectations of youth and adventure, attacking football and, of course, European glory as the benchmark of greatness.

So this return to Munich by a United team was bound to come loaded with history and emotion, and due recognition of this defining tragedy. History is never far away at United, and Charlton, who had been thrown out of the plane strapped in his seat, was on the flight out to Munich. Heading into the Olympic Stadium, the fans sang the catchy, evocative 'United Calypso'.

Manchester,
Manchester United.
A bunch of bouncing 'Busby Babes',
They deserve to be knighted.
If ever they're playing in your town,
You must get to that football ground.
Take a look and you will see,
Football taught by Matt Busby . . .

And, of course, there was the European quest. Busby had led the club into continental competition in the belief that United teams should test themselves against the best, wherever they hailed from. To triumph in Europe was the expectation on any successful United team.

As Ferguson's men played out a 2-2 draw in Munich in the Champions League – undone by an uncharacteristic late Schmeichel error as he rushed out and missed a long Bayern throw-in, to leave United with two points from two games – that burden of history was still very much on these successors to the tragic Babes.

27

Coley

When it comes to nominating famous games from the Treble season, the trip to Southampton on 3 October will not feature on many lists. But talking to Andy Cole it was as big as any fixture. 'It was,' he says, 'a game that changed everything.'

Eleven matches into the campaign, Cole was reunited with Dwight Yorke in the starting XI for the first time since the away trip to West Ham United in August. Alex Ferguson had been trying everything else in attack; Solskjær, Sheringham, Scholes, even Giggs alongside Yorke against Arsenal. It was as if he had written off the Cole and Yorke partnership from one test run but, after trying every other option, had little choice than to give it another chance.

Twelve minutes after they walked out at The Dell, Cole found himself out on the left wing. Turning back on to his right foot, he could see where Yorke wanted the ball playing into the near post and delivered. Yorke's finish was not a clean one but enough to nudge the ball into the net and set United on their way. The second goal was a lovely, confident first-time finish from Cole, cutting across the defence and then opening up his body to shoot after he had been put through by Jesper Blomqvist.

Winning 3-0, United had clicked in a ground where they had encountered problems in recent years, and Cole walked off feeling rejuvenated. There was a new zest in the dressing room, the sense of a team coming together. 'That's where my season started,'

Cole says. 'That was the birth of the Andy Cole/Dwight Yorke partnership. The manager saw something that afternoon and thought, "I'll give it a go." And then after that, for me personally it was poetry. It was something that was meant to be, you know.'

The relaxed, chatty Cole who reflects for more than an hour could almost be a different person from the bristling, prickly figure I once interviewed at his agent's office in Wilmslow, Cheshire about the pressures of being United's No.9.

Cole had won two titles (including a Double) in the three-and-a-half seasons since his startling – I am sure we called it 'sensational' – £7 million transfer from Newcastle United. Ferguson had turned to this slight and angular penalty-box poacher because opponents were increasingly sitting back. He wanted a finisher, a fox in the box. Cole had done that job superbly at Newcastle United – a remarkable 34 league goals in his best season of 1993-94 as a quick and lethal goalscorer off either foot – but he had never looked fully at ease since that big move to Old Trafford.

He was mortified when he was blamed for costing United the title in his first season – I had been among those critics, watching him spurn chances on the final day at Upton Park in May 1995 – and suffered fractures in both legs the following year. Ignored by England, struggling to fulfil all the expectations, he began to try too hard, which made him even more anxious – or prickly to the outside world. I sat down with Cole and, like most conversations with him at the time, it felt edgy and difficult. He was bristling and defiant.

As we were walking out, Cole saw a photograph of himself on the front cover of a football magazine. He picked it up and flicked through the pages. Finding himself, he glanced at the headline, which was something like 'Football's Worst Signings!' Cole chucked the magazine back onto the table and left, without another word. It felt like a brutal summation of his time at United. He was the main striker, but there would be a new rumour every year about a replacement, as if the No.9 shirt could be ripped off his back at any moment. United did not even try to hide the pursuit of Patrick Kluivert in 1998. 'I'll be honest, if Patrick had decided not to go to Barcelona, I don't think I'd have been at United,' Cole says. 'Simple as that.'

Cole smiles about it now – and not just because of how the season unfolded. He has tried to look on the brighter side of life ever since, in 2015, a virus almost killed him. When Cole fell seriously ill on returning from a trip to Vietnam as an ambassador for United, he swelled up to almost 18 stone. His kidney was failing. If he had not been a fit former footballer, he might not have pulled through. His life was saved by a nephew, Alexander Palmer, donating a kidney for transplant. It was a trauma compounded during his recovery by a painful and bitter marital separation. That brush with mortality, divorce and therapy have rounded off some of Cole's sharp edges. It has made him more reflective and grateful for what he has – and for all he had in a partnership which is still, rightly, talked about as one of the finest of the Premier League era.

'Let's be honest, the gaffer stumbled upon it. He was a genius manager but there was no grand plan for me and Dwight.'

As Cole attests, one of English football's most fêted double-acts was not built with brilliant foresight or planning. Nor was it the work of painstaking hours on the training pitches at the Cliff. There was no detailed work on interplay or attacking patterns. In practice games, often England against the Rest of the World, Cole and Yorke would be on opposing sides. They might do some finishing together, but there was no conscious effort from them, or Ferguson, to create a collaboration.

'That's what no one will ever understand,' Cole says. 'I wasn't supposed to be there, so when we were training, it wasn't like I was paired up with Dwight. There was nothing in training together. A lot of people still come up to me and say, "How'd you guys do it?" It was just naturally, we just knew where each other was gonna be, you know. Everything was off the cuff. Me and Dwight, we hardly spoke a word on the pitch and that's what made him better for me. I've never said, "Get in the circle or wherever." Let's just play it how we see it. And, to me, that's what made it poetry.'

This was a harmonious union not just of football skills but personalities. Yorke, as we know, could not have been more loose and languid. Cole was at an extreme of edginess, as a player and person. When he had been dropped after the West Ham game, he went to see the manager, and received a blunt response. 'I can't see you two doing it, so I have got to look at my options,' he was told.

Never a man of many words, Cole retreated into silence. 'When the manager used to leave me out of the team, I didn't speak to him. I refused to speak to him. I'm not sure how many managers would be prepared to accept a player not talking to him, but he knew my character.' It was Cole's way of handling rejection – 'the angry young man I was,' he says – but whereas other managers would escalate the situation into a blazing row, Ferguson shrewdly assessed that Cole was not a man to prod and probe.

'People always worry about the quiet ones,' Cole says, with more self-awareness than people usually give him credit for. 'They always want to know what you are thinking instead of letting you be. That's why Alex Ferguson was so good. He treated you as an individual. He was the only one who wanted to get to know me. Most managers wanted to challenge you, the aggressive thing. They would say, "I'm going to get into your head." I would laugh at that. I couldn't get into my head. My quietness was perceived to be a problem. I've never understood this. A quiet person? He's weak, he's aloof and arrogant or surly. But I don't go around telling people, "Why are you so loud?" Alex Ferguson didn't want to change me. He allowed me to be who I was.'

When it came to that trip to Southampton, Cole understandably felt he was on trial. 'And I took the opportunity with both hands. Even the boys were saying, "Wow considering you two never played together. I mean that was some stuff going on today." Everyone was auditioning for a role to play with Yorkie. And my audition seemed to work out better than everybody else's.'

What was key, Cole believes, is that the pair had quickly become friends off the pitch. When Yorke arrived in Manchester, put up at a drab hotel in Alderley Edge, it was Cole who offered to show the new man around; taking him into Manchester and pointing to Moss Side, telling him it was not a place to venture into; inviting him into his home for dinner with his wife and family; helping him with house-hunting in the footballer belt in Cheshire. Yorke was impressed by the welcome, especially considering he could be taking Cole's place.

They were the same age, born less than a month apart, but very different people, which is perhaps why they clicked so well. Cole was an introvert, a brooder; Yorke the gregarious joker. Cole had once bought a Porsche but did not drive it into the training ground because he felt self-conscious. After Yorke's arrival, they bought identical purple Mercedes convertibles, one digit different on the number plates, like new best friends. 'Polar opposites,' Cole says. 'Yet we understand each other like we were born together. Yorkie brought something out of me that I knew I had in me. This is what I've been waiting for.'

After an awkward, largely silent relationship with Eric Cantona – and open animosity with Sheringham, which we will come to shortly – Cole had a mate alongside him, one who never stopped smiling. Yorke showed him a different way, easing the pressure.

'What I learned from Dwight is that his attitude is very carefree. You know he's always laughing, always joking. I call him Peter Pan because he's never going to grow up. I love him. His attitude and just the way he used to come in, breathe a little bit of fresh air into the dressing room was phenomenal.'

The next five games they started together, United scored 21 goals, with Cole and Yorke sharing almost half of them. In the match after Southampton, they put five past Wimbledon with Cole rounding off the scoring by nutmegging a defender. He was reborn.

Cole and Yorke would plunder 53 goals between them across all competitions in 1998-99, and share 31 assists. To read back my report of flying back from the crushing victory over Brondby in the Champions League group stage, where they helped United rack up six goals in 62 minutes, is to be struck afresh by the transformation in Cole's mood. I wrote of a rejuvenated spirit, a change in his body language. Cole and Yorke were inseparable, giggling their way from airport terminals to hotels to training grounds.

Through a stroke of luck, it was the coming together of 'a beautiful chemistry' according to Yorke. Cole talks of 'pure joy'. Ferguson was not about to deny his good fortune given everyone knew he had chased Kluivert, and had largely ignored Cole in the first two months of the season. Asked if he had foreseen the partnership blossoming into one of the most feared in Europe, he told the *Guardian* in February 1999: 'No, absolutely not, it's a piece of luck. I admit I had no idea.'

28

The feud

Another reason why the signing of Dwight Yorke proved so inspired was that it helped to shift a very awkward dynamic in the United dressing room. It was not just Roy Keane who was refusing to speak to Teddy Sheringham. Andy Cole had stopped talking to his fellow striker for some time, too. In fact, Cole loathed Sheringham.

A bitter feud had its origins back in March 1995 as England were preparing to face Uruguay in a friendly. Cole had been called up to his first senior squad by Terry Venables, but Sheringham recalls that it was antipathy at first sight.

'There were issues, just two characters clashing very early on,' Sheringham explains. 'I don't know whether he didn't like the look of me, or I didn't like the look of him. Even from the first England training session, it seemed like there was a bit of friction. I don't know if he expected me to be more forthcoming because I was already in the England squad and to be good to him, or I expected him to be more outgoing when you come into an England squad and put yourself out there a bit. We just didn't hit it off. There was something in the week leading up that made me think, "You don't want anything from me, I don't want anything from you." That was how it was.'

From a bad start, it would only get worse. In the absence of the injured Alan Shearer, Sheringham started up front against

Uruguay with Peter Beardsley. After 71 goalless minutes, Venables sent on Cole to replace him. Cole was on the sidelines, full of nervous excitement as he prepared to run on for his first senior cap. As Sheringham came close, Cole raised his hand. Sheringham walked past, without acknowledgement. A fleeting moment, something that perhaps no one else inside Wembley would notice – but for a man like Cole, who had felt every slight like a knife-wound since he was a kid, it was a snub that instantly cut deep.

Cole was so mortified that his skin prickled with anger for the 19 minutes he was on the pitch. He says that he could not wait to come off, a special occasion ruined. Instead of pride at representing his country, he felt belittled. In Sheringham's lack of acknowledgement on the touchline, he felt, was a message: 'I'm coming off for *you*?' As far as Sheringham was concerned, he and Cole were already working to a tacit understanding that they were not in the business of handshakes and high-fives.

Either way, the United lads had to smile when Sheringham was signed by Ferguson in 1997. How was this going to play out? It was clear from the start that a strained relationship was not about to be healed as club teammates. Playing a friendly in Milan, Sheringham mentioned something about movement. Cole ignored him. 'I'm only trying to help you,' Sheringham explained. 'I don't need your help, you fucking prick,' Cole responded.

Against Bolton Wanderers in February 1998 – a sombre afternoon to mark the 40th anniversary of the Munich disaster – United had laboured to a 1-1 draw. Cole had scored the equaliser and was furious when Sheringham blamed him for the Bolton goal. Racing up the tunnel, he launched himself at Sheringham as soon as they reached the dressing room, throwing punches. Keane intervened. 'What the fuck are you doing, Coley? Sort yourself out. We're a team.' According to Cole, Keane then turned on

Sheringham and gave him both barrels. As we know, they were not exactly friends.

Ferguson called Cole and Sheringham in for sharp words. He was accustomed to problems between teammates but felt this rift had gone too far, affecting performances. He told them both that if they continued to undermine the team, he would have no option but to sell them.

Yorke was a huge help in easing the enmity between the warring pair. His personality made him a natural collaborator with every teammate, and he became the conduit between Cole and Sheringham, albeit in a very weird dynamic. As Cole recalls, 'I used to speak to Yorkie, who then spoke to Teddy, and then he would talk to Yorkie, who would come back to me. That's how we did it. We never spoke directly to each other at all.'

Yorke told me that he was initially bemused by his role as a go-between. 'I was sitting in between them and at first I had no idea. Then I realise Teddy's passing a message on to me asking me if Coley's coming. And I've got to ask Coley. And then the messages were passing through me because I could be a mediator. It's bizarre looking back at it.'

These days, Sheringham is quite sanguine about the rift – the pair managed to shake hands years later when they bumped into each other – but acknowledges that it had started to undermine the team, until Yorke's arrival. 'There was something about Dwight which brought something out of Andy, and the fact I didn't get on with Andy wasn't ideal for the team. It had made things a little bit harder.'

One of Ferguson's great managerial skills was persuading players to set aside these issues to think about a higher cause, a unifying purpose. According to Sheringham, 'I don't think it's team spirit, it's something different. Just an unbelievable focus, we're here to work, this is what we do, at the pinnacle of our careers. We're here to play for Man United. What an honour, as

Alex always said. Everybody got their heads round that. We're not here to make friends. It would be nice if everyone gets on but it was obvious from an early stage that that wasn't going to happen.'

---

* For a while, Dave Fevre, the physio, was in charge of putting the players together in rooms for away trips and one day he wrote down Cole and Sheringham. He thought he was helping the team by pairing two strikers. Fortunately, Gary Neville saw the list before it could be circulated. 'Dave, don't do that whatever you do,' the defender told him. 'It'll be World War Three.'

If that was a bad idea, Roy Keane did not agree with players rooming together at all. He complained about it furiously in his first autobiography – 'I found room-sharing an embarrassment bordering on insulting,' he said – rightly pointing out that it was treating millionaire elite athletes like kids on a school outing. He had a point, though it was not until the 2000-01 campaign that grown men would be allowed their own room.

29

The Class of '92

One morning at the Cliff, the training session starts as usual, with the players in the boxes; firing the ball at each other as one of them chases around trying to intercept. A world-class game of piggy in the middle. The younger players form one box, while Alex Ferguson joins the older ones. The manager likes to muck in occasionally for a bit of fun and to sense the mood – but on this day the vibe is not at all to his liking. The ball from the younger box keeps intruding. Ferguson becomes increasingly irate.

'Right, the next time that ball comes over here, you lot can run around that fucking university,' he shouts, pointing at a tall building against the Salford horizon. The players all smirk at the manager's temper. Someone cannot resist seeing just how short his fuse is that morning. The ball gets flicked over once more, messing up the older group.

'Right, that's it!' Ferguson rages. 'Get fucking running!'

And so, the day before a league game in the biggest season of their lives, David Beckham, Ryan Giggs, Paul Scholes, Nicky Butt, the Nevilles – serial champions and internationals – run around the streets of Salford on a punishment lap. They are wearing boots, so their studs clatter on the pavement as they jog in their United tracksuits past homes, shops and bemused onlookers, giggling like naughty kids.

Someone is still laughing when, almost four miles later from their tour of Lower Kersal, they turn back into the Cliff and the manager spots them. 'Right, I don't want to see you lot again!' Ferguson rants. 'Fuck off home!'

They still chuckle about it now, and how this collection of home-grown players could be acclaimed as phenomenally successful superstars one minute and then berated by their manager like disobedient children. Perhaps it was a bit of both which made them great.

Many successful sides have been built without a group of friends at the core, but what an advantage to have – not just in the talent but the spirit. To have a brilliant cabal who were bonded by close personal ties; loyal to the club that had taken them in as children; schooled in the expectations of a team and manager who would not settle for second best.

By 1998, the Class of '92 were coming into their mid-20s, to their prime, and they formed an unbreakable core at the heart of the dressing room. There was no one more influential than Roy Keane, but even the skipper had to accept that this group gave Ferguson's second generation of champions its character. As Keane noted in his autobiography, 'At the heart of our club there is something solid, something real, something identifiably Mancunian, an attitude created by the Six Amigos, that is fundamental to the team and its success. When players join United, however much they cost, wherever they come from, it is this attitude they must plug into.'

It was an attitude which had been shaped since they arrived as schoolboys. They had been moulded through the youth teams, sometimes brutally, by the coaches, Eric Harrison and Nobby Stiles. They had seen first-hand from Bruce, Hughes, Cantona and the rest of Ferguson's first title-winning team what it took to be winners, and to withstand the pressures of playing for United.

Gary Neville laughs at memories of that undeniably macho, combustible team ripping into each other, or engaged in furious bust-ups with the manager. 'Proper going for it. "You're a fucking disgrace." It mesmerised me the first four or five years. Warriors like you wouldn't believe, ferocious. And we had to step up. We had to really step up. To be honest, you could say that they weren't the nicest people to play with at times. They were so demanding, so aggressive. You lived or died by it.'

It was an intensity the Class of '92 had sought to maintain as senior players, on into the 1998-99 season. As Neville says, 'England against the Rest of the World on a Friday, you're talking about 22 maniacs. I mean people would do anything to win.'

The manager was a tough parental figure who could be harder on this group than any of his squad. As Neville recalls – the spokesman of the Class of '92 group then as now – that run around the university was not a one-off. 'Once we lost in the reserves at Everton. We were called in by the manager at 6 a.m. to do cross-country, a proper 10-15km through woods and mud. Punishment, basically.

'It was old-school mentality but I really loved the fact that I came through in a world where you experienced those traditional principles. If you don't do well there is a consequence. Whereas now you're talking about sports science and analytics and data. There's been a huge shift in technology and modern approach towards leadership. I don't think you can have that spirit of the '80s, '90s in a modern working environment.' His voice carries an air of regret.

He understands why the world has changed but cannot help but lament the loss of resilience and discipline that came from a robust upbringing. The Class of '92 had come through not only on rare ability – the first United youth team to win the FA Youth Cup since 1964, when George Best was a prodigy – but by surviving the test of character. Plenty failed, which made those who endured feel like the elite of the SAS. They were the ones still standing after Ferguson had weeded out those he regarded as weak-minded.

After the Busby Babes, they had to be given their own moniker, but 'Fergie's Fledglings' is a terrible name because it does not begin to capture the drive embodied by Gary Neville's approach, even as a 14-year-old, that if academy training started at 5 p.m., he would be kicking a ball against a wall by 4.30. Neville knew he had no choice but to work hard, but it was intrinsic to all of them. There was not a harder-working group of teenagers in the country.

In their own ways, they had steeliness too. In his second autobiography, Ferguson expressed his love for strong characters. The manager might want control of his players, but he knew that timidity could not thrive at United. 'Those lads from the 1992 class were never scared of anything,' he said.

To follow this group's rise, tracking their careers from their earliest days, mixing with their families on trips and eventually assisting Beckham and Neville with memoirs – almost growing up in the game together it could feel to me (certainly not to them) – was to be given an education not so much in the talent it takes to reach the top, and stay there, but the depths of persistence, the relentless application.

The idea that Beckham was just a preening peacock, with a bird brain, never did add up. You only had to meet his parents, Ted, a gas fitter, and Sandra, a hairdresser, on the road to understand he had his head screwed on. He might be the apprentice who hankered after leather seats in the first club car, a touch of Cockney flash, but when we spent time together in 1996 at the Toulon tournament in France, where journalists could mix freely by the pool with England's most promising young players, Beckham was almost shy. Certainly not a poseur.

He was seriously focused, and not just in perfecting his right-foot delivery. Helping to write one of his early books (Victoria said it contained 'nice pictures', which was a fair summation of my input as the wordsmith), I told Beckham that the publishers were hassling for some spicy content. 'They'll get what I give them,' he replied. Beckham knew his own worth. In fact, he knew exactly what he wanted, and how to get it, as much as anyone I have met in sport.

That his best friend was Gary Neville spoke well for his groundedness. Neville always has possessed one of the most finely tuned antenna for bullshit; as down to earth as a highly successful footballer at one of the biggest clubs in the world could be. 'The Foreman', as Eric Harrison called him even back in the youth team, had an opinion on everything – but while you might disagree, you could not question his conviction or sincerity.

To know Neville Neville, a former lorry driver who used to start work at 5 a.m. to get his rounds done, and Jill, toiling away conscientiously at Bury FC even as their three offspring, Gary, Phil and Tracey, all excelled at the highest level of sport, was to understand where the work ethic came from, as well as the core of loyalty.

Giggs was much harder to get to know, partly because his manager wanted it that way. Even his teammates would say there were parts no one ever really penetrated. In the early days, he could be as elusive to pin down for an interview as he was on the ball as Ferguson sought to protect the boy-genius. A year older than the rest, he was the phenomenon who became 'the king, the man,' as his manager called him, making his first-team debut at 17 even before lifting the FA Youth Cup as captain in 1992. He seemed reserved but had a hard edge, and would follow Keane in testing new recruits. 'We would bobble balls up, hospital passes, we would smash them if we had a chance,' Giggs said with relish.

Nicky Butt was Giggs's closest friend among the group, and they were fellow mischief-makers. Butt had a streak of jack the lad, which served him well on the field. He had a reputation for fearlessness but when I asked him what drove him on he replied that it was fear – not of anyone (he never had that) but of being left behind. He had seen much more skilful players cast aside at United, but ability on the ball never was the only test, or even the key one, for Ferguson.

Temperament was vital, and Paul Scholes had a character that his manager loved for its anti-showbiz attitude on top of marvellous abilities as a scheming player that seemed so un-English. Except for the complexion, Scholes should have been born in Barcelona. He came into interviews like he was already looking for the exit – but when talent is so eloquent, that is more than enough.

These six were all friends, but they also formed pairs; Gary Neville and Beckham, Giggs and Butt, Scholes with the younger Neville. Phil was full of athletic talent, two-footed, a brilliant cricketer though always mindful that it was Gary, older by almost a couple of years, who expected to have the last word. Phil would always smile at how if he said to meet at 6 p.m., Gary would reply, 'Make it 5.50.'

In *My Autobiography*, Ferguson noted of Phil that if you asked him to run up a hill, sprint back down then cut down a tree, he would respond: 'Right, boss, where's the chainsaw?'" But you would not have found any of this gang shirking the mission.

With the growing tide of foreign players – December 1999 would see Chelsea field the first overseas XI in more than a century of English league football – there was no single way to be successful. The game was opening up to foreign influences as never before. Every club, including United, was increasingly looking to the overseas market which made this home-grown group even more extraordinary. That they came through together, and enjoyed such success over a sustained period, might be the true miracle of United, and European football, in the late '90s. We could call it freakish were it not for the fact that Ferguson had transformed the youth policy at United precisely with the intention of bringing through such a crop.

As Gary Neville explains, 'If you think I joined the academy at the age of 11 in 1986, everything that happened in 1999 was designed 13 years earlier. The manager wanted young players he could mould and bring through, knowing he had loyalty and commitment and continuity. To get them to a level where they're the best in the country, it's phenomenal. Whatever happened in 1999 was the culmination of a vision.'

30

Big Peter

At Manchester Airport one April morning in 1997, the media pack are in our familiar position, loitering near the desk where the United players will check in for our flight to Dortmund for the Champions League semi-final first leg (these are the days when journalists are allowed on the team plane, albeit knowing our place at the rear). It is one of the club's biggest games for years, arguably decades, and we feel short of material. 'You get on well with big Pete,' one of my colleagues says. 'See if he'll give us something.' So off I go to grab Peter Schmeichel for a few words. Decent guy that he is beneath the shouty, angry competitor, he stops to chat as I turn on the tape recorder.

Given all that is at stake, how close United are to claiming the biggest prize in club football, an obvious theme is how this team might compare to the European champions of 1968. Schmeichel readily engages. 'We would beat them 10-0,' he says. Mmmm. That sounds like a story. He is not being arrogant or dismissive – at least not intentionally. Indeed, he goes on to explain how the game has transformed over the decades. 'We probably play at twice the speed they did in 1968,' he says. 'That's why I'm saying we would beat them. Just look at the old videos and see the space and time on the ball they had. That doesn't happen anymore.'

He is careful to acknowledge that Matt Busby's European champions were a great side in their own time. 'But things change. Back in 1968, it was a different world, probably a better world. But you look back and realise they walked football in those days. They didn't run. The game has become quicker and quicker.'

It is a fair debate, and a great talking point, for the eve of a Champions League semi-final. But I can foresee the problem. I have already agreed to share the quotes with my fellow journalists, and in certain newspapers, the story will not be packaged with – how best to put it? – all the nuance of Schmeichel's argument. However tactfully some of my colleagues write it up, the headlines will scream arrogance. I am not wrong.

That 10-0 line is splashed all over the back pages the following morning. 'What Fergie's side would do to Busby stars'; Schmeichel's 'extraordinary claim', and so on. The *Mirror* have sent a reporter to ask George Best what he makes of the idea that he would be spanked 10-0. Unsurprisingly he is unimpressed. 'Insult!' he cries. 'How can he say things like that? Our team of '68 had three European Footballers of the Year in it – Bobby Charlton, Denis Law, and me. He's out of order, gone right over the top. I think he must be dreaming his Danish dreams. We won the European Cup. United haven't even got to the final.'

Players do not appreciate being in the thick of controversy on the morning of one of the biggest games of their lives – especially when United lose to a Borussia Dortmund team they should beat. Worse still, Schmeichel had been injured in the warm-up and forced to watch from the sidelines.

I have a feeling Schmeichel is going to be fuming and, standing in the mixed zone in an underground tunnel at the Westfalenstadion where journalists wait to speak to players after a match, I experience what it must be like for a United defender who has just made some calamitously careless error to let down the world's best goalkeeper. Schmeichel is a strapping 6ft 3ins and he has never seemed bigger as he storms over, clearly furious. Wagging a finger, face reddening, he erupts. 'Bobby Charlton is in that dressing room and you've made me look a fucking idiot in front of him,' he shouts.

There is no defence but I try anyway, pointing out that the articles were fine, it was just the headlines. Off he storms in a rage, which is not soothed when United stumble in the second leg. Another European failure. We do start talking again, but the incident is bad enough for Schmeichel to recall it when we chat for this book almost 25 years later.

If that is one reason for Schmeichel to crave victory in Europe, a much bigger one is revealed in mid-November 1998, catching us all by surprise. At a press conference at Old Trafford, he announces that he is going to leave United at the end of the season. A week before his 35th birthday, a subdued, reflective Schmeichel says that he is starting to feel the physical strain. 'I am enjoying the game as much as ever but it is getting harder to keep pace,' he says. He can come over as a man with a towering ego but there is humility, too.

He is feeling worn out in his eighth season at Old Trafford. After losing a World Cup quarter-final to Brazil with Denmark in the summer, he had just ten days off before returning to training. Ferguson had wanted him back for Champions League qualification. Mentally and physically, he feels shattered. We had seen it in some uncharacteristic mistakes, like at Bayern and letting in a soft free-kick against Brondby.

Schmeichel had taken his concerns first to Martin Edwards, the chairman, and then to his manager. Ferguson had not been thrilled that he was second to hear the news. When Schmeichel went to speak to him at the Cliff to explain his wish to leave, the meeting was short and businesslike. 'You'll go at the end of the season,' Ferguson said. 'But make sure it's a good one, eh?'

They had initially kept the decision quiet but, with questions mounting about Schmeichel's fitness and form, the big goalkeeper wanted to seize the agenda. Reflecting now, he admits that he rushed into a hasty announcement.

It was the end of an era. We marked the news by stating that whatever happened in Schmeichel's final season, his stature was assured. He had helped United to become the dominant force in England with four Premier League titles and two FA Cups, not just through his rare talents but by bringing aggression even to a role between the posts.

Ferguson called him 'an attacking goalkeeper', which was, in part, to do with the goals he scored – including one I saw against Rotor Volgograd in the Uefa Cup in 1995 when he leapt to head in a Ryan Giggs corner – but mostly the way he defended his penalty box, and his goal, like it was a personal insult to put the ball past him. He was huge and intimidating, and his idiosyncratic star-fish saves not only made full use of his big frame, but his ability to psyche out a striker. A photograph of him diving to save at White Hart Lane, almost horizontal high off the ground with the ball cradled in his left hand, is an iconic image of an outstanding goalkeeper's athleticism.

A £550,000 recruit from Brondby in August 1991, he was arguably Ferguson's best-value signing. In announcing they would allow Schmeichel to leave without a fee on the proviso that he did not join another English club, United recognised all the years of wonderful service.

Beneath the belligerence has always been a thoughtful character who had worked in a number of jobs – carpet fitter, cleaning in an old people's home – before becoming a full-time goalkeeper. Schmeichel has always made a fascinating interviewee, with his curiosity about the world. The son of a Polish musician and a Danish nurse, he now had a desire to see more of the planet. 'I was pointing out on a map to my son, Kasper, all the countries I'd been to when I realised I could hardly tell him about anything other than hotels and stadiums,' he reflected as he explained why it was time to move beyond Manchester.

In his column in *The Times*, Gary Neville reckoned that Schmeichel would be harder to replace than Bryan Robson or Eric Cantona (so it proved for a number of years). No teammate, he said, was more obviously the best in the world or had more mastery of his position. Ferguson called Schmeichel the best goalkeeper he has ever come across.

His farewell tour had begun, and Schmeichel told the press conference that he would do all he could to ensure that he left with a trophy. One in particular. 'We have been working towards the European Cup for a long time,' he said. 'And to win it now at the end would be a dream come true.'

Little did he know, sitting at Old Trafford on 12 November, that his fantasies would only be half as good as the real thing.

31

AGM

Fewer than 200 of the 28,000 shareholders of Manchester United PLC might usually be expected to attend the company's AGM. In November 1998, there were more than a thousand straining for access to the Manchester Suite of Old Trafford's North Stand. The atmosphere was as electric as a big game under lights.

Ned Kelly and his men were on high alert. United's burly head of security, who was never short of a story about his previous work in the SAS (and some of those tales might even have been true), was worried by the size of the crowd who had come to protest against the proposed Murdoch takeover. Some of his men tried to stop the rebels handing out leaflets, which inflamed tensions. There was a mutinous air, especially when Martin Edwards started responding to fierce criticism from the floor.

Heckled that the sale to Murdoch was driven by personal enrichment, Edwards replied, 'That's got nothing to do with it. Once you get beyond a certain figure, money does not mean anything at all.' The chairman was not going to win any prizes for diplomacy.

The board had to field questions, or angry tirades, for more than two hours. One by one fans stood up to berate the directors for seeking to sell out, even if the deal was now out of their hands, given it had been passed by Tony Blair's government to the Monopolies and Mergers Commission to investigate.

One fan reminded the meeting that Edwards had once held

talks with the late Robert Maxwell and then Michael Knighton. 'Now Murdoch,' he said. 'What an unholy trinity. Three strikes and you're out. Go, Mr Edwards, go!'

A woman, visibly upset, told him, 'The majority of us have lost faith in you. We believe that all you care about is making money when we want to continue the traditions of Sir Matt Busby.'

Another insisted, 'Please think about what the real shareholders want – without the supporters you are nothing.'

Implied was a threat that supporters could be driven away. But when Edwards looked outside, he could see queues of day-trippers at the Old Trafford Megastore. He could see the long snake of fans at the ticket office. Asked afterwards whether he was surprised by the ill feeling at the AGM, Edwards replied, 'Not really.' It was not that he did not care – but he knew the bottom line told a very different story.

32

The brand plays on

When Manchester United released a new home kit for the 1998–99 season – the 13th jersey in five years, yet still safely predicted to be the best-selling shirt ever – the most obvious modernisation was Umbro's 'revolutionary' zip collar. Fans queued up for hours to be first in line when the jerseys went on sale at midnight at the club shops.

The zip still makes that shirt a coveted retro classic, but a closer look revealed a change of much greater symbolism and significance. The club crest – with its ship from Manchester City Council's coat of arms, and red devil holding a trident – had been altered for the first time in decades. The words 'Football Club' had vanished.

By the late '90s, 'Football Club' was too limiting for the new wave of ambitious marketing men sweeping into Old Trafford. Manchester United was now much more than a team playing football. It was a global corporation and brand.

These days, we take the commercialism of football as normal, inevitable, unstoppable. It was a revolution then, with the launch in 1998 of MUTV as a new subscription channel, United shops springing up overseas, an MUFC credit card and everything from an official lager to chocolate bar. Steven Howard of *The Sun* joined the day-trippers and souvenir-shoppers heading into the new Megastore, which had been added to the Superstore at Old Trafford. 'Fourteen shirts, an exploding Alex Ferguson alarm clock and two books later – *Me and Me Cars*, by David Beckham, and *A Day In The Life of Ryan Giggs's Gerbil* – you spin out of the United Super Mega Mega Super Megastore blinking at the light,' he wrote, with just a dash of cynicism.

You could call it crass commercialism, as many did, but it was working. People lapped up anything with a United logo. Annual turnover from merchandising soared from £1.2 million in 1992 to £28 million in the year to the end of September 1997, and carried on growing. By 1998, merchandise sales had helped United become the world's richest club. According to a report by Deloitte Touche, United's financial muscle was unmatched with a £87.9 million turnover ahead of Real Madrid (£72.2 million), Bayern Munich (£65.2 million) and Juventus (£55.3 million). United's revenues were as much as Arsenal and Chelsea's combined and accounted for almost a fifth of the Premier League's total turnover.

This success created its own tensions. Traditionalists argued that if so much money was being generated, why was there a need to keep increasing ticket prices at Old Trafford, which had seen the cheapest seat rise from £10 to £14 in three seasons by 1998? It was all well and good to keep expanding the stadium – in September the board had submitted a planning application to increase capacity by more than 20 per cent to 67,400 at a cost of £30 million – but the hardcore were increasingly disgruntled by corporatisation. More seats could make the atmosphere worse, not better, if there were too many tourist fans and the prawn-sandwich brigade.

Put the criticism to Martin Edwards and the former chairman is indignant. What was he to do? Ignore the commercial opportunities? Not generate money? He points to the £28 million spent on players in the summer of 1998 to insist that this unprecedented income for a football club was being deployed in pursuit of glory, not just share dividends. As Hugh McIlvanney in the *Sunday Times* put more succinctly than Edwards ever could, 'They argue that they can stay in the business of dreams only so long as they succeed in the business of business.'

Money had always mattered in football – Sunderland were called 'The Bank of England' club in the late 1940s and '50s for their spending – but the league table would increasingly come to represent not just the best team but the richest, too. In taking 'Football Club' off the crest, United were advertising not just their own global aspirations but a wider shift in a game that would become increasingly stratified on financial strength.

Edwards knew the change would attract criticism but pressed ahead anyway. 'People said, "United are so arrogant." But if you think about it, if you are a brand you don't need to put "football club". They don't put Harlem Globetrotters "Basketball Team", do they?' That was not a comparison likely to soothe anyone in the Stretford End – but nor were they about to stop buying the new shirts. Replicas of that 1998-99 jersey, available at £55, are still doing a brisk business from the club's online store.

---

* It was hard not to laugh when the Glazers let it be known in 2013 that they had never liked the 1998 change of crest. Too corporate and too commercial, said the club's American owners, who have, of course, become a byword for corporate and commercial in football. 'I didn't like that change of badge,' said Ed Woodward, the regime's chief executive. 'Joel [Glazer] didn't like that change. We will look at that and have a think about that. We are a football club, not a business.'

In 2021 the Glazers opened the first of five new 'entertainment centres' in China, including the 'Theatre of Dreams' near Tiananmen Square, which offered an interactive journey through United's history and no end of merchandise. A huge United crest was installed over the front. Despite Woodward's comments, 'Football Club' was still missing (as was success). But if you were looking for symbolism, the ship on the badge was sailing in the wrong direction.

33

The Hairdryer

The 'hairdryer' nickname given to Alex Ferguson's bursts of rage showed good imagination from Mark Hughes, that revered Manchester United forward of mighty thighs and thunderous volleys, but it always struck me as greatly underplaying the full force of one of the manager's tirades. To be on the receiving end was never to mistake his fury for simply hot air.

A Ferguson blast was not just an audible assault but a full bodily experience. The reverberations shuddered through you. He would step intimidatingly close, face turning crimson, with a torrent of F- and C-words which drowned out any attempts at retaliation. 'Furious', as his players at Aberdeen knew him, could intimidate the hardest of men without needing to raise a fist, just his voice.

Ferguson always insisted that the deployment of such rage was much rarer than popular legend would lead you to believe, but it could be unforgettable when he erupted. In 1998-99, that occasion came on 21 November in the away dressing room at Hillsborough, as United collapsed against Danny Wilson's Sheffield Wednesday.

A tracksuit-bottomed Peter Schmeichel had let in a soft early goal from Niclas Alexandersson, fumbling a head-high shot backwards – 'straightforward even for the goalkeeper in a pub team on a Sunday morning,' Jon Champion said scornfully from the BBC's commentary gantry – as the goalkeeper still struggled to shrug off his early-season fatigue. The big Dane was completely out of sorts, and his mistake set a chaotic tone. United were level by half-time when Cole and Yorke combined for a brilliant goal – a one-two in which Cole ran on to Yorke's deft chip forward – but that equaliser was not going to spare the players from their fiercest berating of the season.

'What the fuck is that? What the fuck are you lot playing at?' Ferguson demanded to know. 'That is the biggest load of shite I've ever seen. Not one of you can look me in the eye, because not one of you deserves to have a say. I can't believe you've come here and decided to toss it off like that crap you're playing out there.'

The manager was just clearing his throat for the real fury to come. Crimson-faced, Ferguson exploded and kicked out at a medical treatment table in the middle of the room. He always did like to use props to register that his anger was at full blast. A startled Stam, who had never seen Ferguson erupt like this, ducked as drink bottles and medical accessories went flying. Ferguson picked up a stray container and hurled it towards the showers. Then he started singling out players for a verbal battering. They were all in the firing line, including Yorke. 'Get hold of the fucking ball! You're giving soft balls away, allowing people to come through you,' Ferguson shouted.

The blast did not do much good. Even though Wednesday were missing the talented but notoriously volatile Paolo di Canio, serving an 11-game ban for pushing over referee Paul Alcock two months earlier, they were soon back ahead. Ten minutes into the second half, Wednesday pulled United's defence apart with Schmeichel blaming himself for being slow off his line, helpless as Wim Jonk made it 2-1. Another defensive howler led to the third, with Beckham trying to head the ball to Stam on the edge of the United area. Stam's control was clumsy and Alexandersson nipped in to score.

The players were in a foul mood as they came off at the final whistle, not least Beckham, who had been whacked by Andy Hinchcliffe. It all kicked off when the Wednesday full-back taunted Beckham as they entered the tunnel, with Andy Cole grabbing Hinchcliffe by the throat.

It was no less tempestuous across the corridor. Keane was already sounding off as he returned to the dressing room with a clatter of studs and an air of recrimination. Yorke remembers Schmeichel and Keane having to be separated to stop them coming to blows. They never did need much excuse to argue.

Chatting to Yorke more than 20 years later, he could still recall the sense of all hell breaking loose, with Ferguson's fury piled on top of recriminations among senior players. 'That's the first time I really saw the hairdryer. At Villa maybe I'd seen a little stuff like that, but not the battles in the dressing room and players going at each other. Big personalities in that dressing room, big egos as well, and for the first time I witnessed it. That's when it all came out. We all had it in the neck and rightly so, but I just never saw it before where the players got involved.'

Ferguson put on a pretence of control to the media after the game but his words carried a sharp edge. 'Unrecognisable and unacceptable,' he said, damningly of his team. United had not lost since the defeat to Arsenal two months earlier but the manager worried that his players were picking and choosing their battles. 'You wonder whether we are a big-game team now,' he said. 'They let themselves down really because we know that come Wednesday against Barcelona they'll probably excel.'

They did, too.

34

The old one-two

The night before they are due to face Barcelona on 25 November, the United players step out in the Nou Camp for a training session. For some, it is their first visit to a stadium that makes even experienced players look up in awe inside this giant bowl which seems to reach up to the heavens. As United will discover, there are few better sporting venues for immortal deeds.

As they train, the ball zips around on a pitch so slick and true that it feels like you could hit a 147 break on it. Alex Ferguson cannot get his players to stop as they put the domestic bumps behind them to revel on the grand European stage. The Champions League brings the best out of them, an extra edge. This is what makes all the hard work worthwhile, and the players indulge themselves inside an empty Nou Camp with flicks and tricks. Too many for the manager's liking. 'Albert, get those balls in the bag,' Ferguson tells the kitman as the players insist on more shooting practice. They are like kids refusing to listen to the demands of a frustrated parent that they come in for their tea.

At one point, feeling the mood a bit too light-hearted, Ferguson barks at Cole to concentrate. 'Cole, stop fucking about! Focus will you!' he shouts. The instruction is still running through the striker's head when he sees a Ford Focus hoarding next to the pitch. Cole says to the rest of the players that he is going to score in the following night's game and then run over to the sign to celebrate and prove a point to the manager. He senses it is going to be a night for something special.

The one-two, the give-and-go, is among the most basic of football skills but there is something about the way that Cole and Yorke pull it off in the 53rd minute in the Nou Camp that elevates it into performance art. No understanding of football is necessary to appreciate the slick movement, the uncanny understanding and the technical perfection. Like all the very best sport, it is both intricate and beautifully simple.

This is the place to do it, in the home of pass and move. 'The university of the pass,' as the football writer Simon Kuper once called Barcelona's academy. In this wonderful arena, Cole and Yorke pull off a goal that becomes their signature move. They could be the Torvill and Dean, or Ginger Rogers and Fred Astaire, of the football pitch – perfect dance partners with joyous telepathy, an uncanny understanding, a natural flow.

They had pulled off a similar move in United's previous Champions League tie; the 5-0 trouncing of Brondby at Old Trafford which had shown a side playing joyfully unfettered attacking football. Their duet had been the best goal of the night as Cole stepped over an infield pass from Jesper Blomqvist to allow the ball to run on to Yorke – and then collected the return before chipping over the goalkeeper. That stepover part in the build-up was not planned, just clever communication and awareness which would be used to such effect again in the dazzling upgrade in Barcelona.

In another compelling European tie between two teams who seemed incapable of playing at less than full throttle, the score was 1-1 when Keane slipped a pass forward to Yorke. He did the stepover part this time, allowing the ball to run on to Cole. Yorke broke forward to receive Cole's first-time pass, taking one marker out of the game.

With Samuel Okunowo drawn out of defence towards the ball, that left the space for Cole to run into as Yorke hit a first-time return. Cole took one touch to steady himself before assuredly striking a low shot past Ruud Hesp into the bottom corner. It is one of the great one-two goals. And Cole did run over to the Focus sign, with a huge grin on his face.

Cole still loves to watch it back. 'As you retire and become older that goal gets better and better for me every time I see it,' he says. 'The understanding is phenomenal. It wasn't prepared; we just knew. I love that goal. Football is a simple game which is complicated by fools. All these formations and all this messing about. I think the way the manager wanted us to play was to get it, pass it to a red shirt, use the space, just do it easy. So that's what we used to do.'

It was a move to seal the partnership in the minds of the public, and teammates. When he became a coach, Ole Gunnar Solskjær said that he would run sessions of link play with two strikers and see if they could pull off 'the Yorke and Cole'. The pair could have patented it. 'Ah, it was poetry,' Cole says. In ten games they had started together from their pairing at Southampton to cutting apart Barcelona, Cole and Yorke had scored 16 goals.

Not even Rivaldo could overshadow that combination, but the bow-legged Brazilian gave it his best shot. Barcelona needed to win to qualify for the next round of the Champions League and Rivaldo carried their hopes in another contest of thrilling, see-sawing drama. 'A night of complete abandon,' Alex Ferguson would recall.

Four minutes after Cole and Yorke's combination, Rivaldo hit a long-range free-kick past a wrong-footed Schmeichel to make it 2-2. In a game of incessant chances, Beckham whipped in yet another perfect cross for Yorke to head United back into the lead, but Rivaldo was still not done. This time he took the ball on his chest with his back to goal and scored with a bicycle kick. A genius was at work. Rivaldo thundered a long-range shot against the crossbar before the final whistle at 3–3.

Especially for players such as Irwin, Keane, Giggs and Butt, who had been subjected to the 4–0 thrashing by a much superior Barcelona team in 1994, it felt like a major breakthrough. United's players walked off feeling as though, having effectively knocked out the team of Rivaldo, Luís Figo and a young Xavi, they could take on anyone in Europe.

They still needed to avoid defeat against Bayern Munich in the final game – only two runners-up from the six groups progressed to the quarter-finals – but that was accomplished, after some late confusion, with a 1–1 draw at Old Trafford (Ferguson could not believe his eyes when one of the Bayern officials pulled up the other European scores on his mobile phone to confirm United's progress. What technological wizardry!). In the toughest group in the competition, United had finished a point behind Bayern, but they were unbeaten in six matches and had scored 20 goals, and conceded 11. Whatever happened in the rest of the European campaign, it could not possibly be dull.

35

Teddy

On the day that the rest of the players were reeling from Alex Ferguson's tirade in Sheffield, Teddy Sheringham should have been working out at the Cliff as he recovered from a knee injury. The striker had thought he was fit enough to play in Sheffield and was sulking that he had been omitted. It was then that he decided to do something stupid.

Jumping in his red Ferrari, Sheringham skipped the scheduled solitary training session and drove down to London for a night out – as if proving that Roy Keane might have had a point in that drunken rant earlier in the year about the Cockney wide boy in his flash motor. It was a daft move that recklessly underestimated Ferguson's ability to find out all sorts of details that his players would not want him to know.

Sheringham soon heard that he had been rumbled. For a short while, he thought about trying to lie his way out of the problem. 'The manager pulled me in to give me the opportunity to tell him if I went in or not,' Sheringham says. It crossed his mind to try to make up some excuse but, wisely, he decided to confess. Ferguson respected the honesty but still told his forward that he was fined a week's wages and would not be going on the imminent Champions League trip to Barcelona. 'I had never played in the Nou Camp,' Sheringham says. 'Bollocks! I never did that again.'

*

It was a problem Sheringham could have done without in a season of difficulties. As he sits at home, in Camp Nou in Chingford, and chats over a cup of tea, it becomes clear how assumptions of glory and good times for footballers can be misplaced. Sheringham is reflective, and even a little vulnerable, as he talks about life at United and especially the 1998-99 campaign; far removed from the man who once had a reputation for being aloof, among team-mates and media.

'When I do Q&As with fans, it's usually about that season. I get asked what an amazing time it must have been. But I say, "Do you know how many goals I scored?" Five. Ridiculous. People often think I won player of the year or whatever and you look back and think, "What a great ending." Apart from the last two weeks it was probably the worst season of my career.'

Sheringham had endured a tough time at United. He was signed in the summer of 1997 following the departure of a certain Frenchman. Eric Cantona was irreplaceable as a United icon, but it was Sheringham's job to try. His first season finished without a trophy, enabling Arsenal fans to gleefully sing the song about Teddy going to United and winning fuck all. But it was the lack of warmth from United fans which was more troubling. It was startling to read a scathing profile in the *United We Stand* fanzine from May 1998 and to be reminded just how Sheringham was a scapegoat for a trophyless season, even though falling short had many causes. As the piece went:

Least likely to say: C'mon let's get stuck in.

Most likely to say: The transmission on this Ferrari is superb.

Not to be confused with: Eric Cantona

And then there was the dressing room. Sheringham is surprisingly frank about never quite fitting in at United. He does not try to justify his dash to London, but he had a young son who was being brought up in the south, and he never had the circle of close friends in Manchester that he had back home.

As we have discovered, there was Keane not speaking to him; Andy Cole giving him the silent treatment. The Class of '92 gang did not set out to exclude him but they were almost a decade younger and bound by their own close friendships. Talking to Peter Schmeichel, he said that he initially thought Sheringham was arrogant and only realised later that his remoteness was a protective shield.

As Sheringham put it, 'I've spoken quite a lot to my friends about it and they say, "You must have had a great time in Manchester, winning all that stuff, with the players they had." It was fantastic football, but it wasn't the best time of my life socially. I wasn't enjoying myself immensely. There was still that bit missing, "Fuck me, lads, this is brilliant, let's go a bit nuts and enjoy it." There was such a focus.

'When you analyse that squad; three Norwegian boys, lovely but a bit different to my upbringing. Then the Class of '92, younger than me, close-knit. I don't think they realise how close they were, a little bubble come through the ranks together. To try and get into that bubble was very tough. They weren't the most forthcoming even though they would say, "What are you talking about?" It's quite weird. Maybe it was because I was older, from London. Maybe it was a Northern/Southern divide.'

What of the others? 'Roy's Roy. Denis, lovely man, who I still speak to now. David May was a big voice in the dressing room. I played a lot of golf with Dwight. He was still my mate even though he nicked my place. He had a lovely way about him and fun. I didn't get on with Coley. I had no real pals like [at] Tottenham or Forest where we were always grouped together and went out together.'

The arrival of Yorke as a record signing in his position was hardly going to make Sheringham feel more comfortable. He quickly decided that it was not going to help his case by complaining. 'Any other player might have thrown his toys out of the pram but I'm at the best club in the world,' he says. 'You come off the training pitch many times going "wow, what a session". Such a high standard, such high intensity, and that's what you want from your footballing career, you want to be tested every day.'

At 32, he decided to stick at it. United had paid £3 million to take him from Spurs so it was not as though he was an expensive understudy. 'At £10 million I might have had to leave to recoup the money,' he says. Sheringham soldiered on but, by January, he was still fighting to have an impact on the season. He had struggled with another knee injury. He felt under pressure to return but there always seemed to be another setback.

Seeing Sheringham subdued, Ferguson pulled him to one side at the training ground and told him not to rush back. 'Just make sure you are fit for the long run,' the manager said. 'I've got a funny feeling it's going to be a big season.' Sheringham recalls that chat with a smile. 'He saw me looking down and needing a little pep up. It was the perfect chat. I definitely took it to heart. That was good enough for me. And you look back and think, "Maybe he could see what was coming. Wow!"'

36

Pressure

They all felt the pressure in unique ways, but rarely talked about it. Certainly not at the time. It was only later that they would open up that it was fiendishly hard to be a footballer at Manchester United: not in the same way that it is tough to play for Accrington Stanley, nor, indeed, to be a self-employed plumber. But the job brought unique stresses and strains. There were colossal expectations. Constant scrutiny. The rewards were vast – immense wealth, glory on the best days and the chance to live out what so many millions of us would regard as a fantasy existence – but it was interesting to speak to the players and to hear that the pressures could weigh heavily upon them.

In Roy Keane's first autobiography, he talked about the 'savage business' of playing for United. 'You can earn a lot of money and be a hero – whatever that is. But you can also be a failure, humiliated, blasted in the media, jeered by the crowd, or simply left out of the team, a very public slight that hurts not just you but your family, wife, kids, mum, dad, brothers, sisters. The stakes are high, other people's judgements merciless.' Keane might have seemed as impervious as granite to the outside world but even he felt the heat from fans, pundits and the media. 'Bad times are only ninety minutes away. At this club a moment's weakness can lead to shame.'

By the late '90s, every single game was regarded as winnable. Defeat was a shock. Two was a crisis. A fanbase of millions willed on their heroes, but was fickle to any downturn. Andy Cole had suffered from periods of chronic self-doubt. Sheringham, as we have heard, was struggling if not with pressure then the demands of filling Cantona's boots. There will even be a time when Ryan Giggs goes through spells of uncertainty, with the crowd on his back.

Jaap Stam was emerging as a defender of real significance for United, but he put himself under huge strain to justify his fee and reputation. As he explained, 'My wife and I had conversations after my career. "Did you enjoy it?" No. I didn't enjoy it too much because we were always under the pressure of performing, doing better, thinking about the game, thinking about that one mistake, needing to prove yourself until the final game of the season.' Nowhere did that pressure feel as relentless as at United.

Paul Scholes looked utterly bemused when I asked how much fun it must have been as such a talented player at the heart of this side. 'Fun? Perhaps when you are 5-0 up,' he said. 'Or after you've won something.' Fun was something for park players.

'You didn't talk. You cracked on. The stuff inside was your business to handle.' Now that he is approaching 60 and has become a grandfather, as well as going through divorce and a few other life lessons, Peter Schmeichel can reflect on how he bottled up his own tensions.

At the time, he felt a need to be the big, dominant presence. Being an alpha male was part of Schmeichel's character from childhood and one of the reasons Ferguson had wanted him. It felt intrinsic to his success at Old Trafford to be tough, uncompromising – the 'Mad Mullah' as his manager sometimes called him.

He thrived as this intimidating 6ft 3ins, 16st goalkeeper who screamed at teammates for not crossing properly in practice, and hated acknowledging he had screwed up. Schmeichel returned from injury once. 'The operation has not worked because Peter still won't admit it when he has made a mistake,' Brian McClair said drolly.

As reserve goalkeeper, Raimond van der Gouw would watch Schmeichel play even when he was injured and despair at the senior man's refusal to take a day off. It would drive van der Gouw mad. He had huge respect for his abilities but told the UTD podcast that 'sometimes I hated him'. Schmeichel could be selfish and, indeed, 'a pain in the arse'. Van der Gouw recalled a game at Wimbledon where Schmeichel had a hamstring injury which meant he could barely kick the ball yet still insisted on battling on. No weakness.

It was with that same macho pride that Schmeichel had taken the decision to step away from United without first consulting family, teammates or his manager. Reluctant to open up, or ask for help, he had concluded that it was all or nothing. Only after he had publicly announced that he would be leaving at the end of the season did he, finally, show a little vulnerability.

He had gone to see Ferguson in the wake of the Sheffield Wednesday debacle to apologise for a shabby performance. He knew he had not been playing well through a combination of mental and physical fatigue. He was honest about his struggles.

Ferguson's unexpected response was to pull out the fixture list, ask Schmeichel to keep going through the busy December programme, and promise him a week's sunshine leave early in the New Year. A relieved goalkeeper started looking into a family holiday to Barbados and the chance to lie on a lounger soaking up restorative rays. Immediately he felt better.

Schmeichel had shown a little fragility and found a manager who was willing to listen, and adapt. He wonders now how different it might have been had he reached out for help before. But that was not the way you did things.

You carried the strain inside, even if that meant taking it out on your family. As Schmeichel explained, 'At that level of performance, whether it is sport or music or theatre, you don't walk around thinking every day, "oh, I'm under pressure", but sometimes something snaps. It might be an argument with my wife – you love her and you know it's crazy but that's the mental pressure you are under.'

How much of that pressure was self-inflicted is, he says, hard to estimate. By never disclosing it at the time, they were never likely to find out.

37

Strife of Brian, part one

On the night of 2 December, as United prepared to face
Tottenham Hotspur in the Worthington Cup at White Hart Lane,
Brian Kidd could be seen running flustered along Tottenham
High Road less than an hour before kick-off. Travelling to the
match with members of the United board, Kidd's taxi had been
caught in traffic. Panicking that he would not be there for the
warm-up, he decided it was best to jump out and run. The driver
told him it was one mile to White Hart Lane. It felt a lot further
to a breathless Kidd as he dashed past startled fans.

Kidd was a man in a hurry in every respect, contemplating
leaving United in the middle of the season. It was a huge decision
for a figure who had served the club as a distinguished player,
most famously scoring in the 1968 European Cup final on his
19th birthday. Kidd had once cleaned the boots of George Best
and Nobby Stiles as a teenage apprentice, and then fulfilled a
dream by playing alongside them on the greatest night in the
club's history.

As a coach, he had been brought in by Ferguson to work with
the kids at United and then, when Archie Knox left in 1991,
become the manager's assistant, serving at his right hand through
all the glories. It was an impressive rise but he also felt undervalued, certainly financially. Peter Kenyon was earning way more
as deputy chief executive and Kidd shared Ferguson's view that
others, less deserving, were growing rich on their excellent work.

Kidd's head had already been turned by interest from Everton in the summer, and also from Manchester City, when in late November Blackburn Rovers offered him the manager's position. Roy Hodgson had been sacked with the team bottom of the Premier League, but the backing of Jack Walker, the steel magnate, meant they could make an offer that Kidd was struggling to refuse. His salary would be at least £750,000, which was more than three times his income at United.

It was a need to tell the board his wishes to leave, meeting with Martin Edwards, Roland Smith and Kenyon in central London on the day of the Spurs game, that meant Kidd was running late. As Edwards recalls it, United were never going to be able to match Blackburn's offer, or give Kidd any guarantees of succeeding Ferguson. They wanted to keep him but there were limits. 'Blackburn were offering life-changing money and Brian wanted to have a go,' Edwards says. 'I knew we weren't going to match that so he went with our blessing really. I never felt in all honesty that he was doing the right thing, but he wanted to do it. He would have never known if he didn't take the opportunity.'

Ferguson insists that he told the board to do whatever it took to keep Kidd and avoid such unwelcome disruption mid-season but, seeing the manager shortly before the game at Spurs, Edwards said that it was clear from the earlier meeting that his assistant was determined to leave. Ferguson fumed at the news. Asked, after a 3–1 defeat to Spurs, by a reporter from the *Mirror* if it was a difficult choice for Kidd to decide between United or Blackburn, his anger boiled over. 'That's a fucking stupid question,' he said.

No one could know the impact that losing Kidd in mid-season would have on the team, but they certainly felt the emotional wrench. Kidd was the good cop in the United dressing room, an obviously decent guy who was much respected and liked by the players. Even Roy Keane had a good word for him, saying he regarded Kidd as a 'straight talker'. Gary Neville spoke for the Class of '92 when he said that 'right from the start, he was your mate, the guy always looking out for you'. Cole was particularly knocked back. Kidd had been the confidence-builder during some difficult times, with the coach working on his game and his morale.

Asked about the popularity of his departing assistant, Ferguson might have spoken with a dash of envy when he said, 'He put his arm around them and told them they were wonderful. And they all believed him. Me? I was the one who told them they were dropped.'

Ferguson's first concern was a practical issue of who was going to take training. The United manager had always provided the framework for the team, and taken the lead on selection, but it was Kidd who was out there on the pitches every morning. Suddenly Ferguson was going to have to find extra time to think about the sessions, and to take them alongside Jim Ryan, his other assistant.

When Patrick Collins of the *Mail on Sunday* visited the Cliff shortly after Kidd's departure, he had the sense of Ferguson being strained, and grumpy. The manager talked of being 'very, very disappointed' at the club's failure to keep Kidd, and there were references to the amount of money swilling around Old Trafford and being paid to the directors but not being lavished on coaching staff. Collins described a scene of the preoccupied United manager in his boots coming off the training ground, heading straight to his office past autograph hunters, to plot the next match. As Collins wrote, 'Being Alex Ferguson, he puts on the bravest of faces. Yet, I fancy he looked more harassed than usual. And a little more lonely.'

38

So near yet ...

It is 3 December, the day after United have lost in the Worthington Cup to Tottenham Hotspur. Whatever else unfolds this season, the League Cup is one competition United will not be winning. Yet it has still been a night Alex Notman will cherish for the rest of his life.

The young Scottish striker has made his first-team debut for United, starting to fulfil the promise that has made Alex Ferguson compare him, as a short, prolific finisher, to Paul Scholes. After sitting on the bench next to David Beckham, Notman has played 20 minutes up front with Teddy Sheringham and Ole Gunnar Solskjær. He has slipped on that famous red shirt, loving the stage even if he had to watch David Ginola deliver a masterclass capped by a 25-yard blast to give Spurs a 3-1 win.

The next morning, Notman sat on the red seats in the lobby at the Cliff still buzzing about his first-team debut when Ferguson walked in, saw him and sat down. 'Well done, son,' the United manager said. 'You've done excellent last night. I think you can really push on now, get in front of some of these others.' Notman smiles at the memory, and his absolute certainty that this was the launch of a wonderful career at Old Trafford. 'I never played for United again,' he says.

There is the glory of Manchester United. There is the club's unequalled reputation for developing its own players. And then there is the sad story that Notman tells, chatting from his home in Norwich where these days he is an engineer in the oil and gas industry. He recounts his tale without any rancour or self-pity as he reveals how close he came to being part of this era of United greatness – and how far away, too. His story is unique to him but it is also typical of football – very common, even – in the sense that many more talented young players fall by the wayside than make it to the top. Notman was entitled to think that he would be one of the success stories.

Ferguson had personally lured him down from Scotland, where he was on the books of his boyhood club Rangers. The United manager had an empire to run but he still found time to take Notman and his family out for dinner in Manchester. Notman was only a schoolboy. 'Dinner at the Castlefield Hotel,' he recalls. 'It shows you what a guy Sir Alex is that if he wanted you, he'd take the time. That was the difference with United.'

Notman moved down in 1995 as a trainee. It could be a tough existence. The Class of '92 had endured initiation rituals and humiliations as young apprentices, and now they were passing on the same rites of passage. An ominous sound from the first-team dressing room – rather like the theme to *Jaws* – meant that all the first-year apprentices had to gather in front of the senior players. Then the torments would begin. Ryan Giggs and Nicky Butt were the worst.

Singing 'Wonderwall' does not sound so bad – 'come on, hands behind your back just like Liam,' Giggs would instruct them – but that was just the start of the indignities which could be excruciating for teenage boys. As Notman says, 'They'd ask, "How many birds have you shagged?" I was a virgin, aged 15 at the time but didn't want to say that in front of everyone so I said two. They said, "Show us how you do it on the bed." It was a nightmare. You had to pretend you were in a nightclub and chat up girls. "Show us how you do that." A mop was in the corner and you had to walk up to it. Giggsy comes over as this reserved guy but he was one of the ringleaders and Butty. They absolutely loved it. It is what it is and didn't do me any harm, but I don't think they're allowed any of that now.' There was a practice of wrapping a ball in a towel and whacking it over an apprentice's head. 'They were just passing down what Ince and Hughes had done to them,' Notman says.

Training with the first team was no less intimidating. For Notman's first session, he was on the same side as Roy Keane. 'I gave the ball away three times and he shouted, "For fuck's sake, keep the ball! You're better than that!" That was my introduction at 15. At that age, that's daunting. It was a demanding club to be at, but that's the standards they set.'

Notman was a talent. He plundered goals in the junior teams, including at Anfield facing contemporaries such as Steven Gerrard and Michael Owen. Ferguson had high hopes for him. In November 1997, chatting to the *Guardian*, Ferguson talked of Notman and Erik Nevland, a young Norwegian striker. 'They're the best young strikers the club's had, as a pair,' he said.

Notman says that he never lacked belief that he might make it. 'Up to the day I left I always thought I'd be involved and get a chance,' he says. 'I loved it and wouldn't change a single minute of it.' After 86 goals in 121 reserve games, and Ferguson's encouraging words on the back of that first-team debut at Tottenham, he was so close, yet frustrated, too. Crucially he lacked the yard of pace that made Owen so special.

After loan spells at Aberdeen and Sheffield United, Ferguson called Notman, aged 20, into his office and said that Norwich City were willing to pay £250,000 for him. United were happy to accept. It was downhill from there because of a succession of ankle injuries. After countless procedures, Notman was warned by specialists of long-term risks of disability. He had lost his professional career at just 23. One appearance in a Norwich reserve game had invalidated an insurance claim, costing him up to £250,000.

Notman thought about coaching but, through family connections, started working for Halliburton in the oil and gas industry. As we speak, he is about to travel to Egypt on a job for BP, building a new gas plant. He tests parts and systems for leaks, checking pressure. His fellow workers know his past. They will ask 'did you meet, Sir Alex?' Or 'what was Beckham really like?' He tells them about Keane's fierce competitiveness, Giggs's running on the ball and he drools over Scholes. 'I always regarded him as the best I've ever played with.'

It was Ferguson who made the most lasting impression. 'You'd hear him at the training ground before you would see him and the hairs on the back of my neck used to stand up. Honestly, every time. I got a blast a few times. A youth team game away at Blackburn and he's there. I didn't play well. He's in the dressing room and launched straight away going round, shouting and swearing.'

Aware it sounds harsh, Notman tells one more story. Just when he was wondering what to do with the rest of his life after the doctors told him his career was over, his phone rang. It was Ferguson on the line. 'I'm really sorry to hear you had to finish. If there's anything we can do for you here give me a call, come back to the Centre of Excellence there's a job here for you,' Ferguson told him. As Notman says, 'He couldn't do enough, and I can't speak any higher of him.'

Some who have been through Notman's journey might be bitter, but he is appreciative that he had the opportunity at all. He played for Manchester United in a period when they were one of the biggest clubs on the planet. He was part of the Treble season. That it was only one fleeting opportunity shows how ferociously competitive it was to make it into the squad, never mind to establish yourself like a Giggs, Beckham or Scholes. Perhaps we need a story like Notman's to remind us just how special they are.

39

Ooh aah, Eric the film star

The familiar, straight-backed figure walks down a Mexican backstreet. A football rolls away from a group of street urchins to the hero's feet. Eric Cantona nonchalantly steps over it and walks on.

As symbolism goes, the scene is as subtle as a kung-fu kick. The message would certainly not be lost on any wistful Manchester United fan in marking Cantona's transition from footballer to lead actor in movies. He is now officially an ex-player. It is a remarkable transformation in so many ways, not least because it is December 1998 and Cantona is only 32.

In other circumstances, involving a less mercurial figure, Cantona would still be the talismanic forward of this United team; the magnificent and brooding No.7 of a side he had elevated into the dominant English team of the decade. At 32, he would still be striving to lead his team on the final ascent to become European champions, climbing those last steps with his chest out, collar up. He would be fulfilling the promise he had made one afternoon in the Bull's Head in Hale in late 1996, when Cantona had turned to David Beckham and Gary Neville on a team bonding session. 'Together we will win the European Cup,' he said.

But as United continue their quest for the trophy that has eluded them for so long, Cantona has ended up starring in a film with a talking chimpanzee and garnering his worst reviews since walloping an abusive Crystal Palace fan. The film is *Mookie* and it is Cantona's first lead role as a small-time boxer, though *Le Journal du Dimanche* suggests that the Frenchman is in danger of being upstaged by his co-star – the ape. The newspaper publishes a photograph of the chimp and the actor with the caption: 'Which of these two is the more expressive?'

Plans to release the film in Britain are dropped and it appears the country has not been denied a comedy classic. But Cantona is committed to his new life and has dived in with both feet, so to speak. Before *Mookie*, he has popped up in doublet and hose as the French ambassador, Monsieur de Foix, in *Elizabeth* alongside Cate Blanchett, Geoffrey Rush and Richard Attenborough. As *Mookie* appears, he is working on a new film, *Les Enfants du Marais* ('Children of the Marsh'), set in rural France in the 1930s. Playing a psychotic pugilist, there seems a risk of Cantona being typecast.

Cantona, living in Barcelona, is intent on distancing himself from football. 'I know that many people thought I had stopped playing so that I could make a sensational comeback six months later,' he says while promoting his new career. 'They've got egg on their faces now.'

He had walked away. But regrette rien? In his previous starring role at Old Trafford, Cantona won four league championship titles and two FA Cup medals but repeatedly felt the pain of European failure. It was within hours of losing to Borussia Dortmund in the Champions League semi-final in April 1997 that he told Ferguson of his plans to retire even though he had 12 months left on his contract. The following month he was gone.

Ferguson would question how Cantona had lost his way, wondering if he had made a mistake in burdening his star player with the captaincy. Perhaps that made European failure harder to bear. Cantona's retirement was a horrible shock for United followers but he has always said that he quit at the right time, when the passion had gone. Perhaps, as it turns out, he quit at the right time for United, too.

---

* It was in 2009 that Cantona came of age as an actor in Ken Loach's amusing and touching *Looking for Eric*, guiding a United-worshipping postman through a midlife crisis. His best role turned out to be playing himself.

40

Absent

Helping Gary Neville to write his autobiography *Red*, I asked him whether a manager could really make a difference once a game had started. Surely the ranting and raving from the side-lines, the waving of arms and indecipherable hand-signals were all just for show? Weren't they just a manager's pretence of control amid the chaos of a match?

'Bollocks,' he called that theory. As he put it, any player who felt a manager was forgotten once the game started had never had a proper manager. He talked of sensing Ferguson's presence incessantly. 'You can feel him in your head,' he said. 'At the back of your mind – sometimes at the front, too – you'll be thinking, "Christ, I've got to go and face him at half-time. I'd better start playing better or he might rip my skull out." Don't get me wrong, you aren't living in a state of fear. But you know, deep down, that you are puppets on the end of his string. He's in control. He makes or breaks your career ... He controls your destiny.' He went on to argue that 'you could argue that it's the manager's greatest talent – to always make you feel his presence'.

It raised the question of what would happen if Ferguson was absent, which was an experiment which took place for the first time in more than 12 years as United manager on 19 December 1998. Ferguson had his own sad and personal reasons for taking leave. Sandra, his sister-in-law, had died of cancer. Ferguson was close to his brother Martin – Alex had been best man when

Martin and Sandra married – and the younger of the brothers had come to work for United as a scout from 1997. Martin had become trusted eyes and ears for Ferguson in checking out players, including Jaap Stam. Ferguson was not shy around this time of promoting his own family, though it would soon lead him into trouble and conflicts of interest when one of his sons, Jason, became an agent.

The timing of the funeral meant that Ferguson would be absent when United took on Bryan Robson's Middlesbrough at home. He was kept informed over the phone by Ken Ramsden, the club's assistant secretary, who had the unenviable task of explaining that, without the injured Stam, United were a defensive shambles.

By half-time, they were 2-0 down to goals from Hamilton Ricard and Dean Gordon, and walked into a ferocious dressing down from Eric Harrison. The former youth coach had been summoned out of retirement just for the day given the manager was not there, and a replacement for Kidd was yet to be appointed. Harrison showed that he had lost none of his ability to strip the paint off the walls with a half-time talk. 'This fucking defence! We've had to stick three in midfield because, by fuck, don't you lot need protecting!'

Harrison berated a back line in which Phil Neville was struggling at right-back and brother Gary not faring any better as a stand-in centre-half. Then they went 3-0 down. There was an attempt at a comeback but United lost 3-2 and Ferguson was furious when he returned to watch the match video. He waited a few days before putting on the tape in front of the players and telling them some brutal truths. He accused his players of laziness and complacency – the worst possible crimes.

It was not so much the run of six matches without a win – leaving United third in the table, below Aston Villa and Chelsea as they went into the New Year – that annoyed him as the sloppiness that could see his team look as potent as any side in Europe in some games and yet head into the turn of the season with the eighth worst defensive record in the league. This was not, he told his players, the form of champions.

---

* Ferguson missed just three games out of the 1,500 competitive fixtures as United's manager. As well as the Middlesbrough defeat, he was absent for a Manchester derby in November 2000 after telling his son Mark it would be a good date to get married in Cape Town because it was an international week, only for the schedule to be changed. In September 2010, he skipped a Carling Cup victory over Scunthorpe to watch David de Gea playing for Atlético Madrid at Valencia. United did win both of those in his absence.

41

Party time

It seems a little fanciful to talk about a Christmas piss-up as a turning point in Manchester United's season. 'I know, that makes it sound all a bit Mike Bassett,' Gary Neville laughs. But he, and many of the players, are insistent that a blow-out, a legendary one by all accounts, could represent a moment of release, drunkenness and then clarity. One last blast of indulgence before the serious business began.

Could one bender make a difference? Sir Dave Brailsford would not approve but Neville talks about it as a marginal gain. 'That extra 0.5 percent when you think, "I will die for this team,"' he says. 'Yes, it was the manager, it was the fans, the stadium, the history – but it was the party too. That's when you get to know your teammates on another level. Those do's were the best days of my life.'

This one in December 1998 was certainly a belter. It kept them chuckling for weeks, though memories are suddenly – or conveniently – a little blurred over the details. They went on an afternoon bender in a few pubs, including the Old Grapes run by Liz Dawn – or *Coronation Street*'s Vera Duckworth, as she was better known – and Mulligans Irish bar on Deansgate. With a guitarist to accompany them, they sang songs; Oasis covers and, after a few pints, anti-Liverpool chants.

With Neville chivvying them along to his schedule, punctilious even when pissed, they headed to the Reform Club in the evening. Ned Kelly, the security man, had been sent down to ensure the CCTV cameras were turned off, and to sweep the place for any devices. Everyone was searched on the way in. There was a simple rule for guests – free drinks all night but no blabbing afterwards.

Dwight Yorke had distributed many of the 250 guest tickets around Manchester using a simple system, 'Any girl who made me go "wow".' Once the party was in full swing, Yorke pulled out his party piece, balancing a tray of 20 shots on his head and bringing them over to the rest of the squad. The lads loved that.

'It's the one night during the season when we drank as much as we liked, would be sick, fall over,' Neville says. 'You'd see someone be sick at 6 p.m., sleep it off and you'd see them back there at 10 p.m. and there would be a big roar when they came back into the room. You'd find one of the lads slumped in the toilet. We talked about it for weeks, giggling about it.'

The bar bill was reported to be £35,000. No one can remember – it was that good a night – but they all say it was worth every penny. A chance to gather at a mid-point in the season, to let off steam knowing that they would have to knuckle down seriously once they sobered up.

Of course, other teams had their Christmas parties so could United's shindig really count as beneficial? Did it really help to create an unshakeable bond? Perhaps when you hear what happened elsewhere.

If there was an award for the most tasteless footballers' Christmas party of December 1998 – perhaps of all time – it was surely won with exceptional grimness by Newcastle United, who conducted a Secret Santa. Dietmar Hamann, the German international, ripped off the wrapping paper to discover a copy of Adolf Hitler's *Mein Kampf*. Duncan Ferguson was given a convict's outfit as a memento of his time in prison for assault. Apparently he had tried to buy a live llama for Nobby Solano, the club's Peruvian international, but struggled to find one on Tyneside.

The present everyone remembers went to Alessandro Pistone, the injury-prone Italian, who was given a bloody sheep's heart fresh from the butchers. 'It's a heart because you haven't got one,' Pistone was told by guffawing teammates as he opened the grotesque present. 'I'm sure it was a joke,' he later said. But did anyone see the funny side?

Brawls, strippers, arrests, dwarf-tossing; the list of scandals arising from footballers' Christmas parties is long and inglorious and Ferguson would ban them at United after a very messy one in 2007. Many managers came to see them as more trouble than they were worth, but the players all chuckled when I brought up the 1998 festivities. One of the best, they said, and their smiles suggested that I only knew half the story.

42

Countdown

The party was well and truly over. At the Cliff, the players called a meeting. At Roy Keane's instruction, they gathered in the first-team dressing room. Hard truths were said about the inconsistencies of the first half of the season when they could stand toe-to-toe with Barcelona and Bayern Munich then surrender to Sheffield Wednesday and Middlesbrough.

December had yielded just one win in eight matches, and form had been far too fitful. These players knew they had extraordinary capabilities running through the team; Schmeichel ready to rediscover his aura again after unburdening himself; Stam more impressive every week as the defensive rock; Keane the indomitable leader; Yorke as potent as any striker in the league, and Cole rejuvenated alongside him. Thanks to the supply of chances from Giggs and Beckham, United were the highest scorers in England, and Europe.

But eight wins from 18 games was not going to win the Premier League. Enough was enough. After the players spoke about the need to pull together, to work harder to tighten up defensively and to keep better shape, the manager was invited down to add his thoughts. 'The nonsense has gone now,' Ferguson said. 'No more fucking around.'

He told the players that he was going to make training more intense. January was the only month when they would be free of midweek fixtures. He was going to treat it like a mini pre-season, with extra running. 'You'll be tired for the next few weeks but I'm thinking about March and April when I need you to be strong,' he told them. They ran off the hangover.

There was one moment of jollity in the players' meeting. After reflecting on the need for improvement, someone piped up, 'Win the next 33 games and we'll be fine!'

It coincided with a swift upturn in fortunes. After a solid defensive display to draw 0-0 at leaders Chelsea in the last league fixture of the year, United beat Middlesbrough in the FA Cup third round in the first week of January, atoning for their previous dreadful performance. That was followed by a 4-1 thumping of West Ham United and a 6-2 demolition of Leicester City, with Cole and Yorke helping themselves to eight goals in two matches. Amid the dramatic upturn in fortunes, the joke stuck.

'Just 31 wins to go!'

Another victory. 'That's 30 wins left, boys!'

It was Yorke, typically, who picked up the line and ran with it, adding it to his repertoire of ways to lighten the mood in the dressing room. After each game he kept up the running count-down which just happened to coincide with a new resolve.

Up to the Middlesbrough defeat on 19 December, United's form in the league was eight wins and three losses from 18 matches (1.72 points per game) with 36 goals scored, and 23 against. Thereafter it was 14 wins and no defeats from 20 matches (2.4 points per game) with 44 scored and 14 conceded. Those 33 games in Yorke's countdown until the end of the season? United were not beaten in any of them. Jigging around the dressing room – 'Just another 29 wins!' – he was ticking off the matches in the most momentous sequence in the history of English football.

43

Aberdeen

Alex Ferguson can be a hard, ruthless bastard. He can also be a man of touching sentimentality, as could be seen by taking a full-strength United team to the north-east coast of Scotland for a game that has slipped off the records.

Entering such a critical time of the season, with a pressing need for focus and a looming FA Cup tie against arch-rivals Liverpool, it is extraordinary that the entire United squad should fly through a storm into Aberdeen airport in January 1999 to play in a testimonial game for a man none of the players had heard of.

Ferguson had made a commitment to bring a United team for a testimonial for Teddy Scott, who had played just one first-team game for Aberdeen in the 1950s before becoming reserve-team coach, kitman and the guy who, almost single-handedly, kept the club functioning. In Ferguson's time as manager at Pittodrie, he would arrive some mornings and find Scott sleeping on the snooker table in the club bar because he had been working too late to catch a bus home.

The United manager had made a pledge to honour Scott, which was how Schmeichel, Beckham, Scholes, Yorke, Cole and Giggs ended up chasing around on a freezing night in Scotland in front of a capacity crowd just days before facing Liverpool. Scott was estimated to have made £250,000 from the match. When he died in 2012, Ferguson was there to speak at the funeral. 'Loyalty should always be recognised and rewarded,' he said.

It is unthinkable that this testimonial involving a strong United XI would be squeezed into the mid-season calendar now – unless there was a lucrative sponsorship deal behind it – but Ferguson hoped that there was a life lesson for his players. 'It's exactly what United should be doing,' Gary Neville says. 'And it wasn't just that trip to Aberdeen.'

Neville recalled heading to Barrow as a young first-team player on a cold December evening and sitting on the bench. 'I'm thinking, "What the hell am I doing here?"' The answer was that Brian Kidd had briefly been manager of Barrow and had offered United's services to help raise money when the non-League club fell on hard times. As Neville adds, 'That's where I should have been – raising money for a guy that's given his life to football or helping to save a club in need. United should play against a non-League team every year and raise millions. That Aberdeen story bleeds into the history of the club. That's the spirit, the passion of football.'

He pauses. 'Or it was, when you think of the Super League and where we are today.'

44

Character is fate #3

Manchester United 2 Liverpool 1, 24 January 1999

Teddy Sheringham once said that there is no more exciting sight in football than Manchester United chasing a game – but on a Sunday afternoon, 24 January, that excitement came mixed with a deepening fear for the home supporters that their team was crashing out of the FA Cup to opponents they despised more than any other.

United were 1-0 down to Liverpool, of all teams, at home in the FA Cup fourth round. Michael Owen had scored with less than three minutes gone, meeting Vegard Heggem's cross to punish another lapse in the United defence. On the sidelines, Ferguson was thoroughly unimpressed that a 5ft 8ins striker had been given a free header in the six-yard box. Up in the press box, I wrote that the United manager was chewing his gum so vigorously amid the stress that he seemed in danger of gnawing off his tongue.

I also noted that it was an unusually raucous occasion. FA Cup rules meant that Liverpool had 8,000 travelling supporters, many more than for a league match, and the rivalry had rarely felt more noisy or intense. Gerard Houllier's team was in excellent form, and United's resourcefulness was being tested to the full. It was, in short, a humdinger of a cup tie.

At half-time, Ferguson told his players that they were being sucked into attacking too centrally, running into Liverpool's midfield. He told them to build from wide, drawing out Paul Ince and Jamie Redknapp, until they were nearer the box. But when Roy Keane struck the post for a second time, he sensed that it was time to gamble. In the 81st minute Ferguson sent on Ole Gunnar Solskjær for Denis Irwin and switched, highly unusually, to three at the back. He had Yorke, Cole and Solskjær up front, ahead of Giggs, Keane, Scholes and Beckham in midfield. This was the kitchen-sink formation.

Was it ability, spirit, a sense of 'Fergie Time' or the weight of attacking numbers that dragged United back into the game? It certainly felt like a force more powerful than luck. After a foul by Redknapp in the 88th minute, Beckham floated a free kick towards the far post. Heggem was too soft, allowing Cole to head the ball back across goal where Yorke waited to pounce for an easy finish. Yorke's wild-eyed expression as he ran off told not just of his usual joy at being alive but something deeper. He says he had never felt so emotional after a goal; something about the intensity of the occasion and the mounting weight of pressure. Yorke sprinted away, shouting and swearing. 'That really wasn't my style but something got to me that day,' he says. 1-1.

Soon the game was into added time. There had been 70 seconds beyond the regulation 90 minutes when Stam launched the ball forward. Solskjær had been on the pitch for more than ten minutes and could not remember a single touch.

As Scholes took down Stam's long pass trying to find room for a shot, the ball ran to Solskjær. He took a touch with the left then the right to steady himself and struck a low left-foot shot under – or was it through? – Jamie Carragher. Amid all the chaos of a penalty box in the final minutes of a frenzied match, he had pulled off his signature move of shooting through the legs of a stretching defender. The ball flew past David James into the net.

From 1–0 down heading into the closing minutes to 2–1 up at the final whistle, leaving a stricken opponent wondering how victory had been ripped away from them – this was a storyline we would see again.

'The most exciting and ultimately satisfying finish to any game I ever played in,' Scholes reflected. The devastation on the faces of the Liverpool players and fans was a prize in itself. Gary Neville had taken stick off the Liverpool fans all afternoon and ran over towards them to celebrate with unabashed glee. 'That was a big one,' he recalls. 'The impact of beating them with thousands of Liverpool fans behind one goal. That was the first time I went over and gave them some.' It would not be the last.

Solskjær, who had celebrated his winner by clutching the United badge on his chest and brandishing it at the Stretford End, still had a beaming, boyish grin when he was interviewed on television afterwards. 'To beat Liverpool this way is better than beating them 5–0, I think,' he said. 'It's the best way to win a football game, in the last minute.'

A late win fills a dressing room not just with the jubilation of snatching unlikely victory. In coming back from the dead, it can create a sense of invincibility. Ferguson was eager to accentuate that sense of growing belief when he talked afterwards. 'We have been a goal down in both our FA Cup ties at Old Trafford this year and to come back to win in that situation tells you something about the character of this team,' he says. The unrelenting pursuit of victory was, he suggested, something that cannot come from a manager, or a tactics board, but from within the beating heart of his players.

45

'Fergie Time'

Did 'Fergie Time' exist? Did Manchester United enjoy added minutes at the end of tight matches, like that victory over Liverpool, through the intimidating power of one man vigorously chewing gum and tapping his watch?

Later in Ferguson's reign, a few studies tried to establish if there was scientific evidence of 'Fergie Time' – was it fact or faith? – but with inconclusive results. Big teams in general were more likely to see more added minutes when losing, especially at home, but that may have been legitimate if opponents were wasting time trying to cling on to a win or draw. Referees, consciously or otherwise, will also have felt pressure from home fans – and perhaps from the sight of an agitated Scotsman trying to bully them to add extra seconds – yet in a tally of Premier League winning goals beyond the 90th minute across Ferguson's time in charge at Old Trafford, Liverpool were top and United fifth.

'Fergie Time' could not be proven through data but the reality seemed much less important than whether the football world *believed* both in the influence of Ferguson to extend a match through force of personality and the ability and character of his players to keep chasing victory to the last kick. As Ferguson explained in *My Autobiography*, pointing at his watch started off as a complaint and/or demand to the officials but became a psychological ploy aimed at the opposition. He was never actually keeping track of the time, or any sensible measure of the minutes to be added, but felt he could instil fear into United's rivals.

'It was the effect it had on the other team, not ours, that counted,' he wrote. 'Seeing me tap my watch and gesticulate, the opposition would be spooked. They would immediately think another ten minutes were going to be added. Everyone knew United had a knack of scoring late goals.'

Whenever United did rescue a result it strengthened the idea that 'Fergie Time' was real. It gave his own players extra belief that it was worth fighting to the end. Ever since their comeback against Sheffield Wednesday in April 1993 in a famous victory that propelled United towards the first transformative title of the era, the idea had taken hold that this was a crucial quality of Ferguson's sides.

Tapping that watch was about trying to build a sense of inevitability about a United fightback, and striving to make opponents feel like this was a losing battle as Ferguson threw on more strikers in pursuit of a late winner. 'Seeing me point to my timepiece, our opponents would feel they would have to defend against us through a spell of time that would feel, to them, like infinity,' he remarked. Possessing an unprecedented four top-class forwards in 1998-99 added to the sense that resistance was futile.

Of course some opponents did not wilt, but enough succumbed to make 'Fergie Time' feel like more than just a demented manager jabbing his wrist but an irresistible temporal force shaped by unwavering character and conviction. As Ferguson noted of those late comebacks, 'It didn't always happen, but the team never stopped believing it could.' The victory over Liverpool was a stirring revival not just of United's prospects in the FA Cup but the idea that Ferguson's men could shape events to their will. It was the most notable comeback yet in a campaign remarkable for the number of them.

Ferguson could always identify with one of the famous

sayings from Vince Lombardi, the revered coach of the Green Bay Packers, 'We didn't lose the game, we just ran out of time.' Except, in a world of 'Fergie Time', there was the sense that United always would conjure one more chance.

When those late goals went in, especially to beat a team like Liverpool in knockout football, there was no better feeling. 'You score in the last minute or injury time, the dressing room is electric,' Ferguson said. 'The fans are going home and can't wait to get to the pub to talk about it, or go home to tell their wife and kids what it's like to score in the last minute. That's the value.'

A late decisive goal created a dynamic, a momentum, an empowering sense that United were irrepressible. 'Fergie Time' was a belief system and there were not many agnostics left by the end of 1998-99.

46

'94 versus '99

After the victory over Liverpool, Alex Ferguson had been sufficiently roused by his team's comeback that he reached for the ultimate compliment. He compared this side with the Double winners of 1993-94.

Ferguson was wary of ranking his teams – too much like deciding which was his favourite child – but there was no doubt that the '94 vintage had a special place in his heart. He loved them not just for what they won, putting United back on the domestic perch, but for being a squad blessed with indomitable will who battled to establish the reputation that United are never beaten. He loved their pugnaciousness, even if it could often spill over. He loved that they were hard men, like him. Now, he said, he could see similar qualities of character emerging with the '99 side, which raised an intriguing question – which team would win if they faced each other?

From first-hand experience of the 1993-94 campaign, there was something very special about the devastating speed of Andrei Kanchelskis and a young, unrestrained Ryan Giggs, either side of Cantona and Hughes, with Ince and Keane as a central midfield pair that would win not just football matches but every argument you dared to pick with them. Steve Bruce and Gary Pallister were not just very good defenders but impressive men. But I would say this emerging team of '99 had more variation and certainly greater depth.

It is a close call, so I checked with the experts. Giggs had loved the pace and power of the '94 side but felt that it was never going to succeed in Europe. That mission required a team more capable of passing through opponents. Peter Schmeichel concurred and suggested that the signings of Sheringham, Yorke and Stam, in particular, had provided greater sophistication. 'I felt that it was becoming more of an international team,' he said. 'It was built with that purpose.' Denis Irwin, who straddled both, felt the quality of the '94 squad fell away quicker beyond the first XI. Pushed to choose, he leant towards '99 because of so many different options in attack, from the guile of Sheringham and Yorke, to the pace of Cole and rare finishing prowess of Solskjær.

Of course, there would be another contender. When it comes to Ferguson's greatest team, the 2007-08 side won the Champions League with an attack of Rooney, Tevez and Ronaldo, with Carrick and Scholes in midfield and the redoubtable Vidić / Ferdinand partnership at the back.

The best? The 1999 vintage still takes my vote but, much more importantly, it has the blessing of Scholes. He felt there was too much reliance on counter-attacking in '08. 'In 1999 we had a bit of everything,' he said. 'A team is only as good as your centre-forwards and we had the best. And we had four of them. I thought it was the most exciting team. Goals everywhere. Every time you went on the pitch you thought you'd score three or four.' Gary Neville tends to like the last word. He concludes that '08 was the best in terms of technical quality but that '99 was closer to Ferguson's ideal given the core of home-grown players.

United fans will have their own favourite. I am going with '99, for reasons that were still unfolding.

47

Denis

At a Q&A session to launch one of his memoirs, Alex Ferguson was asked to name his best XI from across 27 years at United. 'It's absolutely impossible,' he said, running through the array of talent in each department. To pick Stam and Ferdinand at centre-back would mean ignoring Bruce and Pallister and Vidić. Go for van Nistelrooy and there would be no place for Cole, Rooney or Hughes.

It was a fiendishly difficult question but Ferguson did eventually acknowledge that one man would be straight on the team sheet: Denis Irwin. Or 'eight-out-of-ten Denis' as he was known by his manager. 'At Highbury in one game, he had a bad pass back in the last minute and Dennis Bergkamp came in and scored,' Ferguson explained. 'After the game the press said, "You must be disappointed in that pass back." I said, "Well, one mistake in ten years isn't bad."'

Eight-out-of-ten Denis walks into a bar in Altrincham, nodding to a few of the fellow locals. There never have been any airs or graces about the man who can claim to be the best right- and left-back in modern United history. Has there ever been a more versatile and consistent full-back across the entire Premier League? Nothing ever seemed to be too much trouble for Irwin. Penalties? No problem. Free kicks? Which corner would you like me to put it in? Left-back, right-back? Whatever. Ferguson could have picked him on either flank in his select XI.

Irwin brings the same easy composure as he strolls down from his Cheshire home to order a coffee and to chat about those glory years as one of the most successful Irish footballers in history, with 12 major trophies from his 12 seasons at United including seven league titles. To think he was wondering when he came over to England as a teenager that he might have better prospects as an accountant. Such an understated man, Irwin gives the impression that he would not have been too disappointed if he had ended up balancing the books. In a United dressing room full of egos and noise and sharp edges, Irwin was the amiable sort who could get on with anybody and everybody.

Just do not call him soft. Irwin is a compact 5ft 8ins and, as he sits down, he looks like he has barely put on an ounce since he was working up and down either side of the pitch with supreme dependability. He seems notably slight for a footballer but he knew how to handle himself from a childhood playing hurling and Gaelic football in Cork. Those Irish sports taught him to withstand physical blows. Football was not sanctioned at Irwin's primary and secondary school and so, remarkably, it was not until he was 14 and playing for a club at weekends that the game became a passion for him, but he was already a talented, gritty ball-player.

He needed mental resilience, too, to survive rejection from Leeds United at 20, when he was inexplicably dumped by manager Billy Bremner. Irwin might have given up and gone back to Ireland – and become that accountant – if Oldham Athletic had not come in. He thrived there and, at 24, joined United. Martin Edwards ranks Irwin in the top three signings during his long stewardship, behind only Eric Cantona and Peter Schmeichel. '£700,000 and that was with add-ons,' Edwards says. 'That was for more than ten years, and seven championships. A fantastic player.'

*

As Irwin sits and reflects, it is striking that, like all the United players I spoke to, he loves to talk about the characters more than the medals. He reminisces about training as much as famous matches. He would be as pleased to be back at the Cliff as walking out in one of the great European stadiums. We imagine that footballers must love coming into work; a couple of hours kicking a ball around in the morning. But not all of them have a love for the game or, indeed, for self-improvement. This United squad, to a man, was at the other extreme.

'I used to go with Ireland and there were players who didn't like going in and training,' Irwin says. 'At United, it was the opposite. I loved going in. So that's what I remember, training and the competitiveness of it. I bought into it. You had to. It was in my nature.

'I didn't realise how competitive it was at United until I left and went to Wolves later, and it was a different world. At Wolves, if it happened, it happened. If it didn't, it didn't. At United, there was never any let-up. We used to have five-a-sides, the Mancs, or the English against the Rest of the World. They used to get tasty on the Cliff pitch, but you need that sometimes. There was a huge spirit in that dressing room. The manager led from the front, but you need lieutenants. Roy was no shrinking violet.'

Ah, Roy – the man everyone talks about eventually. Irwin knew him better than most because they were roommates on trips, and they were both raised in Cork. They had their flashpoints but Keane had huge respect for Irwin: for the lack of fuss and the quiet professionalism. Irwin chuckles as he recalls one of Keane's first sessions at United and Ferguson joining in one of the boxes. 'How he [Ferguson] was a footballer I don't know. The ball hit him on the head and the lads had a little chuckle. Keany couldn't stop laughing. The manager turned around and looked at him. Roy got the message.'

Irwin is another player who says that Keane set the mood as the driving force of the team, and the squad. His own role? He is beyond self-deprecating. He is described by teammates as the most reliable they ever came across, but demurs when it comes to praise. 'If you ever want to be a footballer, come back as a forward,' he says. 'Full-backs, we were just pawns on the chess board. Nev and myself, yes, you have to be comfortable on the ball but Becks and Giggsy did the majority of crossing. We were just there as back-ups, decoy runs.'

He laughs: 'You see £50 million full-backs these days, so quick and full of running. We were pawns. Full-backs are now bishops!' The chess analogy is not coincidental. Irwin was a keen player from schooldays and used to challenge his teammates. Cantona was one of the few to accept. 'But Eric wasn't very good,' he says. Irwin ended up having to play on a computer.

He is still involved with United as an ambassador, working with the Manchester United Foundation. He says that he could be out in the Far East every week if he fulfilled every request, but he likes to keep it low-key. He does not have anything on show at home; no shirts or medals and not a single piece of memorabilia.

It is the people he misses, occasionally meeting up with a teammate for a drink. He has had a pint with Ryan Giggs a couple of days before we gather. He looks back fondly on going to training and then for a beer in Altrincham or one of the village pubs around Cheshire where the United players would hang out. 'You could do it back then and try to stay under the radar. I was able to hide away and have a few pints. Brasingamen's in Alderley Edge on a Monday night, Royales in Manchester on a Tuesday, it was changing in the '90s but you could still enjoy yourself.' He smiles at the memories of football in the '90s, and a life before camera-phones. 'It must be hard these days for footballers,' he says. 'You never see them out. Very dull.'

It is getting dark as we leave the bar and a couple of the locals invite Irwin to stay for a drink. 'Ah, go on then,' eight-out-of-ten Denis says, amiably joining them – perhaps the most grounded footballer you will ever meet.

48

Fergie for England

On a January day in 1999, Glenn Hoddle rang me at home, spouted some offensive nonsense about how disabled people are being punished for sins in a previous life, and talked himself out of his job as England manager. He was sacked within days. And so, for at least the third time, the FA hierarchy considered who they wanted to take on the Impossible Job (as it was known pre-Gareth Southgate) and struggled to see past Alex Ferguson.

Ferguson had been coveted when Hoddle was appointed; seen as the outstanding man in every way except for being fiercely Scottish. The issue of nationality did not deter Jimmy Armfield, the FA's headhunter, who made contact with United but found Martin Edwards blocking any approach. Now that Hoddle had gone, the FA clung to the very thin hope that Ferguson might somehow be persuaded, even after Kevin Keegan had initially accepted an interim role for four matches.

It was a job Ferguson was never likely to take but he used to love the speculation that he might manage England, if only for the jibes that he could hurl at us when we gathered at the Cliff. 'I'll take it and get you'se relegated,' he would cackle. As it turned out, Keegan almost pulled that off.

49

Character is fate #4

Charlton Athletic 0 Manchester United 1, 31 January 1999

A wintry, nondescript afternoon at The Valley. Alan Curbishley's Charlton Athletic, fighting relegation, have stuck a five-man defence and a dogged midfield in front of Manchester United in the hope of battling out a goalless draw. With 90 minutes gone, it looks like they have succeeded.

If we are looking for the hallmark of champions then what follows counts as significantly as any of the more glittering and celebrated occasions. Speak to the United players and they all have different defining moments of the campaign, but Peter Schmeichel has no hesitation in naming Charlton away among the most important days. He might have recalled it solely for dislocating a finger were it not for the way that the team pulled off the type of victory that was fast becoming their precious, distinctive quality.

When a team can throw on Ole Gunnar Solskjær to join Yorke and Cole, and then add Paul Scholes off the bench for the last ten minutes, it can always hope to wear down any defence. With the game in added time – in 'Fergie Time' – it was Scholes who slipped past a marker, and curled a deep cross to the far post where Yorke showed the athleticism and resolve to win a header which bounced off the inside of the post for his 18th goal of the season. United had done it again, almost with the very last kick.

With Chelsea losing to Arsenal and Aston Villa also faltering – reeling from Stan Collymore's revelation of depression which was widely greeted in the media, and even by his own manager, as unforgivable malingering in a sign that the mental-health discussion was barely in its infancy in football – victory put United top of the Premier League for the first time, apart from 24 hours in December. After that bumpy period up to Christmas, United had recorded five straight wins in January and, better still, they were making a habit of turning tight matches in their favour.

From the victory against Liverpool the previous week until the end of the campaign, United played 28 matches and 43 hours of football. During those 2,580 minutes, there were only 318 – around 12 per cent – when they enjoyed a cushion of more than one goal. In other words, they were living on the edge for almost the entirety of four months, when every game and every goal counted. That afternoon at Charlton was more evidence that they thrived on danger, and on very fine margins.

50

You're banned!

Alex Ferguson looks out into the car park at the Cliff one morning and sees a reporter skulking around without permission. He charges out and demands that one of the security men throw the journalist off the premises. 'Fucking disgrace, snooping around,' he says, launching into a diatribe of shipyard Glaswegian as the smarting reporter makes his escape.

Just as Ferguson is finishing his rant, he turns around and finds a mother and child standing there waiting for an autograph. Ferguson is mortified that they must have heard his four-letter tirade. 'Sorry about that,' the United manager says, trying to sound more statesmanlike. 'But you've got to speak to these c***s in language they fucking understand.'

One of the great regrets of covering United is not to have kept the tapes of the most ferocious Ferguson tirades. They could be vicious, outrageous, bullying and, often, entirely unjustified. And there was nowhere else you would rather be. These were the stories to dine out on; Ferguson as our foul-mouthed adversary. Our Malcolm Tucker. We were face to face, close enough to physically feel the blast of one of the most remarkable figures in the history of British sport. Close enough to be able to feel his hot rage blowing furiously in our faces. And if the most successful manager in the country was shouting at us then that made us players in this epic sporting show, right?

Ferguson always said in public that he never read the media.

Many times he has trotted out the yarn of being under pressure and wandering past Matt Busby's office one day as the grand old man puffed on his pipe.

'All right, son?' Busby supposedly asked. 'You look troubled.'

'It's the press, they are giving me a terrible time,' Ferguson replied.

'So why do you read them?'

In the fantasy version he peddles, Ferguson takes Busby's advice and never again looks at the back pages – which we know from experience is complete and utter bollocks. Ferguson knew exactly what we had written and frequently told us so with reviews that were scathing. If you had the dubious fortune to work for the *Daily Express*, as I did covering United in the mid-'90s, you were directly in his sights. It was the one newspaper that he had delivered at home.

In the days before the explosion of internet sites and new media, there would be as few as half a dozen of us at a briefing at Old Trafford or the Cliff before a domestic game. There was intimacy. We could ring Ferguson at home to check out a story. We might even wake him up if he was having an afternoon nap.

That access was starting to wane later in the decade as the size of media grew too big and unwieldy for Ferguson to control. Because control was his aim, much more than truth or accuracy. Ferguson's anger was invariably nothing to do with whether a story was factual; indeed the true ones could annoy him the most because they were evidence of a leak. They were a sign that someone within the club was operating beyond his command.

'The rulers of North Korea or Cuba may be able to control their press, but it is sheer fantasy to think that anyone in England is going to be able to do the same,' Ferguson wrote in *Leading*, once he had retired. But it did not stop him trying.

David Beckham stares at the red card against Argentina in the 1998 World Cup that will make him a villain of the nation.

This notorious effigy of Beckham, replete with sarong, was hung from scaffolding outside a pub in south London.

It was Beckham's misfortune that United's first away game of the season was at Upton Park where the abuse was even nastier than anticipated.

As 'Posh Spice', Victoria Adams was more renowned and richer than her footballer boyfriend when they started dating.

A shaven-headed Roy Keane was determined to prove that he was back from long-term injury and even more ferociously committed than ever.

No managerial rivalry in the Premier League has matched the intensity of Alex Ferguson's battles with Arsène Wenger.

After many decades as United's training headquarters, the Cliff gates would open to fans for the last time in 1999.

Sport and politics increasingly did mix in the '90s, with Tony Blair keen to make the most of Ferguson's affiliation to the Labour Party.

No one embodied Manchester's swagger quite like Oasis and singer Liam Gallagher.

The Hacienda club was at the heart of the Madchester scene that made the city a cultural mecca through the '80s and '90s.

Relations between Martin Edwards, the United chairman, and Ferguson could frequently be strained by issues of money.

Supporters campaigning against the proposed £623 million takeover by Rupert Murdoch, which could have transformed not just United but English football.

Brian Kidd had worked successfully as Ferguson's assistant for many years but the relationship would end amid acrimony.

Dwight Yorke not only added goals, assists and irrepressible confidence but brought out the best from a revitalised Andy Cole.

Jaap Stam arrived as the world's most expensive defender and, after a bumpy start, began to assert himself against rivals including Liverpool's Robbie Fowler.

A mural of the Busby Babes shows them lining up in Belgrade for the last time. This brilliant young team would soon be destroyed in the Munich disaster.

The Class of '92, coached by the demanding Eric Harrison, were the culmination of Ferguson's campaign to restore United's reputation for producing outstanding youth.

Beckham's distinctive technique brought him five goals from direct free-kicks, matching his highest total of any campaign at United.

A reunion with Diego Simeone when United met Inter Milan in the Champions League quarter-final ended in a handshake and triumph for Beckham.

Steve McClaren brought bold new ideas to Old Trafford when Ferguson plucked the little-known coach from Derby County to be his new assistant.

Ole Gunnar Solskjær celebrates one of four goals he scored off the bench in less than 15 minutes in United's 8-1 trouncing of Nottingham Forest.

Denis Irwin was loved by his teammates, including irascible captain Keane, for his dependability.

To Ferguson, the world could be reduced to a simple, binary test – are you with me or against me? Journalists had to make their own choice.

To arrive at the Cliff was to walk into a lion's den. Prepare to be mauled. We sat on the red benches in the lobby like patients in a dentist's waiting room, until Ferguson came down the stairs from his office, often whistling or singing. He could be in great humour – and, often, he would stay that way – but out of nowhere he might remember that someone had annoyed him or simply decide that it was a day for sending a message that he was not to be crossed. And he could be nasty, viciously so, when he turned on someone.

Or he might lie. Especially when pushed on detail like injuries or transfers, Ferguson would often cough, which was usually his 'tell' that he was about to be less than truthful. Everyone recognised that cough. He would think nothing of misleading us about a player's injury if he thought it would help his team. He wanted to make the rules; we reserved the right to ignore them. Bans for writing something that upset him were commonplace. 'You're finished! Again!' as he once shouted at me. I would have to ring up his secretary to ask if the suspension had been served. The line would go quiet. 'No, the manager says at least another few weeks.' Still on the naughty step.

One ban went on for months after a couple of us struck extraordinarily lucky one day, knowing Ferguson was away on other business, and snuck down to the training ground to see what we could pick up. We saw Andrei Kanchelskis walking out to his car.

'All right, Andrei?'

'No, I want to leave, I want transfer.'

'What?!'

It was a journalistic fantasy come true. We were hoping for

a 'good morning', and a quick chat about the next game, not a bombshell transfer request. We checked out the story with the player's translator – 'Oh God, I really wish he hadn't said that' – splashed it all over the back pages of our papers and turned up the next morning at Old Trafford. 'You two, outside now!' Ferguson barked, without even sitting down. Up against the wall in a tight corridor, jabbing us in the chest, Ferguson was apoplectic.

'Fucking disgrace ... you never fucking called me ... fucking finished ... stay away from my fucking training ground ...' We tried to get a word in reply, but that only enraged him more. 'I don't want to fucking hear it ... fucking troublemakers ... fuck off and don't come back!' It was a relentless barrage that was intimidating, and thrilling. In every 'fuck off' was a sign that we had done our job.

Ferguson's mantra – 'I can't lose an argument. The manager can never lose an argument' – applied as much to media as to dealings with players. But he could be compelling company, too. He loved to gossip, often with slanderous comments about referees or rivals, and he could be a wonderful storyteller. There would be instances of kindness. When a colleague, John Bean, suffered a heart attack, Ferguson's bouquet was one of the first to arrive at hospital with a handwritten note.

Above all, no time with Ferguson could ever be boring. That was partly his position running the biggest club in the country but much more to do with the man himself, and the scale of his personality and the many contradictory sides of an uncompromising, charismatic leader who could fill our notebooks with gems one day and, the next, tell us to fuck off out of his sight.

One bit of footage that does survive is a 25-second clip of Ferguson ranting at Matt Lawton, of the *Daily Express*, in February 1999. Ryan Giggs had been forced off just 11 minutes into the victory over Derby County, suffering with another hamstring problem.

It was that injury which had forced him out at a critical time – indeed, at almost exactly the same point – the previous season. An outstanding sports-news reporter, Lawton was led by a source to believe that Giggs was a serious doubt for the remainder of the season. He wrote it without seeking the (inevitable) obfuscation from Ferguson, and turned up at the next press conference to find the manager seething.

'You wrote that fucking Giggs is out for the season?'

'I understood that to be the case.'

'You understood that? You ask me that?'

'To be fair, Alex, I can't always get hold of you.'

'Well, fucking, you can fucking try, writing shite like that. Any more you are out the fucking door, right! Fucking rubbish you write.'

That outburst counted as quite mild as they go. 'Get that c*** out of my tunnel,' might be the most succinct abuse he ever delivered my way when I was once, with permission, down near the dressing room at Old Trafford to interview a player.

It is not the most pleasant way to be addressed but we put up with it – indeed, frequently sniggered through it – because we were dealing with one of the most fascinating figures in the history of British sport. We were seeing the charismatic life force up close and personal. Ferguson could be a bully but a captivating one. Being shouted at was better than being kept at a distance, which is how the world of football and media would soon become.

51

Ole

Manchester United were leading 4-1 away to Nottingham Forest on 6 February when Alex Ferguson signalled for a change. Dwight Yorke was on a hat-trick, as was Andy Cole, but the manager wanted to give Yorke a rest, which he accepted reluctantly, running off after 72 minutes to be replaced by Solskjær. The Norwegian striker came on with instructions to keep the ball and play it simple. No need to expend unnecessary energy. This game was already won and a narrow advantage at the top of the table secured. Solskjær had other thoughts, or perhaps he simply could not stop himself.

In the 80th minute, he tapped in his first goal at the far post from a low cross from Gary Neville. Eight minutes later he ran clear of the Forest defence on to a long ball from David Beckham, failed with his attempted chip over David Beasant, who got a hand to the ball, but smacked the rebound like a missile into the roof of the net. His hat-trick came in the 90th minute after Paul Scholes found him just inside the penalty area with a chipped pass, and Solskjær controlled the ball with one touch and, with his second, rifled his shot with unstoppable power. He could make finishing, that fiendishly difficult art, look so simple. There was still time for more. United players were queuing up to shoot in the final moments as Scholes's miscue ran to Solskjær to apply another composed finish into the bottom corner. In his baggy white shirt, Solskjær smiled almost with embarrassment. He had scored four goals in 13 minutes 48 seconds.

At 8-1, United had their biggest away win in 99 years and nine months, since 1899 when the club was still Newton Heath. Solskjær was the first player in the Premier League to score a hat-trick off the bench. 'The best substitute in the world,' Ferguson said afterwards – which was one of those double-edged compliments that a player less smart than Solskjær, or less quietly confident in his own skin, might have taken the wrong way.

The day before he plundered those four goals, Solskjær was spotted buying his own pair of boots in a sports shop in the Trafford Centre. 'We couldn't believe it,' the store manager told *The Sun*. It was one of those stories that contributed to Solskjær's reputation as the most unassuming of footballers.

He did not want to be a substitute. Who did? But he had seen other players sulk and moan about being on the sidelines, and soon be moved on by Ferguson, so he had the wisdom to realise what was the best for his career. Other strikers had a reputation for selfishness, but Solskjær was a team man loved by his colleagues for his humility. He was also extraordinarily effective. Solskjær scored a league goal for every 71 minutes he played in the 1998-99 campaign. It remains an unmatched strike rate in the Premier League among any player who has scored more than ten goals in a season. A hell of a record, in other words, from a striker who could be fourth choice.

Of the 366 appearances Solskjær made for United, 150 were made as a substitute. Of the 126 goals he scored (ninth on the club's all-time list), 33 came during the last 15 minutes of matches. He had scored six minutes after coming on for his debut against Blackburn Rovers in August 1996 and, from the start, this role had become his speciality. 'I'm sure he hates being called a

super-sub, and it's unfair, but the fact is ... he is,' Ferguson said
after those four goals at Forest.

Solskjær had signed from Molde for an initial fee of just
£1.5 million. Coming in a summer when Ferguson had chased
Alan Shearer, who preferred to leave Blackburn for hometown
Newcastle United in a record £15 million transfer, the new
arrival seemed an underwhelming purchase.

His own teammates had been unconvinced. They initially
thought he was a competition winner, walking around the Cliff
in a jumper straight out of Kristiansund, the quiet fishing village
where Solskjær was raised. He was 23 going on 14, with a che-
rubic face and an accent from somewhere over the North Sea, as
if Scandinavia and Manchester were engaged in a tug-of-war for
his next syllable. Coming into this United dressing room full of
noise and egos and merciless stick, he seemed so polite. Too nice.

But as soon as they trained they realised what made Solskjær
so special. He drove Peter Schmeichel mad the way he could
slide a ball through the goalkeeper's legs. Unlike other strikers in
shooting drills, he would not try to take an extra touch for the
perfect finish but practice getting his shots away with whatever
little time and space was available. He had this seemingly innate
sense of finding the gap between the legs of defenders as they
lunged to block.

He always seemed to arrive on the pitch with the same sense of
calm assurance. As someone once remarked, 99 per cent of being
an assassin is the waiting and the planning – and 1 per cent the
kill. This baby-faced assassin, as he became known, understood
how to bide his time, and then strike.

Ferguson had a deep affection for Solskjær and for his willingness to be a squad player. As he noted after the Forest rout, 'If I
ever feel guilty about the teams I pick and the players I leave out, it
invariably centres around him. He really deserves better than the
number of games I give him, but the other factor that influences

me is that he is better than everyone else as a substitute.' After coming off the bench to knock out Liverpool, he was not done there. Solskjær would finish the season with more goals (18) than starts (17) and his status as the world's most effective substitute confirmed, spectacularly.

52

Steve

Sitting on the United bench as Solskjær ran riot against Nottingham Forest was Steve McClaren. One day he would become a familiar figure for the nation's football fans – especially when sheltering under an umbrella – but there was no reason for United's away supporters to recognise the ginger-haired chap in a tracksuit next to Alex Ferguson.

Football's cognoscenti were aware of McClaren's reputation as one of the brightest young coaches in the English game, but this rise was extraordinarily swift. In midweek he had been at Old Trafford as Derby County's assistant coach in a 1-0 defeat. Now he was sitting at the right hand of the most dominant manager in the game. 'Everything has happened so quickly. I am in a bit of a whirl and can hardly think straight,' McClaren told the media.

Two months after Brian Kidd's acrimonious departure, it was a huge promotion for a journeyman player whose career was curtailed by injury. Not many years earlier, he was driving Oxford United's youth team around in a minibus. Now McClaren, 37, had been chosen ahead of David Moyes, the young Preston North End manager, who would have to wait another 14 years for his chance to work at Old Trafford. McClaren could not have enjoyed a more remarkable start as Ferguson's new assistant than watching United score eight at the City Ground. He walked into the dressing room at the end of his first day in the job. 'Not bad, lads,' he said. 'Is it like this every week?'

McClaren has worked as a coach across three decades. He has been to a European final, led an English club to a major trophy, risen to the top of the game as manager of England, albeit not for as long as he had hoped. But nothing was like the training-ground environment he walked into at United in February 1999. McClaren arrived at the Cliff and could almost smell the testos-terone. The whiff was overpowering. It filled the air. 'What I call warriors,' he says. 'Relentless, demanding. A cone out of place in training, a referee decision wrong, oh my God it was war.'

He went to take the boxes in the first week of training. 'Shit control,' Keane shouted. 'Shit pass,' Schmeichel barked. Another bust-up. 'I started off trying to be the referee of the boxes,' McClaren says, 'and I just became the brunt for their conflicts. The best thing I did was actually join in, the best football I've ever played by the way, and tell them to sort it out themselves. At least I slept better at night.'

McClaren had the unfortunate start of being called McClaridge by Martin Edwards, the chairman, at his unveiling press confer-ence. The players killed him for that. 'All new players, especially foreigners, were tested to the hilt verbally and physically. "Are you a man or not, basically?" Oh dear, it could be tough. You would have to win the respect. It was the same for me, little old Steve McClaridge.'

McClaren recalls youth players being sent to join in a prac-tice match and one of them taking a heavy blow, writhing on the ground in agony. 'I'm blowing the whistle and stopping the play for treatment and Roy is saying, "Stevie, leave him, play on."' He shakes his head, smiling at the memory. 'It was a tough school,' he says.

*

McClaren quickly learnt that the secret was to train at an intensity that would be carried on to the pitch. These players hated slowing down. There would be no tactical walk-throughs. They wanted competition – young versus old, Britain against the Rest of the World with forfeits for those who lost – even when they were doing basic fitness work.

'They wanted teaching, they wanted training, they wanted toughness, they wanted discipline, they wanted competitiveness – the players demanded that; it didn't come from the manager,' he says. This is not something that can be taken for granted. It can be easier for players to look cool, and to act like they do not care. 'The players' appetite was insatiable; you could not get them off the training field. I remember on a Friday morning at the Cliff and you know the gaffer's office in the corner with the big window and he's banging on the glass saying, "Stevie, get the players in!" And they wouldn't come in. "One more shot, Stevie!"

'Schmeichel always faced 20 shots on a Friday and he'd fly out in his star-shape, get hit in the head, hit everywhere. He wanted 20 shots and no goals. If one went in, he'd be so mad. That was just the intensity, [the] competitiveness of the characters that were there. They were fierce. If training was too low intensity, it was boring. If it was too high intensity, it became too many fights and conflicts. So you had to keep them in the right band of competitiveness. Schmeichel was very volatile but they all were. They all had a line and once they crossed it, you knew. They'd stand their ground. You couldn't be meek, you had to stand up to that. Anyone who didn't was thrown out.

'Match day was hard because that's exam day, and no one likes exams. But they'd had all week competing against the best. We'd put Butty against Keane and we matched up Gary against Giggsy all the time and Denis against Becks, made it tough for them. Whoever their opponent was would be far easier than playing against Scholesy or Butty or anybody else.'

McClaren says those four months of the 1999 season were the toughest of his professional life – yes, even more than those bruising days as England manager – as he sought to harness that intensity, to feed and nurture it, without it spilling over. Ferguson had not given McClaren any clear instructions. No plans to work on certain moves, or overarching tactical strategy. McClaren had sat in Ferguson's office at the Cliff on his first morning and asked what he should work on. 'Whatever you did at Derby,' Ferguson told him. 'He never said "work on position, work on the back four". It was just, "Go out there and coach." He gave me a clean sheet of paper every day.'

He does not want that to sound like Ferguson was not engaged, or lacked rigour. It was more a case of smart delegation. One of the reasons McClaren was recruited was because the United manager wanted to tap into the hungry mind of an up-and-coming coach, who was a voracious consumer of books and videos about training techniques, including from American sports.

'What's happening? What's developing? Alex wanted to be at the forefront,' McClaren says. Under McClaren, United would become early adopters of data analysis. He introduced Bill Beswick, a sports psychologist, and adapted training to include yoga. Key to implementing new ideas was ensuring that Keane, the skipper, was onside. 'I said to Bill, "If we get Roy then we've got the group." Bill would always talk about Michael Jordan* being a warrior, that kind of environment. Roy loved that. So Bill got accepted – not by everybody – but we were always looking for the extra 10 per cent.'

He had a group of players eager to learn, but they taught him a few lessons, too. In one of McClaren's first games, United won narrowly and he came into the dressing room trying to sound upbeat. 'Well done, lads, great performance,' he told them. 'Roy tore my head off. "We were crap, Stevie! Don't ever tell us we were good when we were crap! We want honesty in here." Every day for me was trying to prove myself to the players that I could do the job. It wasn't until the end of the season I thought, "I might be accepted now."'

---

* If there was a rival 'team of the '90s' to United on global terms, it was the Chicago Bulls led by the incomparable Jordan. In June 1998, he had won his sixth and final NBA championship with the Bulls; a triumph feted in *The Last Dance* series which is one of the very best studies of sporting greatness.

Asked on that documentary whether his desire, his need to win, came at a cost of being perceived as a nice guy, Jordan was fascinating, and uncompromising. As he put it, 'Winning has a price and leadership has a price. I tried to pull people along when they didn't want to be pulled. I challenged people when they didn't want to be challenged and I earned that right because all the teammates that came after me didn't endure all the things that I endured.

'Once you join the team you live a certain standard that I play the game and I wasn't going to take anything less. Now if that means I had to go in there and get in your ass a little bit then I did that. You ask all my teammates, the one thing about Michael Jordan was that he never asked me to do something that he didn't do. When people see this they might say, "Well, he wasn't really a nice guy, he may have been a tyrant." No, that's because you never won anything. I wanted to win but I wanted them to win too.'

No wonder Keane was drawn to Jordan. Those could have been his words. Such different men, and athletes, yet kindred spirits in their unceasing demands on teammates, and themselves.

53

Rotation

On 20 February, Manchester United ran out at Highfield Road to face Coventry City. The line-up, in 4-4-2, was: Schmeichel; G. Neville, Johnsen, Stam, Irwin; Beckham, Keane, Scholes, Giggs; Yorke, Cole.

So far so unremarkable. Except this would be the only time in 38 Premier League games that this XI – everyone's idea of Ferguson's strongest line-up, and one of the most celebrated sides in English football history – would start together in 1998-99. Across the whole campaign, that XI started just one other match together, ten days later in the first leg of the Champions League quarter-final against Inter Milan. This vaunted team ran out together twice. If we compare to the 1993-94 Double season, an XI of Schmeichel; Parker, Bruce, Pallister, Irwin; Kanchelskis, Ince, Keane, Giggs; Cantona, Hughes started 13 games together. Something unusual was happening.

Ronny Johnsen's frequent injuries were partly responsible, with the defender able to start just 19 league games, half the total. Ryan Giggs started 20 league matches because of injuries including those troublesome hamstrings. Ferguson was forced into more changes than he would have liked. But there was another force at work. You could call that Coventry match an interesting quirk or a sign of something broader and more historic. The 1998-99 season was the dawning of true rotation, and Ferguson, through a combination of resources, trust of his wider squad and the courage of his convictions, was at the vanguard.

He understood the growing demands on players and, having already started a trend by using up-and-coming players in the League Cup to howls of outrage, increasingly saw the need for managing his players' physical limits. With no winter break in the English league, he effectively created his own ad-hoc version for tired players, like allowing Peter Schmeichel that mid-season holiday in Barbados, and giving others, including Beckham, Scholes and Gary Neville, periods of rest.

He had built a formidable squad – if nowhere near the stock-piling of today's Super Clubs – and was determined to use it. Nicky Butt was one of those players not in the strongest XI, yet he would be summoned for some of the biggest tests, including all five games against Arsenal, to assist Roy Keane in the physical battles against Emmanuel Petit and Patrick Vieira. Butt would make 47 appearances, including 34 starts, which was only four less than Paul Scholes.

Ferguson's boldness in mixing up his selections, including for some of the biggest fixtures, made it a squad game more than ever, though Butt is unconvinced when I suggest to him that he was as valuable as any of those players who ran out at Coventry. 'Let's be honest, there was an obvious best team,' he says, rattling off the names. 'I'm not stupid. I'm not going to argue with that.'

That response typifies his humility. Butt had the ideal temperament for the role assigned by the manager. He explains how Ferguson would leave him out for a run of games but soften the blow by telling him that he was being kept for a particular contest, like a war against Arsenal. 'I'd still want to know why I'm not playing,' he says. 'I'd go and see the manager, knock on his door. That's how my dad brought me up. One time I got him on a bad day and he told me, "Because you aren't as good as them!" But mostly he'd give me reasons, explain how he was going to use me. He'd say, "You're sitting out these two but be ready for that one."'

Sheringham scoffed when I mentioned the R-word. That was not how it felt for him. As soon as Yorke and Cole clicked, it was obvious that he was going to be deputising. 'It wasn't rotation,' Sheringham says. 'You're listening to Fergie! Yorkie and Cole were his preferred strike partnership. We filled in in the games that didn't mean so much.' But Ferguson kept talking to him, kept him motivated.

It was the same for Phil Neville, who made 44 appearances, including 29 starts, even in a season when he was not only competing with his brother Gary and Denis Irwin but also Wes Brown. Ferguson would tell the younger Neville that he could go to, say, Everton and be sure to start every match but that would be around 45 games and he was getting that at United. 'So what are you complaining about?' Ferguson would ask.

By plotting ahead, telling players to be ready for particular games, Ferguson ensured that no one became alienated. Sheringham and Solskjær knew there was nowhere else with a better chance of winning honours. Butt and Phil Neville had United in their blood. Butt is surprised when I mention that the 'best XI', as he puts it, started just one league game together – 'good pub question,' he smiles – and seems entirely at ease about whether anyone remembers this campaign for a team or a squad.

If any group of players demonstrated that success in the modern game is all about collective strength, and quality off the bench, it was this one.

---

* The rotation that took root in the 1998-99 season became such a norm that, between May 2008 and February 2011, Ferguson went 165 games in a row (in all competitions) changing his starting XI each time. Asked during that run if he could confirm his line-up, he promised that any journalist who correctly predicted the team would enjoy a trip to Loch Lomond at his expense. Ferguson could not resist adding that he would ensure 'the midges were out'.

54

Mr Loophole

On Friday 26 February, Alex Ferguson was driving his BMW 750 along the M602 past Eccles when he found himself stuck in a queue of traffic. A police car saw the United manager drive onto the hard shoulder and skip past the queue of cars. The officers chased him and Ferguson was pulled over, spoken to and subsequently ended up in front of Bury magistrates accused of driving illegally on the hard shoulder.

Ferguson was told by a friend to hire Nick Freeman as his defence lawyer. Freeman explained to the court that, far from being an impatient driver breaking the law, Ferguson had been suffering from severe diarrhoea. Emergency measures had been necessary. He said that his high-profile client had two options while stuck in the traffic jam, 'One is the unthinkable and one is to take evasive action.'

Whether or not this had anything to do with Ferguson being the most successful football manager in the country, the court believed him and let him off. It was a good day for the Scot, but it turned out to be an even better one for Freeman, who thereafter became known as Mr Loophole. It was the United manager who gave him his big breakthrough.

Mr Loophole quickly established a lucrative career out of helping the rich and famous off potential motoring convictions. Later in 1999, after David Beckham was banned for eight months for speeding in his £150,000 Ferrari, Freeman successfully appealed on the grounds that the United star had been escaping a paparazzi photographer. His licence was returned.

When a BMW 750, registered to Manchester United and the same model as Ferguson's, was caught by a speed camera on Derby ring road after United's 8-1 win at Nottingham Forest in February, United insisted that they did not know who was driving. Ferguson was named in a summons but Freeman attended alone and said there was no evidence that the United manager had been at the wheel. The club was handed a paltry fine. Understandably, a local MP asked whether the club was now so successful that it was even above the law.

---

* Shortly after Ferguson explained his case of the runs, a package arrived at his office in Manchester. It was a supply of tablets from Piers Morgan, editor of the *Mirror* and passionate Arsenal fan. 'I sent him a box of Imodium saying that we Gooners knew he was full of crap, and now we've got the evidence,' Morgan told me with a chuckle. 'Fergie didn't take it very well.'

55

Tactics? What tactics?

Alex Ferguson would occasionally pull out a tactics board. He might move a few magnets around. He would gather his players to remind them of the quality of a particular opponent, or how he thought a game might be won. But the genius was never in tactical sophistication. Gary Neville does more detailed analysis on a Monday night for Sky Sports than he ever did in a United shirt. 'None of us would pretend we reinvented the game or out-witted opponents tactically,' Neville says. 'Mostly it was 4-4-2 (or 4-4-1-1) but played at an incredibly high tempo with real quality.'

From our perspective now where we all fancy ourselves as tactically smart – armchair experts on gegenpressing and the low block – it is tempting to look back a little dismissively at the simplistic approach of yesteryear. To talk to United players is to be struck, repeatedly, by how little choreography Ferguson put into his team compared to, say, Pep Guardiola moving a player an inch in his positioning, or tweaking the angle at which he receives the ball by five degrees. Andy Cole talked of Ferguson once struggling to explain a tactical idea, and the movement he wanted. He tied himself in knots before putting the board aside. 'Stuff that, Coley, just get in the box,' he said.

'The manager hated gimmicks,' Cole explained. 'Football is a simple game and will always be. Get it, pass it to a red shirt, use the space, just do it easy. And that's what we used to do. Especially if people were playing well, he always wanted to get the ball to those individuals. So, he'd say to some of the boys, "Just give it to Yorkie and Coley, and let them get on with it." Get it out of Neville into Becks, and Becks used to play it into us. Scholesy and Roy, the first thing they wanted to do was look forward to us. And then we go from there, so we were never starved of the ball.'

According to Dwight Yorke, 'The manager didn't have to do much. In fact, he didn't do any bloody coaching! Steve McClaren did all the coaching.'

That is a little unfair, in the sense that Ferguson was very adept at spotting the strengths and weaknesses of a player, and what he wanted from him. But his approach to training was that he was better off judging from a little distance, walking around the pitches to gauge the mood and having a quiet word. 'Neville, take another touch before you cross it,' he would say. 'Go on, Ryan, run at him!'

He was the boss walking around the factory floor, but he would not lead training sessions. Since his days at Aberdeen, Ferguson felt that he could see more by doing less. He felt that too much instruction could inhibit a player. He wanted clear minds. He hated overelaboration. His tweaks came from sensing which player to pick for an occasion – like Butt for Scholes – to shift the emphasis of his team, but as Ferguson had told the *Mail on Sunday* earlier in the season when talking about how United would approach the final group game at home to Bayern Munich, his job was in setting the tone, which was generally of attacking intent and aggression.

'We're not good at looking for a draw; we're not Italians or Spaniards. We're too honest a people. We'll go at them gung-ho; nine in the box, bags of crosses. It's exciting and it's us, and anyway, you win more than you lose playing it that way.'

It was an oversimplification, almost naively so – and Ferguson would be forced to adjust considerably over time – but it did capture the essence of his approach and the greatest quality of the

1998-99 squad. Boldness had carried United to the quarter-finals of the European Cup, scoring the most goals in the competition – but could it take them all the way?

As United prepared to face Inter Milan, there was a specific threat which occupied Ferguson's mind. Europe was one arena in which he knew, from painful experience, that United's approach could be undone by continental teams with more flexible systems which would create an overload in midfield.

Facing Inter's wing-backs, and knowing that the Italian club would keep only one striker high while Roberto Baggio, waning at 32 but still a stellar name, and Youri Djorkaeff, a world champion with France, drifted into no-man's land, United had to decide whether the centre-halves would come out to close down those roving attackers or the full-backs move inside. Or should picking up these playmakers be the responsibility of a midfielder?

Being outmanned in midfield had been a recurring problem, exacerbated by Ferguson's reluctance to surrender United's strengths of two attacking wide men and two strikers. The threat of Inter had the coaches in conversation about a few little moderations. As Steve McClaren explained, 'Most games, you could get away with Giggs and Beckham being wide and Scholes–Keane or Butt–Keane coping in midfield, and Yorkie also dropping in. But Europe could be a problem. Sometimes tactically, the wingers got a little bit too wide and also Yorkie didn't drop in enough to make the third man in midfield, but that was the only tinkering with the 4-4-2.'

As they prepared to face Inter, Ferguson told the full-backs, Neville and Irwin, that they would need to be more narrow than usual to pick up Baggio and Djorkaeff. It might detract from their ability to overlap but he was confident that Beckham and Giggs would be able to cause problems one-to-one against Inter's wing-backs. It was a tweak, and a nod to the magnitude of the game, but hardly an overhaul or tactical rocket science.

As Sheringham told me, 'Fergie took four training sessions in my time. That's in four years. They were always before European games. It would be, say, to make sure the two central midfield players didn't vacate that area at the same time because a lot of the top European teams liked to penetrate through the middle. He'd get Keaney and Scholes playing from that little area in training and if they went out of it, he'd say, "No, get back here." But there was no system like my Tottenham or Millwall games as I'd been used to. There was none! We train hard, how we want to play, and we take it into games. That's what Liverpool were like at their peak back in the day, a little warm-up, small-sided games and that's it.'

Ferguson was not blind to the need to be aware of particular opponents. In a typical team talk, he would warn his players about the challenge ahead and specific threats. If facing Liverpool, for example, he would make sure his players were fully apprised of the need to track Steve McManaman's running. Against Arsenal, he would emphasise the need for aggression, particularly in the era of Thierry Henry and Robert Pires.

Against Inter, he had his defensive plan and, always, an idea of how the game could be won by predicting the damage that Giggs and Beckham could do with crosses if they could find space behind the wing-backs – but no one would call him an arch strategist or a tactical visionary.

Sheringham adds, 'Before a match Fergie would do his thing on the board about the other team. Like, "the left winger is all left foot", or "the centre midfield player is good but not the quickest so get around him". He would label players but there was no actual tactical training where you'd go, "He's taught me something there." He didn't put too much emphasis on how good the other team were, so you didn't get bogged down thinking "this is Inter Milan, blimey"'.

Or as Ferguson once summed up his approach, 'Tactics are important, but they don't win football matches. Men win football matches.'

56

Pasta joke

There was something else about Inter Milan that preoccupied Alex Ferguson as we gathered on the eve of the biggest test of United's season. The manager seethed with mistrust as he spoke about the looming tie which would indicate whether his side was fully equipped, at last, to travel far in the Champions League. At the pre-match press conference at Old Trafford, much of the chatter revolved around whether the great Ronaldo would start for Inter after suffering with knee injuries. He had not flown over with the rest of the Inter squad, seemingly ruling him out, but Ferguson was deeply sceptical. 'The Italians are the innovators of the smokescreen,' he said, brimming with hostility.

And then he came up with one of those lines that journalists love; Uefa less so, subsequently fining Ferguson for unnecessary provocation. Asked again about Inter's insistence that Ronaldo would be absent, Ferguson replied, 'When an Italian tells me it's pasta on the plate, I check under the sauce to make sure.'

It was a wonderful quote for us, though also evidence that Ferguson was never likely to be initiated into the diplomatic corps. And with Ronaldo not taking to the field, the Italians could reasonably ask which camp had a mischievous Machiavelli as manager.

57

Character is fate #5

Manchester United 2 Inter Milan 0, 3 March 1999

If anyone questions the fortitude, or brilliance, of David Beckham, they should start by looking at the night when he looked Diego Simeone in the eye, shook his nemesis by the hand and then proceeded to play one of the games of his life. The Champions League quarter-final, and sporting fates, had reunited the two foes from St Etienne at Old Trafford. As if there was not enough edge as United faced Inter Milan, Beckham was on a mission of redemption, and revenge.

A blinding flash of camera bulbs as Beckham and Simeone shook hands before kick-off set the scene for another confrontation – and for an exceptional performance. 'The energy and stamina of Steven Gerrard and the delivery and quality of Kevin de Bruyne,' Gary Neville said when I asked him to describe Beckham at the peak of his powers. This was a night when Beckham, unquestionably, looked among the most effective players in the world.

Ferguson's hope that United could open up Inter's 3-4-2-1 system if Ryan Giggs and Beckham could dominate their opposite numbers was quickly vindicated, and by Beckham in particular. Defending Inter's left flank, the right-footed Aron Winter, at 32, was completely overrun. Beckham quickly established himself as

United's main attacking outlet, sending in a barrage of first-half crosses. One chipped cross, hit on the run, after just six minutes gave Yorke the chance to score with a fine diving header. A superbly whipped cross before the interval invited Yorke to rise again to make it 2–0.

Ferguson's plan of the full-backs defending narrowly, with Gary Neville and Denis Irwin picking up Baggio and Djorkaeff, and then attacking with width had paid off superbly in the first 45 minutes.

Never a team to make life comfortable, United surrendered ground in an edgy second half. Peter Schmeichel had to pull off a save which he counted as probably the best, and certainly the most important, of his entire career when Iván Zamorano had a six-yard header. Schmeichel threw himself into one of his trademark star-fish saves, and his left hand held firm. Henning Berg had one of the most notable games of his United career including a crucial block on the goalline. 'The looks of an accountant but a warrior's heart,' Schmeichel would say of the Norway defender.

When Simeone thought he had scored with a header only for the referee to disallow it for a push, this time it was the Argentine's turn to fume about injustice. A promising teenager called Andrea Pirlo came off the bench to replace Baggio but United hung on to keep a clean sheet which inspired a neat line from David Lacey in the *Guardian* that 'the nought was as important as the crosses'. He had a point, but there was no disputing that Beckham had shaped the game with his delivery and domination of one flank. Ferguson gushed afterwards about the way his midfielder had imposed himself, and in such testing circumstances as we studied his temperament on this reunion with Simeone.

As Ferguson told us, 'We have got big-game players in our side and I thought Beckham was outstanding tonight. I didn't say anything special to him about the circumstances of the game, but he distinguished himself out there. No one matched him and there were some terrific players on that pitch.'

As the final whistle blew, Beckham was standing near Simeone – 'It must have been a sign,' he said – and they embraced briefly before the England player initiated a swapping of shirts. 'I will probably frame it,' he told us afterwards, chatting afterwards as though he was at ease with the world. 'That ends it all, I hope.'

58

A boy called Brooklyn

And then they had a baby. Twenty-four hours after displaying such impressive maturity on the pitch, David Beckham became a father for the first time and the world went into a frenzy about the boy born to a star footballer and a Spice Girl. Royal babies have had less attention.

The choice to name their first child Brooklyn after the district in New York where they discovered Victoria was pregnant drew plenty of comment, from the amusing – what if it had been Peckham? – to the insufferably snobbish. Even the *Guardian* asked its readers to consider whether Brooklyn's name represented 'admirable individualism or stunning irresponsibility?'

In his first television interview since the World Cup, Beckham told the BBC that 'a majority of people probably dislike me', but he had been through so much by now that he was at least becoming more adept at handling the vitriol. Facing Chelsea days after becoming a father, with the stick seemingly more personal than ever at Stamford Bridge, Beckham blew a sarcastic kiss at one abuser. Even Chelsea fans had to laugh. Well, some of them.

---

* In 2001, in an interview for Comic Relief, Ali G asked Victoria and David, who had gamely volunteered for the inevitable mockery, what their son would be when he grew up, 'A footballer like his dad or a pop singer . . . like Mariah Carey?' In fact, Brooklyn has become a model, occasional photographer and wannabe chef, with around 14 million followers on Instagram. A celebrity, in other words, though he was that from the day he was born.

59

The end

The day after the invigorating victory over Inter Milan, we joined Alex Ferguson for the launch of his testimonial year at Manchester Town Hall, where he sat alongside Mick Hucknall. The Simply Red singer had agreed to stage a concert in aid of topping up Ferguson's bank balance. The testimonial was the club's way of allowing Ferguson to fill his pockets with cash without having to actually pay him more – but the idea of a tribute year also brought the inevitable question of whether it signalled a man nearing the end.

Was this an indication that Ferguson was looking to wind down? With hindsight, it seems mad that we were asking him as far back as 1999 when he might walk away from United, and from management. But it did not seem so daft at the time. Ferguson's period in charge was already extraordinary after more than a decade running one of the biggest clubs in the world. There was no one with comparable longevity at any leading European side. It seemed reasonable to wonder how much longer he could, or might want to, carry on.

There were also times when Ferguson had hinted at leaving, especially in the constant squabbles over a new contract – and he was embroiled in one of those haggles at the time. Ferguson was embittered that Rupert Murdoch's potential takeover would create vast personal wealth for directors and shareholders while he was fighting for a new contract and a pay rise.

Pay was a constant running battle with Martin Edwards. In the ITV documentary shown earlier in the season, Ferguson had aired his grievance in public. 'You see all this money they are making and it's never reflected in the manager in the way it should be. Whereas you see other forms of business and their chief executives are recognised far more fully. I don't think it will change in football in that respect. You can be successful but not too successful, you know?'

The testimonial was one way for the club to appease him financially, though it was bound to carry suggestions about whether, at 57, he might quit if he did finally win the Champions League at the end of the season. He was not thrilled when one of us asked him that question. 'Are you saying that you wake up the next morning, and all of a sudden your work is finished?' he replied tartly.

Ferguson was not scared of much, but he was very mindful of stopping. He hated the idea of fading away. His father had been diagnosed with lung cancer just a week after retiring in 1978. Within 12 months the disease had killed him. Painful memories of that preyed on his mind. It fuelled the work ethic which his father had instilled in him. Ferguson never could stop, an obsessive with minimal separation between home–life and work. His father had always been out of the house by 6.45 a.m. to be at the shipyard when the gates opened. His mother was a factory worker. Ferguson would sleep for only five or six hours, waking soon after 6 a.m., jumping out of bed to be at the Cliff for 7 a.m.

As he wrote in *Leading* in an ode to the working class, 'Since both my parents worked their fingers to the bone, I somehow absorbed the idea that the only way I was going to improve my life was to work very hard. It was baked into my marrow. I was incapable of coasting and I have always been irritated by people who frittered away natural talents because they were not prepared to put in the hours.'

Ferguson used to say that 'well done' were the two most important words in the English language, but 'hard work' must have run them close. In his addresses to his players, he loved to cite the example of Lew Grade, the TV impresario, who would regularly arrive at his office at 7 a.m. and work 12-hour days even into his 90s. He would talk about Armand Hammer, an American billionaire, and his gargantuan work ethic. The players did not have a clue who these two men were but the message was unmistakable: 'Be proud to say you work hard.' Ferguson regarded hard work as every bit as important as the talent to hit the top corner from 30 yards.

The United manager would lie in bed thinking about themes to inspire his players and often alight on stories he knew of miners, shipyard workers, welders and toolmakers. He would ask them, 'What did your grandfather do? What did your father do?' to remind his squad of their working-class roots.

His players' wealth was soaring, with mansions for homes and a fleet of fast cars in the drive, so Ferguson kept trying to devise new ways to keep them grounded. Phil Neville, son of a lorry driver, told me about Ferguson taking him aside as a young player to advise him on his new contract, 'I'm going to give you £220 a week and your signing-on fee is £20,000. And I want you to give your signing-on fee straight to your mum and dad because they sacrificed everything to get you here.'

Gary Neville went through a typical team talk from Ferguson, and how the emphasis was invariably a narrative of graft. The manager would have a few handwritten notes that he would use as a prompt for a speech that would regularly be built around the idea that the first non-negotiable part of playing for Manchester United was to work harder than the opposition.

As Neville explained, 'He's this Glaswegian union man dealing with a young bunch of millionaires. And he managed to ground us in every team talk. There was always a story to reinforce the work ethic, principles. What would your father say, your grand-father, your grandma think of you if you didn't work hard, didn't get up in the morning, didn't put your shirt and tie on, your blazer on? If the lads weren't wearing their blazers on the plane, or the tie was a little bit down, or the top button undone, it would be, "What would your grandfather say?"

'In a team talk, it could be a story about an entrepreneur who was very rich who still got up at 6 a.m. every morning, or the manager fighting for his fellow workers in the dockyards of Govan in the '50s and '60s. The main message was hard work, groundedness, spirit. That was always the first part of his team talk to connect with us, motivate and make us realise that we were just normal people fighting for each other.'

One of his favourite speeches, which long-serving players must have heard a dozen times, was about Canada geese and how they can migrate thousands of miles by working as a team. They take turns being at the front, head to wind. If one gets injured, a couple drop away to look after it. Ferguson would tell them, 'I'm not asking you to fly thousands of miles, I'm asking you to work hard and look after each other in a game of football.'

Everyone regarded the speech as Ferguson's most important 30 minutes of the week and, while there were messages to be imparted about how they would need to play, it was as much about lighting their competitive fires and reinforcing the expectations of the manager.

Before his team went out of the dressing room, Ferguson would stand by the door waiting for the players to come past. He would shake them by the hand and look them in the eye. He would tell them, 'Don't you dare come back here without giving everything!' It was his last chance to make sure the players were taking that ethos, Ferguson's ethos, of hard work out onto the pitch.

'Make sure you see Alex Ferguson in your team,' one of his

first mentors had told him when he was going through a sticky patch early in management. To the Scot, that meant seeing the work ethic of the shipyards.

Ferguson wanted his own incessant hard work to be rewarded, too, but the United board were making him wait. He had been pushing for a new contract from the start of the 1998–99 season, believing that a basic salary of around £600,000 a year made him, at best, the fourth highest-paid manager in the Premier League at a time when his side were dominant. He had grumbled in public on that documentary, leaked stories to friendly journalists and made sure that everyone knew that he had entertained approaches from English clubs, including Tottenham Hotspur, and European giants such as Inter Milan.

Eventually, in early May, Ferguson secured his new deal with a basic salary of more than £1 million – a three-year deal until July 2002. Of course we speculated that it would probably be his last, and he was happy to concur. 'By that time I will be 60 and you will no longer have to worry about me,' he said. 'I will be out of your lives forever.'

Ferguson eventually retired in 2013, at the age of 71.

60

Treble talk

That beating Chelsea away from home in an FA Cup quarter-final replay struggles to feature among the top 10 key victories in the season underlines all that Manchester United had to overcome.

Chelsea were an excellent side, chasing the title under Gianluca Vialli. They had Le Saux, Leboeuf, Desailly, Wise, Di Matteo and Zola – wonderful players, top internationals, world champions with exceptional quality and their own big ambitions. They had spent a club record on Pierluigi Casiraghi, and their brightest stars earned more than their counterparts at United. Yet, after a goalless draw at Old Trafford when Ferguson had rotated his team for freshness and sent out Phil Neville in midfield to man-mark Zola, Chelsea were killed off three days later at Stamford Bridge with Yorke's two goals taking his season's tally to 26 and prompting plenty of speculation that the striker would soon be crowned Footballer of the Year.

His second was a beauty. Cole hungrily robbed the ball off Desailly and the ball ran to Yorke. His first time chip over Ed de Goey from 30 yards was a wondrous way to bring up United's 100th goal of the season – the first time they had reached a century under Ferguson, and only a week into March.

On the eve of the replay, Ferguson had been pressed on the prospects of a Treble. He responded that it would need a miracle. He called it impossibly romantic. It had never been achieved by an English club for the same reason that it still looked so daunting to United, given that beating Chelsea set up an even tougher tie against Arsenal, the holders, in the FA Cup semi-final. Wenger's side were also on a charge to defend their Premier League crown, and in the midst of their own 19-match unbeaten run. With Inter to be finished off in the Champions League just to reach the last four, there could be at least 16 more tests of United's mettle.

'You can't refuse the challenge,' Ferguson had said. 'Anyone in this position has got to go for it. You know deep down, though, you are not going to do it.' He did not sound defeatist but realistic; mindful of history and the knowledge that, in pursuit of a Treble, just one defeat over the next couple of months could prove fatal.

61

Coming of age

Inter Milan 1 Manchester United 1, 17 March 1999

It was a wild, rowdy night and that was even for those of us who did not have to worry about being brained by oranges plummeting from the sky. Citrus fruit, lighters and water bottles rained down on the Manchester United players as they prepared to face Inter Milan in front of almost 80,000 spectators in the San Siro. There was a touch of mist in the air – or was it smoke?

It was always going to be a tense, tempestuous affair and Ferguson had inflamed matters by following up his pasta comment from the first leg with accusations that Inter would resort to scheming, diving and a full repertoire of dirty tricks back in Italy. When we attended the pre-match press conference, he had even primed an English colleague to ask about the referee so that he could pile pressure on the official to look out for the dark arts.

Ferguson knew it was going to be a test of character as much as skill. In the dressing room, he kept repeating the mantra, 'Take the ball, take the ball.' He always did have the notion that courage in football worked two ways: the obvious bravery to thunder into a 50/50 tackle but also the willingness to take responsibility in possession. His team would need both qualities, especially after Diego Simeone tried his best at intimidation by bellowing at the United players in the tunnel.

Ronny Johnsen had been selected in midfield alongside Keane, which was one of the few notes of caution all season. With the return of Ronaldo to Inter's starting XI, Ferguson felt that Johnsen's speed made him best equipped to pick up the Brazilian if he collected the ball deep and set off with one of those phenomenal accelerations. It was a plan that, largely, worked. Ronaldo had a couple of moments, spasms of a former greatness, but was clearly not fit. Javier Zanetti struck the post with a shot from outside the penalty area, and Inter should have had a penalty when Peter Schmeichel threw himself recklessly in front of Iván Zamorano. Inter were improved from the first game, with a young Frenchman Mikael Silvestre impressing at left wing-back – he would be at Old Trafford within months – but United kept the ball for long enough periods to take the sting out of the game.

The tie was not without its frights. It never was simple with this United team. Nicola Ventola had replaced Ronaldo after an hour and capitalised on a rare mistake by Roy Keane, who misjudged a looping ball over the top of the defence. Ventola scored, to make it 2-1 on aggregate. But any danger of United blowing this opportunity was eased in the 88th minute when Gary Neville hit a high, hanging cross which Andy Cole nodded back into the centre of the goal where Paul Scholes, on as a late replacement for Johnsen, was waiting to apply a first-time finish.

United were in the semi-finals of the Champions League. 'The biggest step forward under my management,' Ferguson said, not so much of the result but his team's maturity. Inter had attempted to wind up Beckham, but when the ball was shoved in his face, he walked away. When Phil Neville was clattered with an elbow late on, United refused to be riled. They had stepped up in one of Europe's most hostile environments.

'You trust the players and perhaps now they trust themselves,' Ferguson noted. They had become the first United team to knock out a leading Italian club, though in the semi-final they would have to beat another one. And Juventus, on course for a fourth consecutive final, were a much tougher proposition.

---

* Sitting at home, gripped to the match, was Rod Hull, the television presenter famed for his partnership with obstreperous puppet Emu. When the picture beamed from the San Siro started playing up in the first half, Hull used a ladder to clamber on to the roof of his home in Winchelsea, East Sussex, to fiddle with the aerial. His son, Oliver, heard a fall and found Hull lying prone on paving outside. Hull was declared dead on arrival at hospital in Hastings. Tributes were paid to the entertainer but, at his funeral, close friend Bill Wallace also felt humour was appropriate: 'Rod would have summed up the tragedy, "I should have known better than to climb up there in the first place – even emus can't fly."'

62

Scholesy

'A scruffy, horrible goal. Was it Gaz who crossed it to Coley? He knocked it down and I think it came off my shin. Luckily the goalie dived out of the way.'

Sitting on a bar stool in Hotel Football in the shadow of Old Trafford, Paul Scholes could be describing a fluked mishit on a Sunday park pitch in Oldham rather than a precious equaliser in the San Siro. But then he always was world-class, not just in striking a football, but in self-deprecation.

Scholes even goes out of his way to say that he was not in the starting line-up in Milan to make the point, against himself, that he was far from the midfielder he needed to be in 1998-99; still developing the all-round prowess which would lead Xavi and Zidane, no less, to call him the complete package. 'I was a bit unreliable in midfield at that time,' he says. 'For European games, we got outrun in midfield many times and I wasn't an ideal midfield player. It wasn't my position growing up. I just wanted to get forward, and I wasn't the greatest athlete and the manager needed real athletes against brilliant teams, brilliant footballers.'

I tell him he is being far too modest. 'No, it's true. I was almost like a forward so positional-wise it didn't come until later in my career. At that time the manager wanted a positional player, more solid, and that was Nicky Butt alongside Roy, or Ronny Johnsen.'

We argue about it some more − as I point out that Scholes finished the season as the fourth highest scorer, while proving the perfect foil to Keane in many defining matches of the campaign – but he keeps deflecting praise on to others. Even if Scholes has proved a much better television pundit than anyone anticipated, talking about himself is as much fun as auditioning to be Ginger Spice.

I remind him that Alex Ferguson once said that he had four world-class players in his time at United; Eric Cantona, Ryan Giggs, Cristiano Ronaldo and Scholes. What an honour! 'What do you want me to say,' Scholes responds, almost pained by the question. 'That's nice of him but in a lot of people's opinion I wouldn't have been.'

You have to speak to the other players to have a full appreciation of Scholes and it is notable how many of them went out of their way to eulogise his abilities. Typical was Jaap Stam when I asked him about who really impressed among his teammates.

'People ask me all the time who was the best player you played with. There's always a discussion. Was it Roy, or was it Giggsy or someone else? I thought Paul Scholes. He was so underestimated. Is it because he doesn't want to be in the limelight? For me, it was his quality on the ball, his touch, his passing, his scoring ability and especially his vision in reading the game. That link between the attack and the defence, spreading the ball and putting players into positions where they can deliver. The front players, they could do well because of the composure behind them. Scholes with Keane, what a combination.'

Put that to Scholes and he looks like he wants to crawl into a hole.

When I arrive, the antithesis of the celebrity footballer is sitting minding his own business. It takes me a little while to find him, tucked away in the corner of the bar to avoid attention. This hotel is part of the empire built by the Class of '92. 'Gary's empire,'

Scholes says. 'Left to me, I wouldn't have done anything. I would have kept myself to myself.'

Scholes was married in February 1999, in the midst of this historic campaign, but there was no massive scramble among the paparazzi, or mega-deals with *Hello!*, or barriers to keep back screaming fans. He drove a Jeep, not a Ferrari. His biggest commercial deal was appearing on the back of packets of Shreddies. He was a master at lying low, even hiding his waspish sense of humour and giving the impression that he was painfully shy.

His teammates knew a very different side. Scholes might not say much, but when he did it tended to be as biting as his tackles. He was unerringly sharp. He could find his target just as accurately as one of those balls he would ping at someone's head on the training ground. Scholes has a mischievous streak, which found one outlet in the dinks he would flick over Peter Schmeichel in the hope of enraging the big keeper. Scholes loved to be on the training ground as long as it did not involve running drills – even his asthma feels characteristically unglamorous – and he still believes that practice matches were ample preparation. In his eyes, then and now, football is a simple game complicated by idiots. 'It's true,' he says. 'Football tactics are a bit boring.'

If Pep Guardiola had arrived as manager, he is certain the 1999 squad could have quickly adapted. They had the technical prowess; Scholes in particular. It has often been said of him, with justification, that he would have been the English player best suited to the great Barcelona side, exchanging tiki-taka passes with Xavi and Iniesta. 'We'd have taken it all on board,' he says of detailed tactics, 'but I don't think we'd have enjoyed it anywhere as much as we did.'

Enjoy how? 'We'd kick lumps out of each other. Blood rolling down your shin.' He says it with relish. Train, play, go home, zero fuss. Scholes thinks he must have learned from his parents. 'They preferred to watch matches in the pub,' he says, when I ask if they were there to see that goal in the San Siro and other great moments. 'I wasn't bothered.'

Scholes was not immune from the pressures. He says that he never detected nerves in Butt or Giggs but would always feel a knot in his stomach before matches. 'If it wasn't, there was something wrong. It brought the best out of me.'

Ask him how much he revelled in the fun of it all, especially as such a wonderfully talented player, and Scholes looks a little taken aback. His reply was surprisingly similar to many of the players and another insight into life at the very top of the game. 'I think I enjoyed it at the time, but I'd never say it was fun. It was so intense. Leading into games, you just felt you had to win every one and that wasn't really fun. It was like going to work and not many people would say going to work is fun. But there were rewards at the end of it.'

Days after his goal against Inter Milan, Kevin Keegan picked Scholes in his first game as interim England manager. Preparing to face Poland in a Euro 2000 qualifier, Keegan summoned an old line Bill Shankly had said to him many years before at Liverpool, 'Son, go out there and drop some hand grenades.' Scholes scored a hat-trick for his country in a 3-1 win.

'If you were a racegoer,' Keegan said afterwards of his modest match-winner, 'you wouldn't pick him out in the paddock. But when it comes to the business end of the race, he will be there. He's a winner.' It was an echo of something once said by Ole Gunnar Solskjær about Scholes, which neatly sums up how his fellow professionals felt about him: 'He's not the quickest, he doesn't run the most, he never wins a header, he can't tackle, but he's the best player.'

Best player? I am not sure that is true, but the more Scholes plays down his many qualities, the more his teammates feel a need to ensure he is properly recognised as one of the greats.

63

Zidane on one leg

Manchester United 1 Juventus 1, 7 April 1999

Manchester United versus Juventus. A Champions League semi-final first leg. Alex Ferguson always knew it was going to be one of those nights that he would be thrashing over restlessly into the early hours, whatever the outcome. He would be replaying the key incidents; measuring a trial of strength against the team that had become a benchmark for European mastery. After Barcelona, Juventus were the last mental hurdle for United to overcome. Some of the players were still scarred by a beating in 1996 which was, somehow, only 1-0 but felt like humiliation. They had felt daunted just looking at Juventus in the tunnel. It was men against boys even before they ran out and failed to muster a single shot on target.

United had fared better since in group-stage matches, but Juventus had an aura. They were striving for a fourth consecutive Champions League final. They had Zinedine Zidane, the maestro of France's World Cup-winning team and unquestionably among the finest footballers on the planet; Didier Deschamps, dependable skipper of the world champions; Edgar Davids, the Dutch pitbull. On the right side of midfield, Antonio Conte was as intense on the ball as he would later become as a manager. The back line was led by Paolo Montero, the tough-guy Uruguay defender on course for the most red cards in Serie A history.

They were true heavyweights but there was also a new vulnerability. Marcello Lippi, a manager much admired by Ferguson, had departed in mid-season to be replaced by Carlo Ancelotti; wily veteran for a rising star of management. But Ancelotti had been in charge for fewer than ten games and had faced antipathy from the Juventus fans for his playing links with Roma and AC Milan. This gilded team had been stumbling in Serie A. It felt like United had an opportunity to go further than they had gone before, which, of course, piled on more pressure and expectation. A meeting with Juventus could only ever feel like it was a special occasion, and this, back near the top of Everest where the air is thin and a sense of vertigo can afflict even experienced players, was one of the biggest matches at Old Trafford in decades.

Sensing the magnitude, Ferguson arranged for the entire United squad to stay overnight in a hotel post-match, which was highly unusual. They drove to Mottram Hall in the Cheshire countryside, even though for most it meant travelling straight past home, and their own beds, to thrash out the implications of a fraught night.

At Old Trafford, we watched Juventus batter United in the first half. Even if Zidane was coming back from injury and playing with a heavily strapped thigh, his roving role caused huge complications. 'If this is what he can do with one leg, you fear what he will do with two,' I typed up in the press box, as we watched Roy Keane become preoccupied by the Frenchman's elegant gliding from attack back into midfield.

With the United captain otherwise engaged, it meant that Davids was free to press forward, protected by Deschamps behind him. The Dutch midfielder was typically forceful, and effective. It was the old problem in midfield as Keane and Paul Scholes found themselves overworked and overrun. United's full-backs were tied down by Di Livio and Conte, who scored a fine first-half goal when Davids slipped the ball to him through Scholes's legs. With one touch to set himself up, Conte, the Juve captain, shot past Schmeichel and ran off for a manic, wild-eyed celebration, with his arms outstretched like he was trying to reprise Marco Tardelli in 1982.

Juventus could have scored several more, and United were grateful for the chance to stabilise at half-time with the tie still salvageable. Ronny Johnsen replaced the struggling Henning Berg, and Ferguson reorganised his midfield with Beckham told to withdraw and sit much tighter in support of Keane and Scholes to try to wrest back some control. It was a strategy that worked, especially as Zidane began to tire after a month out, but United still had no reward for their improvement as the game reached the 90th minute. Teddy Sheringham had come on in place of Yorke, bringing added threat, and he was key to yet another late United comeback.

Trying to cause chaos in the Juventus box in the last thrust of attack, Beckham hooked the ball into the area, Sheringham won the battle for the header, and it was knocked on into the goal-mouth. Finally it fell to Giggs, who blasted his shot into the roof of the net. Schmeichel reckoned the roar which greeted that goal was as loud as any he ever heard at Old Trafford. Another late goal, and a precious lifeline.

Back at the hotel, Ferguson felt the need to have a full-blown analysis with his players. It was not his usual style – best not to say too much in the post-match emotion – but this ceaseless run of big games demanded that they were on top of any issues quickly, ready to learn and move on. Ferguson emphasised to his players that he had wanted to be bold, and true to the team's nature, but that they had erred by Giggs and Beckham both bombing forward in the first half. He had told them that one should be mindful to support the midfield when the other was attacking. In the adrenalin of a rousing night at Old Trafford, they had been too gung-ho, which had allowed Zidane and Davids to take charge.

It was an impassioned Ferguson who spoke to his players, according to Steve McClaren. 'He was very emotional, and he was kind of upset with the result because 1-1 at home felt like a big advantage for Juventus. But Alex was convinced by his methods. He did not want to dilute the game plan. People were screaming at him to change, to put an extra man in midfield. He said, "No, I'm going to fight this, and you've got to fight it with me." He said, "This is what I believe in, these are my principles." He talked a lot about the attacking traditions and Sir Matt and the legacy. Further down the line, when there were some disappointing years in Europe, he had a rethink and reinvented the team with new tactics and won it again. But at this time he had his methods.'

Ferguson needed the players to be smart and adjust to the demands and some of the hard realities as they faced the best sides in Europe, but there was going to be no turning back from the spirit of adventure – especially as they were now going to have to score in Turin to make it to the final.

64

Monopolies 1 Murdoch 0

Two days later, at 3 p.m. on 9 April, Stephen Byers, the trade secretary, announced that Rupert Murdoch's bid to buy Manchester United had been blocked. For all the speculation that the Blair administration might find it difficult to stand in the way of such a powerful media tycoon, Byers had little choice, given the findings of the Monopolies and Mergers Commission that the bid was not in the public interest. And so concluded what Michael Crick, the journalist and anti-takeover campaigner, called the worst PR campaign in corporate history. BSkyB and United's board had failed to win over any key party. It was a comprehensive victory for those fans who felt they were fighting for the heart and soul of United, and English football, though it would hardly be the last battle in that war.

The lessons from Murdoch's unsuccessful attempt were clear enough. Byers said the deal would have reinforced 'the trend towards growing inequalities between the larger richer clubs and the smaller, poorer ones'. Did anyone take notice?

An editorial in the *Independent* celebrated the decision to block Murdoch but warned, 'If soccer is to thrive as a business, it must thrive as a sport, which requires it to nourish its roots and to pay attention to the non-commercial loyalties of the fans.' Did anyone take heed?

Murdoch's bid was a precursor to so much that would unfold; the growth of the Super Clubs, football's wealth inequalities and, in particular, very rich men trying to buy big clubs for their own interests, which could encompass anything from vanity to exerting soft political power, to extracting cash and dividends.

If Murdoch was a warning, no one really listened – not even to each other. In 1999, Crick urged United fans to buy up shares to prevent another potential takeover. He thought that if the 28,000 individual shareholders, representing 23 per cent, could double their shareholding then it would put off outside investors and effectively give the fans a veto. But supporters either did not see shareholding as attractive or felt they were already sinking enough money into United. The club would remain available to be bought by whoever wanted it, and for whatever means.

65

A word, Ryan

The day after Manchester United had drawn 0–0 against Arsenal in the FA Cup semi-final at Villa Park, taking the tie to a replay on the same ground and adding another huge fixture to a daunting run-in, Alex Ferguson told Ryan Giggs to come by his office at the Cliff. It is tempting, given caricatures of the United manager, to assume that the summons was for a bollocking. But that would be to underestimate the subtleties of his leadership.

Ferguson wanted to offer advice and encouragement to a player who, at 25, felt at the crossroads of a career in which the years of sprinting at full-backs had been compromised by vulnerable hamstrings. Giggs had been developing a broader game, less reliant on dashes along the touchline, but his manager had a nagging worry that the attempt at versatility had gone too far. In that first drawn game against Arsenal, Giggs had spurned a few opportunities to run at the defence, looking for a pass or chipping the ball forward rather than offering direct penetration through that thrilling combination of speed, balance and intricate control that had made him a wunderkind.

Ferguson felt that Giggs was playing within himself but, as the winger settled into the chair on the other side of the desk, the manager was not about to dwell on failings. He wanted to fill one of his match-winners with the daring to be his boldest, and his best. He wanted to remind Giggs what underpinned his greatness, and tell him that aspiring to be a better all-round

Peter Schmeichel dives to save Dennis Bergkamp's penalty, and to keep the Treble dream alive, in the epic FA Cup semi-final replay at Villa Park.

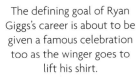

The defining goal of Ryan Giggs's career is about to be given a famous celebration too as the winger goes to lift his shirt.

© Matthew Peters./Manchester United via Getty Images

One of the most dramatic domestic football matches ever staged also featured a number of jubilant pitch invasions.

Just when it seemed that another European campaign was about to end in failure, the captain dragged his team back into the contest with this header against Juventus.

© Ross Kinnaird/Allsport via Getty Images

Keane obeyed all his competitive instincts when he tackled Zinedine Zidane, but the yellow card came with drastic consequences.

© Etsuo Hara/Getty Images

Schmeichel celebrates the Champions League semi-final victory that Ferguson would describe as one of the finest performances under his management.

© Paul Popper/Popperfoto via Getty Images

Andy Cole lifts the ball deftly over Ian Walker to score a brilliant, decisive goal on the final day of the league season, and claim personal redemption.

One down, two to go as the United players celebrate lifting the Premier League title at Old Trafford.

Sheringham and Scholes loved playing together and never more so than in helping each other to goals to beat Newcastle United in the FA Cup final.

Mehmet Scholl turns away, convinced that he has just scored a vital second goal for Bayern Munich in the Champions League final.

In desperate times in the final, agonising moments at the Nou Camp, Schmeichel leaps to meet Beckham's corner.

Sheringham had endured a difficult relationship with th United supporters, but one goal off his shin transforme everything.

The ball rises into the net off Ole Gunnar Solskjær's boot
for the most celebrated goal in United history.

Solskjær's knee slide is the iconic image of the Treble.

The delirious United fans inside the Nou Camp celebrate the most famous comeback of all.

No image captured the stunning turnaround quite like Samuel Kuffour's distress as the Bayern Munich defender beat the ground in anguish.

The moment the team of 1999 passed into legend as Ferguson and Schmeichel lift the European Cup.

The celebratory cigar never left Yorke's mouth during several days of partying.

The United bus turned into Deansgate in Manchester and into a great sea of fans.

Instead of leading United to glory, Eric Cantona was starring in a film with a monkey and receiving worse reviews than the ape.

Among the many honours showered on Ferguson after the Treble was a knighthood at Buckingham Palace.

Some of the legends of 1999 had aged better than others when they gathered for a reunion match twenty years on.

player should not come at the expense of the unique skills that had blown Ferguson away the first time he saw him floating over the ground, drawing gasps from even Bobby Charlton.

Ferguson told Giggs that he was the attacking player that Premier League defenders least wanted to face; that they carried a fear of him into every game. He had to grab every opportunity to give them reason to be worried, which would not come from playing safe. As Ferguson later told Hugh McIlvanney, the great Scottish journalist, about this meeting, 'If he does not make frequent attempts to do something apparently undoable, he is not being true to himself.'

Giggs had heard the advice before but recognised that a reminder could be necessary. It had been a while since he felt fully comfortable running flat out. It was partly a sense of self-preservation, but he did not argue when Ferguson told him that he needed to utilise his greatest assets to avoid becoming a useful midfielder rather than a match-winning winger. Ferguson planted the idea that Giggs had unique abilities and 'an absolute right to attempt feats of extravagant brilliance'.

Two days later United returned to Villa Park for another confrontation with Arsenal. After 61 minutes on the bench, Giggs ran on to take his place in one of the most epic domestic football matches ever staged.

66

Character is fate #6

Manchester United 2 Arsenal 1 (after extra time), 14 April 1999

A strange feeling came over Gary Neville in the game that stands, unarguably, as one of the greatest matches in English football history. 'It was the only time in a football match where I ever smiled when I was playing,' he says. 'I was thinking, "This is unbelievable, this." Out there on the pitch, we just knew this was something special.'

The players knew it. We all knew it. Everyone felt it. This was an epic, an Ali versus Frazier of a game. The Thrilla at the Villa. This felt not just for a place in the FA Cup final but the heavyweight championship of the world, with two great teams battering each other for 12 rounds. No single game could define the season, but this was as close as you could get to a decider – a night when it felt like the entire campaign was teetering like that bus at the end of *The Italian Job* from success to disaster and back again.

Put it among the greatest games of football I have witnessed, decided by one of the most sensational of winners.

'Don't watch it alone,' Alex Ferguson said in the build-up, as if he knew that it could not be anything other than historic, and not just because this was the last FA Cup semi-final replay. The

United manager was on edge given his team's workload: perhaps the most intense period of games in the club's history. A European campaign in the balance against Juventus; a Premier League to defend against a buoyant Arsenal; and now this, a second FA Cup clash in four days with Arsène Wenger's men, who had not conceded in more than 11 hours of football. United had not beaten them in six games.

United were sure they had enjoyed the better of the first meeting, but a linesman had flagged for a highly dubious offside to deny Roy Keane a goal. That decision had added further heat to the rivalry and another game to United's packed season. It was then that Ferguson dared to make perhaps the boldest selection of his entire career. Sometimes the directors would come into the dressing room pre-match to wish everyone good luck, see the team-sheet on the wall and struggle to express their alarm. 'It's written on their face,' Ferguson recalled. 'What on earth is he doing now?' This was one of those occasions.

Yorke and Cole had started the first game; now neither was in the team, and Cole not even on the bench. There was no place for Ryan Giggs. Denis Irwin was omitted. Ferguson felt he had to trust his instincts by resting key players, including his first-choice attack, in what was already United's 53rd game of the season including the Charity Shield. It was a colossal gamble against an Arsenal side at full strength. If United's strongest team could not beat Arsenal, how could a lesser XI just four days later?

If this went wrong, United would not only have surrendered any chance of a Treble but Ferguson would be guilty of a gamble too far. The man had more nerve than a poker player in Vegas.

Despite all the changes, United looked the superior team in the first half. Solskjær and Sheringham showed good movement, and it was the latter who flicked the ball back to Beckham after 17 minutes. He could have been placing a golf ball on a tee.

Beckham had a chance to shoot and eagerly took up the invitation with a whipped shot which curled away from David Seaman's outstretched dive. 'We'd always joked about giving him the eyes when we were in training with England,' Beckham told me of shaping up to shoot to one side, before bending it to the other.

United had the lead but Arsenal responded, especially after the arrival of Marc Overmars to replace Fredrik Ljungberg just after an hour. It felt like a turning point in this epic tussle. United were pushed back and, in the 69th minute, Dennis Bergkamp was given room for a long-range shot which deflected off Jaap Stam's knee past Schmeichel. 1-1.

By now, reaching the FA Cup final felt almost incidental in this gripping arm-wrestle. 'Sometimes you invest so much of yourself in a game that it acquires a significance way beyond the prize at stake,' Keane reflected. His commitment was as intense as ever; proof of his own remark once that he had to be at his angriest to be at his best against Arsenal. When Overmars escaped again down the flank, Keane came flying in but mistimed his tackle. Already booked, he did not bother waiting for David Elleray to run over and show a second yellow card.

Now United were down to ten men, without their leader and trying to resist a brilliant, dominant opponent – unbeaten in four months – in a breathless contest. As one commentator put it on TV, 'This match has had everything. If a pantomime horse were to gallop across the pitch, you wouldn't be surprised.'

With more than 91 minutes gone we were all gasping for a breather when Ray Parlour ran at Phil Neville, who was playing left-back in place of Irwin. As Parlour cut to go outside, Neville lunged and tripped him. Penalty to Arsenal. It seemed like this tie would be wrapped up quickly, and in normal time, after all.

'I think I've spoken about that tackle more than the birth of my children,' Phil Neville says. I ask him to recall exactly how he felt lying down on the pitch, head in hands, and then standing up looking like a man watching his house burn down. 'Honestly, I thought my United career was over,' he says. 'It was that big a moment. It was like, "My life is over. Kill me now!"'

It might sound ludicrously melodramatic but, in that moment, Neville knew he would be forever tarred not just with ending an FA Cup run but potentially wrecking United's season. If Ferguson's men failed against Arsenal yet again, what would it say of the balance of power? How could it not drastically affect the confidence of both teams heading into the final run of league matches?

As Neville puts it, 'Those games against Arsenal were life and death. That's how the manager made you feel – life or death, us or them. When you think about the words we used to use – win at all costs, kill the opposition, fight until you drop – it was beyond football. The pressure, expectation, intensity, you couldn't avoid it. And now I am thinking Arsenal will go on to win the FA Cup, probably the league too. I'm devastated.'

The clock read 91 minutes 55 seconds when Bergkamp, the reigning Footballer of the Year, stepped up with the job of scoring from 12 yards. You would back Bergkamp as much as any footballer on earth, given that he was a man who did not just pursue excellence but perfection. But, of course, a penalty brings its own theatre, its own pressure.

The modern trend is for goalkeepers to talk about how they have studied penalty takers, and shifted the odds in their favour, with statistical analysis. Schmeichel had nothing other than his instincts. His method was to decide which way to go, throw himself to that side and hope. At least then, in his own mind, he had been decisive. In that moment, Bergkamp was deciding too. After placing the ball and walking back, he picked his spot, to his right. But in his memoir *Stillness and Speed*, he explained, 'But here, Schmeichel's got – like a cat, you know? – a better reaction than I expect.'

Bergkamp knew in an instant, even before Schmeichel's giant hands pushed the ball away, that he had failed. 'Yeah, it was a bad moment,' he said, still pained by the memory when I interviewed him years later as a coach at Ajax. Tony Adams, the Arsenal captain, would call it 'a trauma' that would put Bergkamp off ever taking a penalty again. On the pitch, the United players ran to Schmeichel to congratulate him. Clenching his fists in a mighty roar of relief, he urged them forward.

'I owe Peter a debt for the rest of my life,' Neville says. 'And he knows it. Whenever I see him, on TV or we meet up, all I can think about is that penalty, because I felt as if he'd saved my life. It's like when people pull you out of a fire. It still gives me goosebumps. Nothing has ever come close to that game. The best, most dramatic I've ever been involved with. One minute I'm thinking my United career is over, my life is ruined and then it becomes the best. If you can play in that game, you can play anywhere.'

When the Arsenal players had seen the team-sheet before kick-off, they had been surprised at the number of United changes. Someone said to Lee Dixon that he could count himself lucky that Giggs had been rested. 'Lucky?' he replied. 'Blomqvist will tire me out and Giggs will come on fresh after an hour.' He was only a minute out.

Giggs came on in the 61st, sent on by Ferguson to run at Dixon, but he had made a poor start. His first four or five touches were ragged. He felt edgy. 'I'm having a nightmare here, I can't pass the ball so I'll have to be more direct,' he concluded.

When the game went into extra time, what he did have was fresh legs. And when a tired pass from Patrick Vieira arrived at his feet 10 yards inside the Arsenal half after 109 minutes, he set off at a gallop towards the goal, propelled by instinct and that demand from his manager that he be true to his gifts. A little nudge, a clip of the ankle perhaps, or a tug on his shirt would have stopped Giggs on his run towards goal, and into legend. But tired Arsenal legs could not get close enough.

Vieira could not recover the lost ground. As Giggs hurtled towards the penalty area, Dixon missed once and came back for a second attempt, but Giggs slipped between him and Martin Keown as if he was a child skipping through the daisies. Dashing inside the box, four internationals were left in wake of this balletic, shimmying winger who was summoning all the wonder of George Best. Next came a thundering Tony Adams, with a desperate lunge.

About the only conscious thought that Giggs remembers from the entire run was arriving into the penalty box and telling himself, 'Just hit it.' As Adams slid towards him, the ball was already rising irresistibly past a sinking David Seaman. The roof of the net bulged like a windsock in a gale. And then Giggs was off running with a shirt over his head, whirling it around in a frenzy and parading the hairy chest that would be the cause of ceaseless stick once the game was over. He had taken 12 touches to create the goal that would be the first on his highlights reel for the rest of his life.

Scholes had the best view. As he put it, 'I was actually trying to keep up. He's got the ball and gone past about ten people and I'm sprinting trying to keep up with him. I always said he should have squared. I was free in the box.' Scholes laughs at what happens next: 'Giggsy runs away peeling his shirt off and, for some reason, I start doing the same thing. Luckily I stopped myself or everyone would have seen a little fat belly.'

As a great roar went up inside Villa Park, Martin Edwards wondered what on earth had happened. The United chairman was so nervous at 1-1, watching 10 men toil, that he had gone for a walk. He was somewhere in the stand when he heard the United fans erupt.

Up in the press box, one of my colleagues had bent down to retrieve a pen just as Giggs collected the ball, and looked up to see the winger running around Villa Park being mobbed by pitch invaders. 'Did I miss something?' he asked, dumbstruck. Someone piped up the droll reply, 'Just the greatest goal in FA Cup history.'

Just over ten minutes later, the final whistle blew and a match that had everything had a pitch invasion, too. Delirious United fans ran on to mob the players, and to breathe alcohol fumes all over them. Beckham was carried shoulder-high from the field as some tried to relieve him of his boots and kit. 'I'd never had so many kisses,' Gary Neville recalled, 'sadly all of them from pissed lads.'

Ferguson was beaming almost beatifically as he made his way through the supporters and back into a dressing room where champagne was spraying everywhere, including over Bobby Charlton. Eventually Giggs made it back inside but only after hobbling off the pitch. He had damaged his ankle in the closing moments, a blow that would rule him out for a month.

Up in the press box, we tried to make sense of all that we had seen. 'One always suspected that it would take a genius, penalties or the toss of a coin to separate Arsenal and Manchester United and, fortunately, it fell to the genius,' I wrote. I would not change a word now.

We spoke to Ferguson afterwards and tried to put the goal in context. It was a challenge. The way Giggs had floated across the turf and through Arsenal's defence felt like an act not just of athleticism but levitation. It was the embodiment of all that Ferguson had told Giggs in that conversation at the Cliff. 'He has been trying to embrace all parts of the game,' Ferguson said, 'but you can never take away the genius.'

If that chat had emboldened Giggs, Ferguson was careful not to take too much credit. 'It would be madness to say I even dreamt he could give us that ecstatic climax.' He had the grace to say that what Giggs had done was uncoachable, 'The ultimate expression of the incredible natural gifts he has always had since the day he came to us as a 13-year-old.'

To listen to Ferguson talk afterwards was to listen to a man become almost lyrical with joy. He knew this was so much more than a victory, or progress to an FA Cup final. It was symbolic of all that he wanted from his teams in risk and resilience and attacking intent – and defiance given the loss of their captain and talisman.

These were players whose legs should have been sapped to the point of exhaustion. A few days later they would have to defend their place at the top of the league. Then they would be flying to Turin to face the mighty Juventus in further pursuit of a Treble, which was now on everyone's minds. We asked Ferguson about it afterwards, but he was still caught in the drama of an unforgettable night.

'People keep questioning whether we can do it but it is all nonsense,' he said. 'It may blow up in our faces, we are aware of that. We have game after game after game. But the most important thing is that nights like this are the ones you never forget. People would pay fortunes to watch that and whatever we achieve, you cannot erase the memories. They are embedded in your mind forever. We have shown fantastic courage and the players will be flying after that. It will be hard to get them down again.'

As if to prove it, Yorke was dancing around the dressing room. 'Ten games to go!' he told his teammates. Ten steps to greatness. The players all talk about this night at Villa Park as the victory which convinced them, to their core, that they might pull off something special.

'Sometimes even Manchester United need the kind of confirmation that comes from a victory like this,' Keane reflected of a win which had made them believe that anything was now possible. Arsenal had been an immovable object for them. Now United had a sense of irresistible force.

Ferguson had a knack of summoning the right words on the biggest occasions and he did not let us down. 'We never gave up,' he concluded, 'but the time to give up is when you are dead. The time to reflect is when you are in a coffin, not on the football field.'

67

If

The chance for an unprecedented double Double for Arsenal had just gone up in smoke, and in circumstances that were shattering, when Tony Adams entered a jubilant Manchester United dressing room at Villa Park. 'When I walked in, I think they thought I was after a fight,' Adams says.

Perhaps the Adams of a few years earlier might have wanted one – certainly a drink, or ten. Something, anything to take off the edge of crushing disappointment as the losing captain in one of the most tumultuous battles in English football. But this was a sober Adams. This was a man capable of shaking his opponents by the hand and saying, 'Lads, congratulations. Outstanding. I just want to wish you all the best in the final.'

It was a gesture which the United players – at the time, and reflecting on it now – found deeply admirable. 'They were a bit open-mouthed,' Adams says. 'They were like, "Wow!"' It was a sign of great sportsmanship but also of the journey that Adams had been on to sobriety through Alcoholics Anonymous since 1996.

'What's that quote?' he says. 'You know, winning and losing and treating them with the same respect, or words to that effect? With dignity and you'll be a man my son ...' He paraphrases Rudyard Kipling and explains how building his own self-esteem meant that he could be generous in defeat. 'I thought it was the right thing to do,' Adams says of congratulating the United players. 'Though, in hindsight, thinking about what they went on to, maybe I wouldn't have been so courteous.' He says it with a smile born of hard-won perspective.

Adams knew that he had been involved in a spectacular duel in that semi-final replay, but it was only after he changed and went to see his sister in a lounge at Villa Park that he realised quite how special. An Arsenal fan, she was deflated by the result but her first reaction took him aback. 'She said something about it being a perfect storm and a beautiful entertainment. So much talent that it could have gone either way. So I am not saying it didn't hurt to lose, but it made me think when she kept saying it was a phenomenal match.'

It was a game befitting a special rivalry. 'It's like Connors and McEnroe,' Adams says. 'You want to pitch yourself against the best. We thought we were the best and they thought they were.'

Despite the rivalry, and enmity between the managers, he had huge admiration for the United players, and not just those like Scholes, Beckham and the Nevilles he knew through England duty. He once took a coaching course with Roy Keane, and they played on the same five-a-side team. 'Instant chemistry,' Adams recalls. 'I got why he was one of the best players in the world at that time.

'Technically Scholesy was a more gifted player but you are putting Roy Keane in your team first. He understood football, how it works. If your right winger is out of the game, all of a sudden he's slotted in and you don't even have to tell him. It's just an awareness. Football intelligence is the only way to describe it.'

How about a composite XI of the best of Arsenal and United? 'That's a really good question. There was not a lot that I'd swap. Do you swap Giggsy for Marc Overmars? That's a tough call.' He ponders, going through all the difficult dilemmas. 'I guess United had more options up front,' he concludes. 'They ultimately had

Sheringham, Solskjær, Yorke and Cole. At the end of the day, maybe they had a little bit more firepower than us.'

Adams certainly has no hesitation in lauding Ferguson, who once described him as 'a United player in the wrong shirt', and twice tried to lure him away from Highbury. The Arsenal stalwart is certain that he could have enjoyed the experience of playing under the Scot.

A few years after the Villa Park epic, Adams met Ferguson at an awards evening. 'Alex was getting a lifetime achievement award. And I said, "You know in '99, we should have done the Double. You know that, don't you, Alex?" I think he'd had a couple of bottles of red wine and he said, "Tony. But you know what? In '98, we should have done the fucking Treble." OK, touché! What a nice way of seeing the rivalry. Perhaps it all could have been the other way round. But it was what it was.'

Back to Kipling – and *If* – Adams's mind drifts back to that remarkable night at Villa Park. He thinks about his lunge to block Giggs just as the winger was pulling back his left foot to shoot. 'I'm not that far away from Ryan and then the course of history goes out the fucking window,' he says. 'And if Dennis gets the penalty, blah blah blah. It's ifs and buts, swings and roundabouts. What was it my mother used to say? Pots and pans and ifs and ands ...'

68

The gallops

It is the morning after the tumultuous night before. United fans are still sleeping off their hangovers when Alex Ferguson heeds a 5 a.m. alarm call, heads to Manchester airport and climbs on a plane bound for Stansted. A fast car ferries him to Newmarket and, before the world has woken groggily, he is watching another set of thoroughbreds. To be standing on Ed Dunlop's gallops was Ferguson's escape from the strains of a night like the one at Villa Park, and the looming second leg against Juventus. 'You're out there on the gallops and nobody can get you. You're watching the horses train and taking in the fresh air. And I'd come back into training on the Friday and be fucking buzzing!'

That crisp, revitalising morning, he watched Candleriggs, a sprinter he had bought in October and named after a street in Glasgow. Later, there will be visits to the stables of Henry Cecil and Sir Michael Stoute before lunch at the Newmarket races where Ferguson was in an understandably convivial mood.

Ferguson's involvement with the racing industry had grown in the two years since he and Cath decided to celebrate their wedding anniversary at the Cheltenham Festival on Gold Cup Day. They loved it. Well, most of it. The Fergusons were in a box next to Lord and Lady Lloyd Webber, who erupted in celebration when their horse, Uncle Ernie, won the Grand Annual Chase as a 20-1 outsider. A deflated Ferguson looked on, cursing his backing of a different horse. 'That's the last fucking musical I ever go to,' he growled.

Owning horses became an addictive thrill, and Ferguson quickly gathered a financial interest in half a dozen, including Queensland Star, named after a vessel that his father helped build on Clydeside. He had horses with Stoute, Charlie Brooks at Lambourn and two highly promising two-year-olds under the care of Aidan O'Brien. Ferguson would talk lyrically about his visits to O'Brien's Ballydoyle stables in Co. Tipperary. 'You are looking for some of the same qualities in a good horse and a good footballer,' he said. 'They are both athletes but it is the heart that counts, most of all.'

Those trips to Ballydoyle brought him into the orbit of the Coolmore mafia; John Magnier, Ireland's most heavyweight racing figure, who owned the training facility and Coolmore Stud, and his partner J.P. McManus, a fanatical United fan. Ferguson loved to mix in the company of powerful men, vast wealth and private jets. He could not have known then just how much he would come to regret the entwining of these worlds.

Just five weeks earlier, on 8 March 1999, a foal was born that would change United's history and reveal Ferguson's misconception of his own power. That exceptional horse would come to be known as Rock of Gibraltar. A bitter row with Magnier over the horse's ownership, which Ferguson was never likely to win, caused the Coolmore crew to sell their significant stake in United to Malcolm Glazer. 'A misunderstanding,' Ferguson subsequently called the episode in *My Autobiography*. One that he, and any United supporter, still has cause to regret all these years later whenever they curse how the club is being run.

69

A happy ending?

On the morning of the biggest game of his life, Alex Ferguson sat in a hotel room near Turin airport with a notepad and pen. He made handwritten notes, adding to more than 200,000 words he had already scribbled about his life story. He reflected on a boyhood in Glasgow's tenements and making his way in the game in Scotland; forging his way as a sharp-elbowed striker into the national team for four caps; all that he had done as an iconoclastic manager smashing the Old Firm with Aberdeen; overturning the established order of things in England by knocking Liverpool, as he would come to say, off their fucking perch.

He had written about his credo, his approach to life and, this being Ferguson, there will be some score-settling with anyone who dared to cross him. He will write about loyalty being the anchor of his life – indeed, he will choose it as the very last line of his book – while leaving others to wonder why they had not deserved it from him in return.

A publisher had paid at least £1 million for Ferguson's autobiography, due to come out in the autumn, and, while the United manager had called on the exceptional services of Hugh McIlvanney to be his ghostwriter, he wanted to immerse himself in the project. Downtime on European trips provided opportunities to delve into his sharp memory and to make handwritten notes to be weaved into the book which will be called *Managing My Life*.

Sitting in that hotel in Italy, Ferguson reflected on all that had carried him to this point, standing once more on the brink in Europe. He knew that if United did not win in Turin later that evening to reach a first Champions League final the book was going to be incomplete. His career was going to be incomplete. For all that he had built the modern United, he would have fallen short again. Overcome Juventus or the book will not have the final chapter he craves.

70

Character is fate #7

Juventus 2 Manchester United 3, 21 April 1999

The Stadio Delle Alpi was not a venue that anyone would choose for a defining performance. Even the Juventus fans hated it. Less than a decade old, by 1999 an ugly ground stuck in the north of Turin was already doomed. This concrete bowl, with its running track around the pitch, was often half-empty. But the night of 21 April was different. In the stadium of Gazza's tears and Chris Waddle's penalty – had it landed yet, we wondered, nine years on from that epic World Cup semi-final against West Germany – we took our seats along with more than 60,000 for the first sell-out crowd of the season at Juventus, sensing that you could stage this game anywhere in the world and it would crackle with anticipation.

After the 1-1 draw in the first leg, United had arrived with bullish confidence from the triumph over Arsenal. At Villa Park, an Italian journalist had asked Ferguson whether his team would suffer with the fatigue of all these big games. The United manager had responded aggressively. 'By the time we get to Turin, we will be chomping at the bit. We will be eating people by then,' he said. 'Never underestimate British endurance. Make sure you write that in your newspaper. You will need to run a million miles to beat us in Italy.'

On the eve of the match, he had once again referenced the character of his players as much as their ability. He talked of those who want to settle for an easy life and others, like his team, who were always striving for more. 'That's the kind of human being I want to have here at United. There are some people who don't always want to win. I can't understand them.' It was stirring stuff, fighting talk, but it felt like empty bravado when United were 2-0 down inside 11 minutes. Up in the press box in that shabby stadium, I started writing the obituary to another European campaign.

We thought it was over. Ferguson wondered, too. 'Another case of suicide,' he sensed as Filippo Inzaghi scored twice in the light mist that hung in the air after a day of rain. Gary Neville was at fault for the first. When Zidane used a short-corner routine to whip in a cross from the left, the full-back was not sure it would reach the far post. It did, and Inzaghi pounced. The second was desperately unlucky as Inzaghi's cross-shot struck Jaap Stam's boot and looped over Peter Schmeichel. That made it 2-0 on the night and 3-1 on aggregate. Against a side of this quality, in their own stadium, who could possibly see a way back from this?

'If he pulls this one out,' Ron Atkinson told viewers watching at home on ITV, 'it'll be the greatest achievement since he's been at United.' Lesser teams would have folded, their confidence shattered. They would have looked up at the task and felt it too monumental. Overcome Zidane, Davids, Deschamps and the rest from this position? As much as a test of ability, it was first about conviction. 'Anybody looking to throw the towel in now had the perfect opportunity,' Roy Keane noted in his autobiography. 'Anybody seeking to prove that they were worthy of playing for Manchester United also had the chance to fucking prove it.'

What followed was one of the most rousing, gripping halves of football ever played by an Alex Ferguson team. To watch United clamber back off the canvas in Turin might even have topped the triumph over Arsenal as a breathtaking display of resolve. It was all the more impressive for the way that United did not panic. They did what they always strived to do when under the cosh; quicken the tempo, squeeze the opposition, move the ball quickly. Dwight Yorke, in particular, was causing Juventus problems with his movement, collecting balls from midfield and linking with a lively Andy Cole. Yorke should have had a penalty when Ciro Ferrara grabbed him around the neck.

With a two-goal lead to protect, Juventus started dropping off and relying on Inzaghi's running on the counterattack, which encouraged the United full-backs to be more adventurous and gave another attacking outlet. 'The next goal is the most massive of the season,' Ron Atkinson said, as David Beckham ran over to take a corner in the 24th minute. He was not wrong.

Roy Keane was first to meet Beckham's inswinger with a perfectly timed run, rising to glance his header sweetly after Zidane had failed to intercept and Angelo Peruzzi, the Juventus goalkeeper, was caught in no-man's land. It was an unusual goal from a player not renowned for set-piece headers but beautifully finished and, above all, a signal that this contest was back on. That message was evident in Keane's no-nonsense celebration, briefly acknowledging Beckham as he continued his run straight back to the United half for the restart. There was a job to be done. Get on with it. United knew they were back in the hunt. Beckham ran back to take his place and turned to Neville, brandished a clenched fist and barked, 'Come on, we can do this.' Fighting spirit coursed through the team.

Up in the press box, we paused those obituaries. We were back, as so often with this United side, on another wild rollercoaster. It was not over. With this team, it never was.

*

Juventus were looking ragged, United on top when, in the 32nd minute, Jesper Blomqvist, playing for the injured Giggs, knocked a nondescript pass inside in the middle of the pitch. Seemingly it was intended for Nicky Butt but it ran on to Keane. The captain had time to control it but, perhaps sensing Zidane close by, suffered a brief lack of concentration allowing the ball to run away from him. As Zidane took possession and sought to attack, Keane obeyed his instinct to go for the recovery tackle. He knew from the instant that he felled the French maestro that he was in trouble.

Keane had already fouled Davids, and pleaded for forgiveness knowing the consequence of a yellow card. This time, there was no mercy from Urs Meier, the Swiss referee. Booked for tangling with Iván Zamorano in the first leg of the quarter-final against Inter Milan, Keane now had a second caution which meant he would miss the final if United made it. That first booking was more regrettable given it was a silly reaction to provocation, but Keane had little time to think and process. He waved an arm angrily at Blomqvist and remonstrated – 'Pass the fucking ball,' he snapped – and then turned back to the action.

Up in the press box, we knew the circumstances could hardly be more poignant. This was the stadium where Paul Gascoigne famously had cried in that World Cup semi-final in 1990, knowing he would miss the final if England beat West Germany. We could hardly miss the connection, but there were no tears from Keane. He really was not the type.

'I was so much into this battle that the consequences of the card barely registered,' he later reflected. Such strength of mind seemed hard to believe until we watched Keane redouble his efforts. After all, his booking would be an irrelevance, a footnote, if United did not reach the final, though there was every reason to believe they might two minutes later.

Yorke had not scored in his last seven appearances, the first mini-drought of his United career, when, in the 34th minute, Neville stole the ball off Di Livio and knocked it forward for Beckham who headed it down to Cole. The cross from the right was perfect in evading the Juventus defence but it still required a special finish. Yorke twisted himself into a spectacular diving header and scored a superb goal to make it 2-2.

In Yorke's rejuvenated performance, striking the post with another chance before half-time, and the eager running of Cole was the reward for Ferguson's boldness in leaving out his two main strikers against Arsenal the previous week and the subsequent league victory over Sheffield Wednesday. United had the fresher legs and now the away goals that would take them through if Juventus did not score again. The drama had been unrelenting in a breathless half of football that had yielded four goals, and promised many more. Zidane had been limited to flashes of his brilliance, Davids to very little at all. Keane and Yorke had not only scored the goals but, against opponents of the highest calibre, been the outstanding performers on the pitch.

Ferguson kept telling his team at half-time that Juventus were 'gone'. He drilled it into them until they believed him. He told them to take responsibility for every pass, for every tackle. 'Don't fucking leave it to someone else,' he said. The mood was focused and upbeat, and rightly so. United had dominated the game after recovering from those two early goals. They deserved to be level.

In the Juventus dressing room, they set about a recovery mission. Carlo Ancelotti brought on an extra striker in Nicola Amoruso to make a switch from 4-4-1-1 to 4-3-1-2, sensing that the game was running away from his team without a change of strategy. He brought on Montero to stabilise a shaky defence, even though the Uruguayan had been struggling with injury. But United would not buckle. Stam was among the United players who rose magnificently to the occasion, recovering from those early blows with an immense display in the second half. Especially with Juventus bringing on a second striker, Ferguson had to ask Stam and Ronny Johnsen to go one-on-one against the forwards. They defended tenaciously.

In a game so finely balanced, the controlled nerve that ran through United's performance was deeply impressive. This was not a Juventus team at their very best but they still possessed immense class, especially in Zidane. Nicky Butt laughs at the memory of trying to steal the ball back. 'It was like it was stuck to his feet,' he says. 'Then you'd try to go in hard and just bounce off him.'

After 68 minutes, Ferguson sent on Paul Scholes for Blomqvist to help keep control of a more narrow midfield. It made sense but it was a fateful change. Eight minutes later, Scholes won the ball off Davids but, as it ran away from him, launched himself into a two-footed tackle. Scholes still shakes his head ruefully and pleads innocence about the challenge. 'Deschamps does this big yelp,' he says. 'It was his scream that made the referee book me.' He had taken the ball but also, undeniably, a Frenchman's ankle, too.

Also on a booking, Scholes knew immediately that he was in trouble and the yellow card duly came, also ruling him out of the final. If ever there was a man less likely to burst into Gazza-esque tears than Keane, it may have been Scholes. He gave one anguished look, received an empathetic pat on the head from Keane and then, like his captain, returned to the business of trying to win the game.

In a contest of thunderous competitiveness, every action might prove defining. Schmeichel saved with his legs from the endlessly elusive, if infuriatingly theatrical, Inzaghi. On a foray forward, Denis Irwin struck the post with a shot from just inside the area. Cole and Ciro Ferrara almost came to blows. Beckham and Davids were engaged in a running battle – the latter was booked for a scything tackle – which spilled over into some verbals. And then, in the 84th minute, Schmeichel belted a long punt into the chilly night sky. We looked on, still wondering which way this game might go, as Montero tried to clear it first time but miscued the ball to Yorke 40 yards out. The striker headed straight for goal.

Yorke had Montero and Ferrara to beat, and tried to take them both with a shimmy and drop of the shoulder. For his boldness, he deserved the generous ricochet off his chest that carried him through both defenders and on to the next challenge of beating Peruzzi in goal. Yorke pushed the ball to the left of the goalkeeper who dived too late and upended the United striker. Just as the United fans screamed 'penalty!' the ball ran clear for Cole, who was following in. Meier played a good advantage. The angle seemed tight but Cole, another player who had excelled on the night, had never looked more confident with a finish. He slipped it into the net. United, having never won a match in Italy, had come back from 2-0 down to lead Juventus 3-2 and, finally, to reach the Champions League final.

Ferguson thought it the greatest performance under his management, which was an extraordinary accolade. Given the magnitude of the occasion, the recovery, the quality of the opposition and the assurance with which an historic victory was delivered, who could argue? There were exceptional performances in every department; from Stam's resolve and forcefulness at the back, through Keane setting the tempo, Beckham's incessant running down the right, and the energy and movement of Yorke and Cole which never allowed Juventus to settle. But, above all, this was a collective triumph of will and fortitude. This was not some last-minute comeback born of desperation – there had been a few of those – but a calculated display, once they had recovered from the early setbacks, of all that made this team great.

United were in the Champions League final, and the United players ran over to the bank of fans to celebrate, Gary Neville brandishing the badge on his chest. The photo he has of himself and Beckham in that moment is one of his most treasured possessions.

Afterwards, we went to speak to a beaming Ferguson, who gushed with praise about his team. There was only one sour note. That Keane and Scholes would be missing the final was, the United manager said, 'a tragedy'. It was not a word to be used lightly in a sporting context but, in the circumstances, it did not feel inappropriate.

71

The Postman

There is a caricature about Roy Keane's TV persona these days – Roy of the Ragers – which obscures the superhuman impact that intensity could yield on a football pitch. His fury is seen now almost as a comedy act. There was an era at Manchester United when it was one of the most powerful forces in the global game.

In the chemistry that makes champions, Eric Cantona will always be revered as the catalyst of the great United era from the early '90s. But if there was one player who ensured that the success did not fizzle out, it was Keane. He won seven titles in 12 full seasons at Old Trafford and you will not find a single teammate who regarded him as less than talismanic – vital, essential – throughout that period of dominance.

Others had more flair, or more eye-catching showreels, or more chants sung for them on the Stretford End. But in the dressing room, they knew that to strip away Keane was not just to lose the pivotal, steadying figure in the heart of midfield. It was to surrender the energy – the dynamite! – that could feel as instrumental to the team's character as the manager's leadership.

Keane could be tyrannical, intimidating – 'frightening to watch,' as Ferguson once said, 'and I'm from Glasgow' – with a brutal tongue, but he was also a team man at heart and one of the great influences of modern English football. It seemed inexplicable that when a side was chosen to mark 20 years of the Premier League in 2012, Keane was omitted from an XI that had

Steven Gerrard and Paul Scholes in midfield. Both extraordinary players, but Keane was something else. He was a force of nature who yielded to no opponent on earth.

Even if, like Scholes, he could hardly complain at the decision for his booking in Turin, Keane's stature and importance for United made his yellow card all the more cruel. He had been on the pitch for every minute of the 12 European games that had brought them to the final. He had more than played his part; in Turin he had been heroic. And now, on what could be a crowning moment for him and the club, he would be confined to a suit and a seat on the bench rather than leading out this team in his warrior uniform.

Keane let his feelings out only after the game was over. You can see a glimpse of it in footage from the spartan dressing room in the Stadio delle Alpi which, although largely focusing on the celebrations, captures moments from Keane that give away his sense of loss. As players clasped each other and shouted 'Barcelona!', and Dwight Yorke went round high-fiving everyone – 'Yeah, baby!' – and everyone slapped each other on the back, Keane raised a half-smile but declined a hug from Peter Schmeichel. If he wanted consolation, it would not be from the big goalkeeper.

Knowing that Schmeichel would now be captain for the final in the Nou Camp cannot have done wonders for Keane's mood. They did not get on. 'As far as I could tell, he and Schmeichel absolutely hated each other,' Yorke once reflected. They had brawled on a pre-season tour in the Far East in the summer of 1997, leaving Schmeichel with a black eye, fallen out again a year later when the goalkeeper had to be ordered by Alex Ferguson to give back the captain's armband after Keane returned from injury in August 1998, and the dressing room never felt big enough for two such dominant personalities. They worked together for the United cause but it was an uneasy truce.

Now Schmeichel and the rest of the United players could celebrate victory but Scholes sat on a bench with a distant stare as he tried to come to terms with knowing that he would be a spectator in Barcelona, and Keane struggled to make sense of the swirling emotions. He had another dig at Blomqvist – 'I think that pass was the only reason he mentioned me in his book,' the Swede smiles now – and as the squad travelled back to Manchester, Keane sat on his own, brooding in silence. He had given his all, and to what end?

Keane has played better games than that night in Turin. I think he was more instrumental in the 1996 FA Cup final, which is often remembered as the 'Cantona final' for the Frenchman's winning goal against Liverpool after returning from his long ban – but it was Keane who was the outstanding player at Wembley, and by a distance. But his performance in Turin went into legend for what it symbolised about the man. It was sport's equivalent of a military commander sensing that there was no way he could expect his troops to run into enemy fire unless he was first willing to sacrifice himself. Keane was not going to play in Barcelona, but he deserved a medal for gallantry.

He had been key in steadying United after the shock of those two early goals. He had taken the fight to Zidane, Davids and Deschamps. His passing, often underrated because of its deceptive simplicity, had been urgent and progressive. He had set the tempo which Juventus could not match. 'Na na na na naaa, Keanoooo,' the fans in Turin sang, to the tune of 'Hey Jude', in recognition of the captain after he had scored that transformative goal. And, of course, there had been the unmistakable contrast, post-booking, to Paul Gascoigne and those tears. Keane had contributed one of the ultimate captain's performances just when it was needed. If it is a defining quality of great sports people to shape key moments to their will, Keane had delivered emphatically on one of the most famous nights in Manchester United's long history.

At the time of Keane's tragic-heroic performance, Ferguson could not have been more effusive. The United manager could hardly fail to note how Keane not only applied himself but appeared to redouble his efforts after he was booked. Speaking to Hugh McIlvanney for the *Sunday Times* soon after the game, he mentioned the great warriors that he had been privileged to work with, 'Individuals who had no need of Alex Ferguson, players with such inner resources that they don't have to draw any strength from a manager.' Keane, like Willie Miller and Bryan Robson, was among the very best of them.

'As you develop a team, you try to get your drive and ambition and the playing principles you believe in to enter into their personalities. You hope they will soak up your values, as if through their pores. But, if you are lucky, you encounter one or two men who are natural mirrors of your commitment, who are such out-and-out winners that you consider it an honour to be compared with them. That's how I see Roy Keane.'

In the memoir he was writing, Ferguson would summarise it this way, 'I didn't think I could have a higher opinion of any footballer than I already had of the Irishman but he rose even further in my estimation at the Stadio Delle Alpi. It was the most emphatic display of selflessness I have ever seen on a football field.'

To recollect such boundless, and fully justified, praise makes it all the more sad that the two men should have such an acrimonious falling-out in November 2005. This bond of manager and captain, two men who saw life and football through the same prism of ferocious competitiveness, was broken amid bitter feuding.

The split had been coming for a while towards the turbulent end of Keane's time at United, but it exploded in the infamous meeting in Ferguson's office in front of the entire squad. Keane turned on Ferguson and particularly Carlos Queiroz, the assistant manager, with savage, personal criticism. He was shown the door and a bitter enmity was born, which was the reason Keane was a notable absentee at the 1999 reunion match at Old Trafford and why he did not figure on the list of world-class players Ferguson once cited, even though he had told us enough times that Keane was the outstanding midfielder in the world – and meant it.

The feud affected Keane, too, and spilled over into a strange argument about his heroics in Turin. In December 2013, the Irishman was interviewed by Gabriel Clarke for an ITV documentary, *Keane and Vieira*. Clarke reminded Keane of those gushing words from Ferguson. His response perhaps marked a moment when he started slipping into angry caricature.

'Stuff like that almost insults me. What am I supposed to do? Give up? *Not* cover every blade of grass? *Not* do my best for my teammates? *Not* do my best for my club? To be honest, I actually get offended when people throw quotes like that at me as if I'm supposed to be honoured by it. It's like praising the postman for delivering your letters. He's supposed to, isn't he? That's his job. My job was trying to win football matches for Man United.'

It was wonderful, compelling stuff – great television, just like Keane provides as a pundit most weekends as he works himself into a fury – but it felt, to me, to be trying too hard to prove a different point, namely distancing himself from Ferguson. It truly *was* a great and selfless performance in Turin. In trying to rubbish Ferguson's praise, Keane was almost diminishing his own great work. A more accurate description, I would suggest, came from Keane in his first autobiography in 2002. Then he offered a more emotional and seemingly heartfelt account of all that he went through that unforgettable evening.

As Keane noted, 'When Andy Cole scored our third, I knew there would be a final to miss. I didn't care at that point (although later I would). I was proud of our team that night. I was, for once, proud of myself, content that I had justified my existence and honoured my debts to the manager who'd placed so much trust in me. The Champions League final was where I believed Manchester United should be. I genuinely felt that was so much more important than whether or not I would be there. When that euphoric feeling evaporated . . . I was gutted.'

In that version, Keane sounds human, conflicted but, above all, proud of his team, his manager and himself. Away from the spotlight, and any personal feuding, perhaps that is how it still is.

---

* A heartbreak XI of players suspended from major finals would make up a stellar side, including Michael Ballack (2002 World Cup final), Pavel Nedved (2003 European Cup final), Xabi Alonso (2014 European Cup final) and Keane as a formidable midfield. The rules would be changed to avoid a lengthening list.

FIFA had already softened its regulations around bookings in semi-finals by the time that Uefa, under pressure after six players from Chelsea and Bayern Munich had missed the 2012 Champions League final, followed suit. From the start of the 2014-15 campaign, yellow cards were wiped out upon the completion of the quarter-finals so that a single yellow card in a semi-final could not lead to suspension for the showpiece game. Too late for many. Much too late for Keane.

72

Echoes of the past

You can never escape history at Manchester United. They could probably find a significant anniversary for every day of the year (the modern, rapacious marketing department may already have done so). In Turin, the echoes were unmistakable. A 4-3 aggregate victory over a mighty continental foe, heroically retrieving a lost cause to reach a European Cup final? It was like the team of 1999 were deliberately paying homage to the ghosts of 1968.

Facing Real Madrid 31 years earlier, Matt Busby's team had also been forced to fight back from falling 2-0 down away from home. In the cathedral of the Bernabéu, they too were trying to topple a side of much grander European pedigree. 'A great and glorious fighting comeback that will rank among the all-time epics of football,' Ronald Crowther wrote in the *Daily Mail* of how Busby's team rallied and Bill Foulkes, a Munich survivor, dragged them into the Wembley final with the equaliser in a 3-3 draw. 'Morale decided this game. United simply wanted it more,' Eamon Dunphy wrote in *A Strange Kind of Glory*. The words could be transposed straight on to a display of unwavering conviction in Turin more than three decades later.

As Bobby Charlton embraced Ferguson in the dressing room at the Stadio delle Alpi, the sense was unmistakeable that these players were not just writing their own remarkable story but adding to the legend created by their forebears.

After all the striving, United were back in the final – the club's first since 1968, and English football's first since 1985 – to face Bayern Munich in Barcelona on 26 May. The date was hugely significant, a special anniversary: were Busby alive, it would mark his 90th birthday. Only the most sworn ABU could be immune to the romance and poignancy.

73

Sir Alf

On 28 April 1999, the news broke that Sir Alf Ramsey had died, aged 79, from prostate cancer. Never an emotional man – preternaturally unmoved at the moment England won the World Cup in 1966 – Ramsey seemed very much of a different age. We marked his death not just by celebrating his pivotal role in creating the high point of English sport but all that had changed in the game and in social mores.

Football breeds nostalgia and, for all the boons of the '90s explosion, there was the start of a backlash too against the new celebrity and soaring wages, and a longing for the good old days when players lived next door and were paid a pittance. Watching the black-and-white footage from 1966, it seemed as if Ramsey might be a figure from another game altogether. We mourned not just for England's most successful manager but for lost values. But then I came across a quote that I had not seen before.

'Players don't remember what you say in team talks or practices – what they do remember is how you made them feel,' Ramsey had said. It was a remark that revealed something timeless about outstanding leadership. And it was exactly something Alex Ferguson might say.

I found that quote in a book, *Belonging*, written by Owen Eastwood, a highly successful leadership coach whose approach is based on establishing healthy cultures in organisations, including sports teams. He has done notable work with Gareth Southgate's England, helping to reinforce a new connection with supporters and sense of pride in the shirt.

His ideas are built around the theme of belonging; creating a cause bigger than the players. He talks of the narrative of a tribe – in England's case, one that has endured for 150 years and featured great men like Ramsey – and a historical thread so that a player might feel his mission was not only about winning (otherwise that dooms most to failure) but honouring traditions and ensuring the shirt is left in a better place.

Sitting down with Eastwood, it became clear that he regarded Ferguson as one of the supreme exponents of this method, even if they had never met. He had heard from Manchester United players how Ferguson would sell not just the chance of trophies, and a fat salary, but a cause that linked them to Busby and daring football and famous triumphs and all the history. Rather than Ferguson's motivation-based approach sounding old-school, Eastwood felt that the United manager had tapped into something that lies at the core of the greatest teams, in sport and beyond.

As Eastwood explained, 'I think Ferguson was actually ahead of his time in many ways. A lot of his former players say he was like a father figure. That might sound antiquated but it doesn't to me. They are young guys spending every day at the club, spending more time with coaches than their families. Some have left home at 16. I hear the same thing from athletes today. When you ask them what they want from a leader, they want someone who cares about them as a person and not just a footballer, and use that language about a father figure. I think it is natural to want that type of leadership that he was so strong about.

'I'm sure Alex Ferguson didn't have training in team dynamics but he had an incredible intelligence around groups, and person-alities. He was able to create a chemistry around a complicated group full of alphas, and all sorts of different people: to build multiple teams, all through this constant thread of the team being bigger than any one individual. One thing I say is that to create a champion team is a spiritual exercise. Secondly, it takes profound emotional communion between people. To me, you can't be a real high-performing team achieving your full potential unless you have both.'

Ferguson might recoil at the word 'spiritual' but there is no doubt that story-telling, belonging, and being a loyal member of the tribe were at the core of his ethos. He embraced the tribe's ancestors, especially Sir Matt Busby and Sir Bobby Charlton. Busby had given Ferguson precious advice when he came down from Aberdeen; Charlton had been a source of reassurance when the manager's position was imperilled in those early years. Far from being threatened by these great men of the past, Ferguson tapped into their wisdom and celebrated their stature as venerated elders.

As Eastwood put it, United is not just a football club but a living narrative. It thrives on myths and legends and one generation connecting to another. Like any tribe, it grows stronger when people find common ground and purpose. Or as Ferguson explained in that ITV documentary shown at the start of the 1998-99 season, 'In most cases, a cause is the best form of motivation – religion, your country, Manchester United, against the world. We use it, I use it, from time to time.' Frequently, in fact.

Did any manager ever create as much of a tribal feeling as Ferguson? Gary Neville would talk of being 'indoctrinated'; Nicky Butt of the manager creating the sense that United was an island which they must defend with their lives. He told them that the world was out to get them – opponents, referees, the football authorities – so all the more reason to bind together. This siege mentality could create an antipathy far beyond the ABUs, but it was also highly effective in winning the players' hearts and minds.

He would knit the fractures between them by giving them a

unifying cause beyond football. As Gary Neville puts it, 'It was almost like we would die out on that pitch as a group of people for the club, for the team, for him, for each other.' Ask any player what they remembered about Ferguson and it was always the lessons he passed on about life and teamwork more than specifics of football. It was about how he made them feel as they ran out on a Saturday afternoon.

As we marked Ramsey's death, we inevitably wrote about his tactics, the wingless wonders, but perhaps we underestimated all that he had transmitted in creating a cause for his players. After all, had he not predicted England would win the World Cup back in 1963 when no one else gave the host nation much chance?

How do you make players believe they can conquer the world? That was exactly Ferguson's mission – to show that his ambition was limitless so that his players believed that anything was possible. 'Psychology is someone else's word,' he said. 'I call it management.'

The cutting edge

In early 1999, Ramm Mylvaganam sat opposite Alex Ferguson at the Cliff and sold him a footballing revolution. The United manager, he explained, was the ideal man to propel the game into the 21st century.

In Ferguson's office was a TV and video recorder into which he would slip a tape of a recent match played by opponents for his research and analysis. He would watch the footage and take mental notes about individual strengths or a team's style. It was slow, time-consuming and highly subjective. Mylvaganam explained that the digital revolution offered so much more. It could bring science and data to football; a proper understanding of how players moved in matches, and where they touched the ball and how often.

In a modern age when Manchester City have appointed a Director of Insights and Decision Technology with a PhD in computational astrophysics, and even the man in the pub can access XG and PPDA (expected goals and passes per defensive action), this might all seem very basic stuff. But Ferguson's willingness to sit and listen to Mylvaganam proved a transformative moment in propelling football into a new world.

He is a fascinating man, Mylvaganam – as full of enthusiasm for new possibilities in the game now as when he started to drag football into its data infancy. An immigrant from Sri Lanka who had come to England to study chemical engineering, Mylvaganam had walked into Derby County in 1997 as part of a consultancy selling Finnish chairs which used sound technology to aid physical recovery. These days the chairs are as obsolete as the ZX Spectrum, but his introduction to professional football proved far-reaching.

What Mylvaganam found inside Derby was, to a smart businessman, ludicrously antiquated. It would have been the same in any club in the country. There was no analytical process for examining matches, no statistical measurements; just managerial hunch and a coach, Steve McClaren, in a cramped cubicle transferring match clips from one VHS tape on to another to show the players. Even that was a laborious process and not a particularly useful one given the limited footage contained no off-ball movement. There were no patterns to discern unless picked up by the naked eye. This former marketing director at Mars told McClaren there had to be a better way. What if they could convert these videos into 2D animation to create an objective overview of positions? And then work out how to track the movements.

Mylvaganam had contacts in the technology world who understood image recognition, but they would need much more data to work on than a simple match video. Eight cameras were installed at Derby's Pride Park to track every player from more than one angle. Algorithms, based on logic sequences, were created to differentiate when players came close together. They could work out where a player moved all game; how much ground he covered. Analysts could input touch statistics, but they, too, would become automated in time.

As Mylvaganam explains, 'So this is the first time that a coach has ever been able to sit down with a player and say, "You ran 12km last week but only 10km this week." It's the first time he can say "you spent this amount of time in this part of the pitch" or "you had these touches in this area". We built a complete event list of everything that happened on the field of play. Good passes or bad passes, simple algorithms like that. We could draw pass maps. We were able to ask what happens in play transformation, how did a move break down and what happened next. And because we created a playlist, we could start to do it at the touch of a button.'

He recruited sports scientists from John Moores University in Liverpool to break down the data, and spoke to Jim Smith, the Derby manager, and McClaren about what information they required, and how best to present it visually. Data collection was not easy – 'One megabyte of data you needed a fridge freezer-size machine,' Mylvaganam says – and some tasks could only be done the old-fashioned way. All the video footage had to be rushed by motorbike courier to Prozone's HQ in Leeds; a warehouse borrowed from a friend in the rag trade filled with computers. But it was revolutionary.

'Effectively we created two key areas of analytics – physical and tactical. Nothing like that had ever been done before so, yes, I'd say revolution is probably the right word for it.' The feedback allowed McClaren to help players with individual analytics sessions and with collective messages about strategy, all backed up by visual affirmation.

McClaren loved it and was quick to sell the advantages to Ferguson as soon as he arrived at United early in 1999. The manager was on board from that first meeting in his office, and sent Mylvaganam to haggle with David Gill. The businessman wanted £100,000 to set up Prozone at Old Trafford. Gill struck a deal that United would pay £50,000 if they won a trophy in 1999, and a promise to keep it on.

The agreement meant that Mylvaganam was heavily invested in United's success as they went into the critical weeks of the season. With the cameras installed at Old Trafford, Mylvaganam remembers his analysts spending a lot of time examining the first leg of the Champions League semi-final against Juventus to assist Ferguson and McClaren ahead of the return in Turin. 'How Zidane played, where Inzaghi made his runs,' he says. 'That game in particular stands out.'

The work of Prozone must have been valued because the next time Mylvaganam saw Ferguson, the United manager took him by surprise by handing over two complimentary tickets for the Champions League final. 'I won the lottery when Steve went to Manchester United,' Mylvaganam says. Football's data revolution had been launched.

75

Bend it like ...

Gareth Southgate explained afterwards that Aston Villa had spent all week thinking how best to thwart David Beckham if he was lining up a direct free-kick. From a certain distance, they would put a man – namely Southgate – on the line to give the goalkeeper extra cover. It had worked in the first half when the centre-back headed away one effort.

Defending a free-kick from a longer range, Michael Oakes, the goalkeeper, opted for no wall in order to be clear-sighted. So much for that. The ball left Beckham's boot 30 yards from goal and seemed to turn sideways in the air before dipping into the far top corner. Feet stuck to the floor, Oakes moved only his neck in order to follow, perhaps admire, the flight of a wondrous shot.

Make that five direct free-kicks – three in the Premier League, two in the Champions League – in the 1998-99 campaign, which was as productive for Beckham from set-pieces as any season in England. Almost two decades since he left English football, Beckham still boasts the most successful direct free-kicks in the Premier League by a remarkable margin. His 18, spread over seven seasons, put him ahead of Thierry Henry and Gianfranco Zola (12 each), though he might yet be challenged by James Ward-Prowse (14, and counting).

'Sometimes you just have to hold up your hands and say it's all down to a fantastic piece of skill,' Southgate said afterwards. 'At the moment he's the best in the world at it.' As the winning goal in a 2-1 victory over Villa on 1 May, putting United two points ahead of Arsenal with four league matches left to play, it was not just a spectacular strike but a vital one, too.

It is easy to forget how exceptional Beckham was as a footballer. Perhaps that is his fault. These days he is so famous for being famous that you might need reminding that, as Southgate said, he was once better at performing certain feats with a football than anyone in the world. There was not a better crosser and few, if any, could match him for dead-ball accuracy. He could strike a ball with endless variety; fizzing with spin off either inside or outside of the boot, or whipped on the run on to the head of a striker. Beckham was also the fittest player at Old Trafford. With the arrival of Prozone, it was no longer a question of observing Beckham's energy. Now they could measure that no United player covered more ground; the legacy of teenage years as a middle-distance and cross-country runner.

It seems worth restating those truths given that the Beckham story would become obscured – not least by himself – in all the celebrity and stardom.

Alex Ferguson's concerns about Beckham's priorities had taken hold as soon as he started dating a pop star – and they would mount with each season – but in 1998-99 the gains far outweighed any reservations for the United manager. When Ferguson had a private word with Beckham in April, just like he had taken aside Ryan Giggs to remind the winger of what made him special, it was nothing to do with his private life but simply to advise a committed player not to try too hard.

Ferguson told Beckham to be wary of overelaboration in his determination to excel, especially in this season of all seasons as the abuse continued at every away ground. Beckham had designs on becoming a playmaking central midfielder but Ferguson wanted him to concentrate on the thrust down the flanks and delivery which had produced so many crucial goals. 'That's when you are at your deadliest,' Ferguson told him. 'Nobody strikes a ball as well.'

The United manager knew what those skills were founded on. In that book he was writing, he would note, 'David Beckham is Britain's finest striker of a football not because of God-given talent but because he practises with a relentless application that the vast majority of less gifted players wouldn't contemplate.'

Starting with countless hours as a kid trying to swerve free-kicks around his dad in a local park, Beckham had honed that extraordinary angle of attack; almost striking the ball at right angles to the goal, using that distinctive body-shape with left leg ramrod straight and sharply angled that would eventually become a brand logo.

The curl and dip – side and topspin – would, by 2002, be celebrated in a movie, *Bend It Like Beckham*, though free-kicks would change in the new Millennium, with Juninho Pernambucano starting to popularise the knuckleball strike in Europe after he joined Lyon in 2001. Perhaps nothing is new in football – the Brazilian Didi was said to have used a version of the knuckleball called the *folha seca*, or dry leaf, back in the 1950s – but the modern ball optimised the wobble in the air.

That was not part of Beckham's repertoire but perhaps he never had a need for it. Still only two players have scored five direct free-kicks in one Premier League campaign; Beckham in 2000-01 and Laurent Robert, for Newcastle United, the following year. And if Ward-Prowse ever does surpass Beckham's tally, he can even take some of the credit for that. 'Beckham was the one for me,' Ward-Prowse told the *Guardian*. 'He was the guy I looked up to and thought, "Wow." He had that effect on me and inspired me to try and take free-kicks.'

76

Ref rage

Asked why he stuck at refereeing despite the relentless abuse, David Elleray would often cite the classic FA Cup semi-final replay between Manchester United and Arsenal as the best possible explanation. 'People say to me, "Do you remember the Ryan Giggs goal?" And I can say I was about ten yards away when he started his run and ten yards away when he scored. How can you beat that apart from actually playing?'

What a perk, but taking charge of games involving United, and Alex Ferguson, could also be a bruising – even scarring – experience. 'I describe Ferguson like someone who gets behind the wheel of a car and becomes a road-rage monster,' Elleray says. And that monster was awoken on 5 May as we were enthralled by a tumultuous clash with Liverpool at Anfield.

Elleray was in the middle of the maelstrom as United went 2-0 ahead within an hour; another magnificent David Beckham cross to Dwight Yorke at the far post, and a penalty despatched with characteristic composure by Denis Irwin to seemingly take United a confident step closer to the title. But it never could be simple.

Jesper Blomqvist was harshly adjudged by Elleray to have fouled Oyvind Leonhardsen. Penalty to Liverpool. 'One of the least likely penalties even Anfield has seen,' Ferguson fumed afterwards. Jamie Redknapp scored. Game on. With just a few minutes left, Karl-Heinz Riedle turned Stam, and the ball fell to Paul Ince, of all people, to make it 2-2 in front of an ecstatic Kop. Ince's celebrations were 'gloatingly excessive' according to an irate Ferguson, who cut short his press conference, but only after he had already boiled over.

It was a painful concession for United, a draw that left them three points behind Arsenal with a game in hand. But that was not all. Late on, as United tried to cling to their lead, Irwin had dribbled the ball out of play and, as the linesman flagged, kicked the ball away. Elleray went to take out his yellow card for deliberate time-wasting. He is still not sure if he would have changed his mind had he remembered that Irwin was already in his book. As he reached again for the yellow and then the red card, he felt bad – he is human, despite what you may have heard – but he was sure that Irwin was trying to waste precious seconds.

The consequences were significant given that Irwin would be suspended for the FA Cup final. As Elleray left the field, he was pursued by a furious Ferguson – 'angrier than I'd ever seen him' – down the narrow Anfield tunnel. A bulky policeman helped to usher Elleray to his changing room before Ferguson could start up the hairdryer or, in this case, flamethrower.

Elleray knew what he was in for. 'Steve Bruce used to say that one of his main roles was to put Fergie in a headlock and drag him away from people at the end of the game,' he recalls. 'It was all part of his emotion and his, I'm sure, slightly longer-term tactic of intimidation. He was one of those that if you are strong and professional, he'll respect you. But if you're weak and try to be clever-clever, he'll eat you for lunch.'

There was little respect on this occasion. 'We will not let this man deny us our title,' Ferguson said on television afterwards, and United did not leave it there. In the *Mail on Sunday* the following week, Martin Edwards was vicious in his criticism, 'If Arsenal or Chelsea win the Premiership this season by either one or two points, I trust they will strike a special commemorative medal for

Mr Elleray because he will have done it for them.' It was a highly inflammatory comment with alarming consequences.

It was no secret that Elleray was a teacher at Harrow School, where he ran one of the boarding houses. He was easily targeted, and not just by nasty letters and phone calls. 'I was being abused in the supermarket and when I was walking from my boarding house to my classroom, and a couple of times cars would stop and people would get out and throw abuse at me. I was told there had been a number of death threats. One or two were slightly credible – most people knew where I taught.'

With the United hierarchy stoking fan fury, Elleray was visited by senior police officers and a Home Office panic alarm was installed in his private quarters. 'You only need one lunatic. If someone tried to do something, throw a petrol bomb through the window or whatever . . .' This was not undue paranoia. After awarding two penalties, one mistaken, against Chelsea in the 1994 FA Cup final, a group of fans had descended on Harrow. 'They started hammering on my door. The boys were very good. They said they'd got the wrong house and sent the fans up the hill to a rival boarding house. A few years later, I was attacked by some random person when I was shopping in Harrow, some guy who was mentally disturbed. It brought it home that one person can do something to you.'

Edwards subsequently apologised, making a conciliatory call, but the ramifications lasted. Elleray was down to officiate Arsenal's final game of the season, with the title still on the line. He pulled out, fearing that he would be embroiled in a terrible controversy that would overshadow the outcome. 'One side of me thinks, "Did I bottle it?" Should I have gone and done that game? I thought it was a ridiculous appointment.'

Then there was the FA Cup final in May, which was being officiated by Peter Jones. Elleray wanted to show support for a colleague and friend, especially with Wembley just down the road from Harrow, so went to the lengths of approaching the school drama department for a disguise. He still has the photograph of him looking like a bad hitman; baseball cap, false beard and moustache with wraparound sunglasses. He even carried a tube of glue in case his beard slipped. Just as well. 'When I got there, my tickets were in the United end,' Elleray says.

Elleray, who retired from teaching/refereeing and went on to work as technical director to the International Football Association Board, overseeing the implementation of VAR (so hardly a quieter life), did not officiate another United game for quite some time. When he did return to Old Trafford, it was to witness Roy Keane taking brutal revenge on Alfie Inge Haaland.

'I sent off Roy four times and none of them could really be disputed,' he says. 'The great thing about Roy is that, unlike a lot of players, if he was going to do somebody, he did it for the whole world to see. It wasn't sly and off the ball.' When Elleray retired, Keane sent him a signed shirt and an amusingly wry letter. 'I am so pleased to hear that you are at long last hanging up your boots and red card,' he wrote. Elleray laughs about Keane once seeing him in the tunnel and saying, 'I expect you've got my name in the book already.' Elleray responded, 'Yes, and I know what it'll be for. All I have to do is fill in the time.' Keane laughed, sort of.

There were lighter moments, but the situation was out of hand when a referee was installing a panic alarm and fearing for his physical safety. What Elleray, and other officials, endured was one reprehensible aspect of Ferguson's siege mentality.

77

A blink

After 36 games, United and Arsenal were level on 75 points. They also had the same goal difference of plus-42. The title race had come down to a thrilling test of nerve in the final week. Who would blink?

Arsenal stepped up first. From 20 December to 11 May, when they travelled to face Leeds United, they had played 26 games and lost just one; that epic FA Cup semi-final replay to a wonder goal from Ryan Giggs. In 19 league games, they had won 15 and drawn four. In that run, they had let in just six goals. Even if United held the narrowest of advantages, on goals scored, Arsenal were showing title-winning form.

As Arsenal took to the field at Elland Road, some of United's players were watching at home on television, though Teddy Sheringham is among those who says that he could barely bring himself to look. In a frantic game of nine bookings, 'tempers threatening to snap like taut piano strings' as I noted, Arsenal created enough chances to win but found Nigel Martyn in excellent form and a teenage Jonathan Woodgate impressing in defence. Nerves were shredded when Leeds won a penalty shortly before the interval, but Ian Harte smashed his kick against the crossbar.

Then, in the 86th minute, Arsenal cracked. Harry Kewell skipped away from Lee Dixon and crossed for Jimmy Floyd Hasselbaink to head home at the far post. Nelson Vivas, who had only been on the pitch for five minutes as a replacement for the injured Nigel Winterburn, was the nearest marker but he could only wave a leg forlornly. After all they had done to hunt down United and defend their title, Arsène Wenger feared the consequences of defeat. 'I know Leeds are supposed to hate United, but maybe they hate us more,' he lamented, before attributing the blame. 'We made a huge tactical error, which is unusual for us to make a mistake like that. Nelson Vivas was in a very bad position at the far post.'

Popular legend has it that Wenger was so upset that Vivas never kicked a ball again for Arsenal. Even Tony Adams remembers it that way. 'Arsène knew in his heart of hearts that Nelson would never play again for Arsenal,' he told me. It is not quite true – Vivas stayed at Arsenal for another two years, albeit in a peripheral role – but the power of this campaign was that it did not just make careers, and reputations, but break them too.

78

Strife of Brian, part two

Brian Kidd is one of the game's more genial souls. While the United players were delighted by Steve McClaren's training sessions and positive energy, they never forgot Kidd's warm advice and sincerity. You struggle to find anyone in football with a bad word to say about this down-to-earth Manc – though it is revealing that Alex Ferguson was the exception. When Kidd left United to manage Blackburn Rovers in December, Ferguson saw not personal ambition and betterment but a lack of loyalty. On the night of 12 May, revenge would be served not just cold but with a large side portion of scorn.

There was not much Kidd could do about it. After walking away mid-season from a United team chasing glory on three fronts, he was facing immediate relegation, and with Ferguson having the chance to inflict the killer blow. When Blackburn and United met on a Wednesday night at Ewood Park in the penultimate game of the league season – 24 hours after Arsenal's loss at Leeds – Rovers needed to win to save themselves.

On a night when Ryan Giggs returned from injury to strike the post with a header from one of the game's best chances, they could only scrap out a goalless draw. For United, it was a point which kept the title in their hands going into the final day. For Blackburn, just four years after they had been champions of England, it was a result which condemned them to a humiliating relegation.

Ferguson must have known, yet, after a curt handshake with Kidd at the final whistle when the United manager did not even look at his old sidekick, he initially feigned surprise on television that Rovers had gone down. Yeah, right. Subsequently, he had a dig at Kidd's selection of one striker, Ashley Ward, and suggested that his former assistant had prioritised trying to thwart United over saving his own team. He described going into Kidd's office post-match and being surprised to find his former assistant in a chipper mood. Was it a front, he wondered? Or maybe Kidd felt relegation was not his responsibility. Kidd had no option than to take the barbs. Little did he know that worse was to come.

Ferguson was the most successful manager in the country, and Kidd had been relegated. That could have been the end of the matter, but Ferguson was never one to miss the chance to settle a score, justifiably or otherwise.

In *Managing My Life*, published later that year, he portrayed Kidd as a moaner and insecure. He brought up Kidd's reservations about signing Yorke, and his pushing for John Hartson. He portrayed Kidd as a solid coach but certainly not a leader capable of making the tough decisions that were Ferguson's daily fare. Publicising the book, he expressed serious reservations about his former No.2 ever taking charge at Old Trafford. This time, Kidd felt a need to defend himself. 'I believe Walt Disney is trying to buy the film rights to the book as a sequel to *Fantasia*,' he said. He explained that he had chosen to respect a decade of working with Ferguson. 'Clearly he hasn't.'

Not long afterwards, in November 1999, Kidd was sacked by Blackburn with the team struggling in the second tier, though he believed that Ferguson's public attack had hastened his downfall. The United manager had been justified in his doubts about Kidd's ability to do the top job. But it also said something about Ferguson's bullying streak that he had to kick a man – a former ally – when he was down.

79

Character is fate #8

Manchester United 2 Tottenham Hotspur 1, 16 May 1999

Manchester United (4-4-2): Schmeichel – G. Neville, Johnsen, May, Irwin – Beckham, Keane, Scholes, Giggs – Sheringham, Yorke. Substitutes: Butt, Cole, P. Neville, Solskjær, Van der Gouw (gk)

Tottenham Hotspur (4-4-2): Walker – Carr, Scales, Campbell, Edinburgh – Freund, Anderton, Sherwood, Ginola – Iversen, Ferdinand. Substitutes: Young, Dominguez, Sinton, Clemence, Baardesen (gk)

On the final day of the Premier League season, the fans pour into Old Trafford in a carnival mood, giddy with excitement. Three games, eleven days, to watch their heroes make history. To win a Treble never achieved before by an English club. Or not.

It is the 'not' that you can read on the faces of the United players as they gather in the tunnel. Faces are fixed with grim seriousness – apart, inevitably, from Dwight Yorke, whose beaming smile manages to emerge, like sunshine, even from behind these clouds of stress and strain.

This is what elite sport comes down to, if you are good enough. The cusp of glory. The chance to prove you are a winner, a champion. No off-day allowed. You have to turn up and deliver. You must deal with the expectations, the heavy legs, and the pressures that put the butterflies in your stomach however many times you have walked this path to the summit. Ryan Giggs admits to feeling nerves like he has not known for years. Even Roy Keane can see the headlines if it all goes wrong: 'UNITED BLOW TREBLE BID' or 'THE NEARLY MEN'. The closer they are to the dream, the worse the nightmare if it all goes badly from here.

Ferguson tries to contain the emotions, but it is not easy. Arriving at the Cliff the day before the league decider, he had found Danny McGregor, United's commercial manager, distributing T-shirts to all the staff with '3 to go' on the front. McGregor had cheerily told Ferguson that he already had the next ones printed and ready to hand out – '1 down, 2 to go' – and so on. Ferguson had winced.

In the team talk, as his players ready themselves to face George Graham's Spurs, Ferguson attempts to reduce the momentousness of the occasion to a game of football, like any other. He wants to stop anyone running ahead with thoughts of a potential Treble and to focus their minds on the task at hand. 'Remember who you are,' he tells the players. 'Remember that you are Manchester United players. Remember what you did to get here. Now go out and do it one more time. And you'll win.'

He knows that some will be carrying the scars of 1995 when United lost the title on the final day, so he goes around the dressing room shortly before kick-off with more encouragement. 'The only way we lose at home is when we beat ourselves,' he says. Win the immediate battle with your direct opponent, he tells them. Wear them down, break their spirit. Then the result will take care of itself.

Out on the pitch Russell Watson, the tenor from Salford, is on the pitch singing 'Nessun Dorma' to entertain the fans. And then, just as Arsenal run out to face Aston Villa at Highbury, the United players emerge with hearts racing. A point ahead at the top of the league, the title is in their hands. It is theirs to win. And theirs to lose, too.

*

When Les Ferdinand scores for Spurs after 25 minutes, looping a shot over Peter Schmeichel, who stumbles awkwardly into the net in his final game at Old Trafford, it becomes clear that, once again, United are not going to make it easy for themselves. 'We so often make a crisis out of a drama,' Ferguson reflects later. Out on the pitch, Beckham can feel the tension, 'How could we have come this far and be playing this badly?'

To fall behind might rattle a lesser team, but United have Roy Keane back from an ankle injury, imposing his authority. Plenty of time left. Keep applying the pressure, stepping up through the gears, squeezing the opposition. 'Make the bastards work,' as the captain puts it. 'Wear them down.' United are creating chances but, as Old Trafford gasps and wails at another opportunity flying wide, or coming back off the post when Ian Walker in the Spurs goal whacks a clearance straight into Yorke, they cannot find the finishing touch. And then Beckham steps forward.

It is yet another top-class goal from United's No.7, and atonement for missing earlier with a point-blank header. Three minutes before half-time, the ball is fed across the United attack on the edge of Tottenham's area. Paul Scholes finds Beckham, who has room inside the box to size up his shot. There is one place to aim – inside the high, far netting – and his whipped strike is perfectly judged as it swerves past Walker. On the final day of the league campaign, as on the first, Beckham's right foot has executed just when his team needed it.

Watching it again later that night, Beckham is shocked by the look on his face as he turns to celebrate and the tension pours out of him. 'That desire, wanting to win so badly; it looked like fury,' he says. United are level, but it still might not be enough.

At half-time, Ferguson senses that they need a jolt. 'Any chance of you fucking scoring?' he asks Scholes as the midfielder walks in. Scholes holds up his hands in acknowledgement of wasted opportunities. Ferguson has already decided to make a change. It is the boldness of a manager who is not going to wait another 15 or 20 minutes, as most would. He wants more cutting edge up front and if that involves a ruthless decision, so be it. 'Teddy, you're coming off. Coley, get on,' Ferguson says.

Sheringham is taken aback, and feels it a very harsh decision. He thinks that he has been contributing with every appearance in the closing weeks of the season. Ferguson sees that he is crestfallen, and has a quick word, but it is not the time for worrying about individual grievances. If it seemed odd to be leaving out a goal-poacher like Cole in the first place, given the stakes, the striker had known that he was going to be dropped when Ferguson wandered up to him in training. The manager had muttered something – 'you don't seem yourself' – which was one of those coded ways of bracing a player for bad news.

Cole objected but the manager's antennae had, as usual, been spot on. It had been more than a month since Cole had been splashed with Yorke all over the front page of the *News of the World* – 'Millionaire Manchester United idols used a besotted teenage fan as their sex toy for a wild three-in-a-bed orgy' – and the ramifications were still being felt in his domestic life. Despite Cole's protestations that the story was false, his wife was still seething, and he was walking on eggshells at home.

A footballer's confidence can be influenced by forces entirely unknown to the millions looking on. Equally, it can be transformed by one moment of game-changing brilliance on the field. Cole has been on the pitch for less than three minutes when Gary Neville chips a ball forward with his left foot, more in hope than expectation. 'A bit of a long punt and I had to do the dirty work,' Cole says. He has spun off Sol Campbell and as the ball drops, he pulls it down with his right foot. As it bounces up, he takes one touch to control it and then lifts it over the advancing Walker. It seems more like the wondrous deftness of Dennis Bergkamp than a typical finish from Cole, but that just makes it all the more special.

In Cole's celebration as he sprints away is not only delight in the execution but the relief from four years of hurt. No one had felt a deeper sense of responsibility for failing to win the title in 1995, given the chances he had missed at Upton Park on the final day. 'You are told you will get your rewards if you stick at it,' Cole told me. 'That was my moment. That was my redemption for '95. I was so joyful. That goal meant a hell of a lot.'

With a lead to protect, it is hard not to sit back. It will only take one incident, one decision, a moment of bad luck to cost United the title – especially when the news comes that Arsenal are ahead with more than 20 minutes left. Everyone inside Old Trafford senses the fragility. As Keane reflected, 'Your mind is distracted, your emotions running out of control, you realise how desperately you wanted this ... and how close you are to failure.'

The United players feel like they have been clinging on for an age when Graham Poll finally blows the whistle. They are first hit by the sense of relief. Then come the emotional waves of jubilation. Ferguson sprints down on to the pitch beaming. He has equalled the number of league titles won by Matt Busby. It is United's fifth since 1993, but this one is different. It is the first to be won on the pitch at Old Trafford. The domestic crown has been reclaimed from Arsenal. And it has been done with yet another comeback, which has piled drama on top of success.

United go off the field then come back on for the presentation. Keane lifts the trophy. Stam pulls on a red, white and black wig. Schmeichel looks around deeply satisfied that his last game at Old Trafford has finished in triumph. 'You will always be in my heart,' he tells the crowd in a touching valediction. Sheringham's disappointment at coming off has turned to delight as he clasps the trophy he came to win. 'You beauty,' he says. But minds are already racing ahead. Russell has returned to the pitch and sings the anthemic 'Barcelona'. As the champagne is sprayed around the dressing room, Yorke is not finished, 'Just two more wins to go, lads!'

80

Under arrest

Approaching the end of a season when he has dedicated himself as never before, with an intensity that few athletes on earth could muster, Roy Keane needed a blow-out. He had earned one. He was carrying a sore ankle but he had only one game left to worry about. With no Champions League final to concern the suspended captain, there was a lack of restraint about Keane as he launched into the celebrations of the Premier League title. An unrestrained Keane can be dangerous company.

After Sunday night festivities at the Marriott Hotel in Worsley – notable for Giggs and Butt doing Elvis impressions on the karaoke machine – the players arranged to regroup on Monday afternoon in Mulligans in Manchester city centre at 5 p.m. Keane could not wait that long. He decided to sink a few early. He met the former United player Norman Whiteside, a man who likes a pint, at The Griffin in Bowdon and was already flying by the time he caught up with his teammates.

'Oh God, look at the eyes, this is trouble,' Gary Neville said to Peter Schmeichel as the captain arrived in the pub. Keane painted a happy scene in his autobiography, though could not resist a swipe at a couple of his favourite targets: 'Peter Schmeichel is posing (what's new?) and boring the arse off people. Dwight Yorke is bubbling with good humour and mischief. Teddy is being cool. He's from London! Denis Irwin and Paul Scholes, the quiet men, are coming out of their shells.'

The drinks flowed, with Ned Kelly, the club's security guard, and two of his best men, Alvin and Graham, watching on. One minder went to check out Henry's, a smarter wine bar, and came back to report that a couple of tables had been reserved. But as the United contingent moved on, they were followed by a guy and a couple of women. The man hassled Keane to buy the girls a drink. 'Piss off and leave us alone,' Keane said. Voices were raised; accusations thrown; and then a glass chucked at Keane, catching him just below the eye and drawing blood on his cheek. He lunged. All hell broke loose. 'What follows is a blur,' Keane said.

A police van appeared, lights flashing. Keane was arrested. He could already see the headlines as he was taken to Bootle Street police station and put in a cell to sleep off the booze. With sobriety came remorse and regret. Alex Ferguson arrived in the morning to clear up the mess. 'I'll get you out,' Ferguson said. It was not a time, yet, for bollockings. A grateful Keane was released without charge and bailed to reappear in July.

Back at the Cliff, it was the squad that Ferguson berated. 'Why didn't you ring me? Why didn't you tell me this was happening? You've all gone home and got into your beds and left one of your teammates on his own!' Teamwork was essential, even when on the piss.

The news broke just in time for United's media day ahead of the FA Cup final. 'Are there any questions about the FA Cup final now?' Ferguson snapped as we tried to eke out more details about the fracas. The story rumbled on for a few days. The two women were reported to have called a tabloid newspaper even before the police arrived. Their wilder allegations that Keane attacked them – 'He had evil in his eyes,' one said – were eventually dismissed. It turned out that Keane was guilty, at least on this occasion, only of being someone people like to wind up – though, as he would admit himself, that was never difficult.

81

Because I'm not worth it

On the Thursday night before the FA Cup final, we gathered in the banqueting hall of the Royal Lancaster Hotel in west London, as tradition demanded, to honour the Footballer of the Year, chosen by the nation's sports writers. After decades of largely British winners, the foreign invasion of the Premier League had been recognised in victories for Jürgen Klinsmann, Eric Cantona, Gianfranco Zola and Dennis Bergkamp in the previous four seasons. They were all stellar recipients of a prestigious award.

So who was the outstanding player of 1998-99, and this very special season? For the record, I voted for Dwight Yorke but wrote that Roy Keane and David Beckham were very valid choices – which is my way of quickly distancing myself from the embarrassment of what unfolded.

The player who stepped forward, with a flick of his beautifully coiffed hair, was David Ginola – just as he had done as the players' choice at the end of April, when Yorke was second and Emmanuel Petit third. *Quelle horreur!* Ginola was an extraordinary player – two-footed, almost unstoppable on his best days, wonderfully balanced for a man over 6ft, and key to Tottenham's Worthington Cup success – but perhaps only he, in the entire universe, could think that his best moments amounted to more than Keane, Yorke or Beckham's contributions. Or Jaap Stam's, for that matter.

His win revealed a few things; mostly, that voting had closed daftly early, long before the season had concluded. Also that United's vote had been split, though that detail was lost on Alex Ferguson, who, in his fury, banned his players from attending the awards dinners. He was no great fan of Ginola in any case, calling the Frenchman a diver.

Keane would never have admitted being miffed about individual honours but, more than 20 years later, Yorke drops his usual sangfroid when I remind him of missing out to Ginola. 'It's ridiculous,' he says. 'Talk about being deprived of a once-in-a-lifetime opportunity.' He points out that he not only scored 29 goals but contributed 20 assists, behind only Beckham. 'I'm still pretty cheesed off,' he says. 'The gaffer was furious about it.'

Indeed, Ferguson was still complaining about it (eight) years later. 'Did you know that in 1999 they picked David Ginola for the football writers' award. We won the Treble that year. In fact, the only thing we didn't win was the Boat Race – and they still gave it to Ginola! Can you believe that?'

---

* There was no award for players' player of the year at United until 2006, but the majority of those I spoke to were quick to nominate Keane. Yorke and Beckham also picked up plenty of votes. Gary Neville put Stam ahead of Yorke in his top three. But it was the captain who was the clear winner.

'The most influential player I've ever played with,' Gary Neville said. As Beckham put it, 'Our captain, the man, the one who drove us on in every single training session.' Keane was rightly awarded the Sir Matt Busby player-of-the-year award, chosen by the United fans, and presented with the trophy in September.

But it was Beckham who was fêted by the rest of the world. In December 1999, he finished second in the Ballon d'Or behind Rivaldo (and ahead of Andriy Shevchenko, Gabriel Batistuta and Luís Figo, with Roy Keane sixth). Rivaldo also won FIFA world player of the year, with Beckham second. Beckham was voted Europe's most valuable player by Uefa, chosen by the continent's leading coaches. He finished ahead of Zinedine Zidane and Keane, and perhaps benefited from having a more glamorous, eye-catching repertoire than his captain.

Keane would eventually receive due recognition with both PFA and Football Writers' Association awards the following season. Those prizes should have come with an apology.

82

Two out of three

Manchester United 2 Newcastle 0, 22 May 1999, FA Cup Final

Manchester United (4-4-2): Schmeichel – G. Neville, May, Johnsen, P. Neville – Beckham, Keane, Scholes, Giggs – Cole, Solskjær. Substitutes: Sheringham, Stam, Yorke, Blomqvist, Van der Gouw (gk)

Newcastle United (4-4-2): Harper – Griffin, Dabizas, Charvet, Domi – Lee, Hamann, Speed, Solano – Shearer, Ketsbaia. Substitutes: Ferguson, Glass, Marić, Barton, Given (gk)

It seems ridiculous to say of an FA Cup final – especially when victory mattered so much – that there was more drama in the build-up than in the sunshine at Wembley as Manchester United faced Newcastle United. But it is probably true.

A keen desire among the United players to be involved in a showpiece game collided with Alex Ferguson's need to prepare for a Champions League final four days later – conflicting interests which were bound to lead to some fraught conversations. Players were desperate to be involved in every match by this point – Gary Neville and David Beckham had refused the manager's offer of a rest for that penultimate league game against Blackburn – and the Cup final was special. There was still some uncertainty about exactly how United would line up against Bayern Munich, so there were also places to fight for.

In the United hotel, Ferguson went on a tour of rooms impart-
ing bad news. Dwight Yorke was one of the first to hear that he
was being held back from the starting XI at Wembley. He knew
that it would do no good protesting, but tried in any case. Nicky
Butt could not even be risked on the bench. He had to spend the
day in a suit. He knew why given that, in the absence of Keane
and Scholes in Barcelona, he had never been more precious, but
there was a short to-do with the manager. Butt would have to
join the suspended Denis Irwin in missing out. Ferguson told
Andy Cole that he could start but would come off after an hour.
When Cole argued back, the manager snapped, 'Well you either
come off or you can start on the bench.'

Jaap Stam was particularly unhappy. A sore Achilles tendon had
been troubling him, allowing David May to come into the side in
the closing weeks, but he was eager to play his first big cup final
in England, and at Wembley. 'Jaap was fuming,' Dave Fevre, the
physio, recalls. 'I think he could have knocked me out. He's an
intelligent guy, a rational guy off the pitch, but when it came to
playing, he was the opposite. He was desperate to play but I said,
"Your Achilles won't stand up to it." The manager was great, and
backed me.' Stam was on the bench.

Finally, Ferguson knocked on the door of Teddy Sheringham
to say that he would not be starting, even though Yorke was not
in the line-up. After being hauled off against Spurs in the final
league game, it felt like another heavy blow. 'I was devastated
inside,' Sheringham says. But not for long.

Sheringham did not even have his boots on. He was sitting on the
bench behind Ferguson, McClaren and the kitman topping up
his tan as the 1999 FA Cup final kicked off, with Prince Charles,
Tony Blair and Posh Spice looking on from the Royal Box. The
game was only a few minutes old when Roy Keane was clattered
on the ankle by Gary Speed. The captain tried to struggle on but

it was clear as early as the eighth minute that he would have to come off. Sheringham assumed that Jesper Blomqvist would be summoned into midfield. 'Then the manager says, "Teddy, get yourself changed, you're going on." And I'm thinking, "What, for Keaney?"'

Ferguson sent Sheringham up front with Cole, shoving Ole Gunnar Solskjær out to the right and David Beckham into central midfield. It was not the obvious scenario. As Sheringham recalls, 'I'm half-questioning what the manager is doing. Then I'm thinking, "What are you doing, you idiot? Get yourself ready and get yourself on the pitch." So I put my boots on and within two minutes I've scored the first goal of the FA Cup final. What a turnaround. Amazing.'

Sheringham's goal, from a neat run in midfield and an interchange with Scholes – they always did love playing off each other – concluded with a low first-time shot under Steve Harper who had rushed out of goal. Roles were reversed for United's second. Sheringham, with his back to goal, laid the ball in the path of Scholes, who hit the ball firm and low with his left foot from the edge of the area.

For United players, it was a game of almost inexplicable comfort. Ruud Gullit's Newcastle should have known that United would be weakened but, apart from Speed leaving that early mark on Keane, they made very little impression. Cole was happy enough to come off after an hour, his job done, to allow Yorke to have 30 minutes. Ferguson could send on Stam for a late cameo, the chance to play at Wembley and for a little match-sharpness ahead of the looming test against Bayern Munich.

It was a strangely easy win after so many weeks of gruelling battles, though after overcoming Liverpool, and both Chelsea and Arsenal after replays (third and second in the league respectively) just to reach the final, it was not as though the FA Cup had been a simple addition to the league title. As Keane led the players up the Wembley steps to receive the trophy from Prince Charles, they could reflect that it had taken United 106 years to win their first Double. Now they had a third in six seasons.

They celebrated in a London hotel with families, though nothing too raucous, before they retreated to the Burnham Beeches Hotel in Buckinghamshire to begin preparations for the climactic game of the season.

Two down, one to go. The United squad were lurching from one defining contest to another. There was barely time to digest it all at the time, but Sheringham can reflect now on his own emotional rollercoaster. As he told me, 'I've gone from the high of being selected against Spurs in the final league game of the season to being hauled off. Dropped for the FA Cup final then coming on and I score and I'm man of the match. I've won the FA Cup. Then it's off to Barcelona. Fucking hell, my 11 days . . .'

83

The meaning of the Cup

The oldest cup competition in the world celebrated 150 years of glory, upsets and whatever we mean by its 'magic' in 2022. It endures. But if that famous trophy sparkles a little less than in the era when we would watch hours of television build-up as kids and memorise the result of every final (I can recall the dramas of, say, 1979 and 1981 much better than any in the last decade), the '90s was when it began to lose some of its lustre. It was never quite the same after 1999.

United's eye on the Champions League meant that facing Newcastle was the first time any manager had fielded a weakened team in the final. United's position was symbolic of a wider preoccupation with expanding European competition. The FA Cup was no longer central to the national conversation. With so much more football on TV, appetites were shifting to something more exotic.

During the '90s, upsets in the FA Cup became notably less common as Premier League wealth started to create a gulf from the lower divisions. Talent, particularly from abroad, was concentrated at the top. There were less of those famous shocks. Ticket prices were rising, making fans more discerning about which games they paid to see, and the Cup began to lose out. In the '80s, gates had been higher for a Cup match than the equivalent league fixture, but that was no longer the case by 1999.

Given these unarguable trends, the FA demonstrated reckless

disregard for its own heritage when it enabled United to pull out of defending the trophy the following season. United took terrible stick, but it was the FA, in a hopelessly naive attempt to win votes for hosting a World Cup in England, who not only allowed United to pull out but positively encouraged them to fly to Brazil for FIFA's inaugural Club World Cup in January 2000 instead of playing in the third round. It was an act of short-sightedness, and self-harm, which could only further diminish the Cup's status.

In 2001, in an attempt to make the Cup more relevant, the FA announced that prize money would be available in every round for the first time, with the winners amassing around £4 million. 'The £30m prize fund to save the FA Cup' as the headlines put it. Throwing money at the problem was all too typical of football's direction and could only have a limited impact when the FA was fighting irresistible modernising forces.

The Premier League and Champions League were filling the airwaves, leaving the FA Cup gasping for room to breathe. But one thing remains true: try winning the Treble without it.

84

Barcelona

And so to Barcelona. When the United squad flew out to Catalonia on Concorde, Alex Ferguson was taken into the cockpit before take-off and stuck on a pilot's hat for the photographers. The jaunty wave belied the tension that was bubbling within.

The nerves showed when United reached their base in Sitges, 30 miles down the coast. The stylish seaside town is renowned for its gay community, as *The Sun* gleefully informed its readers under headlines like 'Hello Nou Campers!' and 'United Away With The Fairies'. Homophobia, 1999-style – and a sign of the times. This was the season when Graeme Le Saux complained about being called a 'poof' and 'faggot' on the pitch by Robbie Fowler, as the Liverpool striker stuck out his backside, only for the Chelsea defender to be booked for time-wasting.

As the United team arrived in Sitges, the hotel was rammed with fans. Parents and kids loitered for photos and autographs, and Ferguson soon realised that it would be bedlam for the next 48 hours if he did not intervene. Security were told to clear out the lobby. His players needed clear heads.

There was lots of time – almost too much – to think about the momentousness of the game that awaited them. On Monday evening on the balcony of their hotel, the Class of '92 gang shared their nervous excitement. It was not fear – certainly not the dread they would feel with England, worrying about the consequences of defeat – but more the feeling that they had come so close to the summit and could not be sure they would ever be in touching distance again.

All the while, Ferguson was plotting how best to fill that huge hole in central midfield left by the suspensions of Keane and Scholes. Nicky Butt was obviously going to start, and the manager's hunch had been to put Giggs alongside him. After inspiring Giggs to skewer Arsenal with dazzling wing play, Ferguson was now tempted to turn to the Welshman's expanding range in midfield. His passing was adept and running from a central position could cause problems, especially for Bayern's ageing libero, Lothar Matthäus.

It was with that plan in mind that Ferguson had told Jesper Blomqvist in the week leading up to the FA Cup final that he would be starting in Barcelona. Steve McClaren was surprised that Ferguson had committed so early to a man in indifferent form, but Ferguson liked to keep a player involved and give him time to prepare. But now the FA Cup final had created a fresh dilemma. Beckham had revelled in his preferred central position following Keane's early withdrawal, and Ferguson started to think that his passing range could prove valuable there. With Butt and Beckham, Ferguson felt that this pair's combination of tackling and passing could handle Jens Jeremies and Stefan Effenberg.

With that selection in central midfield, Giggs could have stayed on the left and Ole Gunnar Solskjær taken the right flank where he had spent most of the Cup final – but Ferguson had made his promise to Blomqvist and he was not about to break it.

And so Ferguson came to a team which had Giggs starting on the right for one of the few times in his life and only the second time all season. Filling in there for Beckham in the Champions League trip to Brondby in October, Giggs had told us gnomically that it was 'like playing on the left, except it was on the right', but this was a very big, late change of role. The United manager now convinced himself that Giggs's running could cause problems for Michael Tarnat, Bayern's deputy left-back who had come in for Bixente Lizarazu, a world champion absent with injury. Beckham would be granted his central role.

Peter Schmeichel was not the only United player who felt it was a mistake to have compounded the loss of Keane and Scholes by drastically altering the roles of Giggs and Beckham, who had provided so much vital width all season. The entire regular midfield was now shaken up. The outcome was a starting XI for United that had never played together – and would never do so again.

As we watched training in the Nou Camp on the eve of the final, Ferguson stood out in his red football shirt with a white round collar – a retro-jersey which paid homage to United's history and, in particular, to the Busby era. There was no escaping the context of this game; United's first European Cup final since 1968.

It had been such a long time and we were so unused to the idea of English clubs conquering Europe that we peppered Ferguson at the pre-match press conference with questions about the consequences of falling short again. It had, after all, been the theme of so many previous years when United had stumbled against lesser teams than Bayern. Ferguson responded by talking about all that he had achieved as a manager. He said that he had been 'blessed' to have enjoyed a great career. Meeting the question with one of his own, he asked, 'Why should I look upon the failure to win the European Cup as a tragedy for me and a failing in me as a manager?'

He said that he would be deeply upset if United lost – 'It would be a terrible disappointment, I would be gutted because I think we have a great, great chance tomorrow' – but he was doing his best to play down the idea that, win or lose, this was a match that would define his place in history. We could understand his perspective but, as we wrote up our previews, it was hard to avoid the narrative that United, and Ferguson, had to win this game if the quest for European glory was to feel not only an obsession but a curse.

At the final training session in the Nou Camp, a familiar figure came to chat to Ferguson. Steve Archibald, a striker who had been a leading member of Ferguson's first championship side at Aberdeen almost 20 years earlier, had lived in Barcelona since he was a player there; one of the team managed by Terry Venables which had reached the European Cup final in 1986. They had lost to Steaua Bucharest on penalties. Defeat hurt, but what had particularly stayed with 'Archigoles', as the Catalans had come to know him, was the memory of having to walk past the trophy – one of the most magnificent and easily distinguishable in sport – and not being able to touch it. To be six feet away but separated from it was a torment, a punishment for losing.

Ferguson was taken with the story, and what the occasion had meant to Archibald, but feared it was a little downbeat to relay to his players before the game. 'I cannae tell 'em that – it's far too much pressure,' Ferguson told Archibald. He had to send his team out brimming with their usual conviction to attack, to win. But those words – and that image of having to walk past the trophy – stuck in Ferguson's head.

Back at the hotel, the players tried to sleep. Blomqvist, in particular, was not finding that easy. The run-in had been difficult for him, with injuries and intermittent performances. He had not been involved in the previous three matches and Ferguson's advance notice that he was starting had done little to soothe the nerves.

Blomqvist struggled to fight off negative thoughts. He tried writing out notes with positive messages, repeating them to himself as a mantra. 'You can do it ... you are faster than the rest ... you are in good shape,' he told himself. It was only a partial success. 'You want some nerves,' Blomqvist says, 'but this was on the limit.'

Tossing and turning in his bed, Andy Cole felt that he was going for a pee every ten minutes. Even Dwight Yorke was struggling to relax. Denis Irwin's sleep was interrupted by Roy Keane, who remained his roommate even though the Irishman was not involved. Keane was trying to put a brave face on his omission, but it felt torturous. He talked of an invisible partition between himself, the captain, and his team.

Ferguson had told Ned Kelly, United's head of security, to keep an eye on Keane, especially after the furore leading up to the FA Cup final. He did not want any more dramas involving the Irishman, who, inevitably, turned to beers to try to soothe the aching dismay which seemed to be deepening with every hour closer to kick-off. Keane was the last to go to bed after sitting up with Paul Scholes, the injured Henning Berg and some family and friends until 4 a.m.

As the rest of the players stirred on match day, there was a nervous energy at breakfast. They had the rest of the day to kill and went for a stroll on the promenade in Sitges and then back to the hotel to pass the time. Yorke rang Graham Taylor, the man who gave him his big break in England as manager of Aston Villa and nurtured him through those difficult early times in a foreign country. As he prepared for the biggest night of his career, Yorke wanted to tell Taylor how much he appreciated all the backing.

Ole Gunnar Solskjær had rung one of his oldest friends back in Norway, a nurse, who said that he was not sure he would be able to watch the whole game because he was on a night shift. Solskjær told him that he had good vibes about the match. His roommate Jaap Stam tried to read a John Grisham novel but realised he was turning pages without registering a word.

Ferguson took some time to sit on a veranda looking out over the Mediterranean. He added some more thoughts to his autobiography, but in the whistling and humming as he moved around the hotel, the players could tell that he was as nervous as they were. The manager's family could sense it too. On the way out of the hotel in Sitges to board the bus for the ride to the Nou Camp, Jason Ferguson told his father, 'Dad, if you don't win tonight it won't change things. You will still be a great manager and we all love you.' It was a lovely message for any father to hear, but insufficient to banish the notion in Ferguson's head that he had spent his whole career preparing for this game.

Wearing their bespoke grey suits, and charcoal ties, which had been designed for the occasion by Donatella Versace at the request of Beckham – who else? – the United team boarded the coach. Ferguson had given them a short team talk before they left for the ground. The tactical work, such as it was for a disrupted team, had already been done, so this was about reinforcing strengths, and emphasising how proud he was that they had reached this point. McClaren remembers that, as with all Ferguson's messages, it was about shaping a narrative, a mood, of ambition.

As McClaren recalls it, 'This is the reason why we are here, this is the reason why we have to win this game, this is the reason why we are in football, this is the reason you could be writing your name in history. This is the reason most people dream of things, of flying to the moon. You have the chance to fly to the moon, to land on the moon tonight.' Start the engines!

Ferguson tried to fill his team with confidence, 'There isn't a team in the world that plays as well as you,' he told them. 'And that's why you mustn't be afraid. I'm very proud, and honoured, about what you've already given me and the club.'

Speaking to the players, few could remember those words. They were too wrapped up in their own nerves and preoccupations. It was an unusually quiet, almost subdued, journey along the coast. Even Ryan Giggs and Nicky Butt, who would normally be pranking someone or taking the piss, were hushed. They were all more nervous than they had ever been. Jaap Stam had played in a World Cup semi-final less than a year earlier but admitted that he had never felt churned up like this.

On a perfect day of May warmth, we came in from our own coastal base in Castelldefels, half-way between Barcelona and Sitges, to find a city that seemed to have been occupied by fans in red. Supporters of United were reckoned to outnumber Bayern fans by two to one. It certainly looked that way. Many did not have tickets, and looked around for touts. There were tales of many forgeries. Fans stood in fountains and loitered on the Ramblas.

We made our way inside in good time. For many of us, this was the biggest occasion of our reporting careers. The Nou Camp has always been a venue to savour and, for once, the pre-match ceremony was worth catching. Montserrat Caballé, the Spanish soprano, was driven out onto the pitch on a cross between a Pope-mobile and golf buggy, standing up to sing a duet with the late, great Freddie Mercury, whose face appeared on the big screen on top of the stand. It was as if he was looking down from the heavens to sing his heart out. As these ceremonies go, this one had rare emotion as Caballé's soaring soprano and Mercury's baritone joined in harmony. The lyrics felt very apposite too: 'I had this perfect dream ... I want all the world to see ... A miracle sensation ... Come alive, and shake the foundations from the skies, Shaking all our lives.'

The song finished and we prepared to start typing into our computers as the players of Manchester United and Bayern Munich appeared in the tunnel. In the Nou Camp, the players walk out to the pitch past a chapel, but it was too late for prayers. They emerged to a deafening roar. The two captains – two goal-keepers, unusually, in Peter Schmeichel and Oliver Kahn – went through the formalities and we wondered which of them would be lifting the trophy by the end of the night. Everything suggested it was going to be a tight game, including the two draws in the group stage. United had beaten every team they faced all season with the exception of Barcelona and Bayern.

Bayern had their own history to chase. They sought their first European crown since 1976 when Franz Beckenbauer had lifted his third in a row as captain. Der Kaizer was up in the stands of the Nou Camp, sitting just along from his old foe Bobby Charlton in the VIP section. A sense of history and anticipation filled us all.

In his last interview to ITV before kick-off, Ferguson told the millions watching back home that he was expecting a rollercoaster of a match. By this stage, everyone felt like Blomqvist, who had still not banished those nerves, 'My legs weren't responding as normal. I looked around the Camp Nou and they felt like jelly,' he said. And then the 1999 Champions League final kicked off.

85

Character is fate #9

Bayern Munich 1 Manchester United 2
26 May 1999, Champions League Final
   Manchester United (4-4-2): Schmeichel – G. Neville, Stam, Johnsen, Irwin – Giggs, Beckham, Butt, Blomqvist – Yorke, Cole. Substitutes: Solskjær, Sheringham, May, P. Neville, Brown, Greening, Van der Gouw (gk)
   Bayern Munich (1-4-2-3): Kahn – Matthäus – Babbel, Linke, Kuffour, Tarnat – Effenberg, Jeremies – Basler, Jancker, Zickler. Substitutes: Fink, Salihamidžić, Scholl, Helmer, Strunz, Daei, Dreher (gk)

FIRST HALF

Perhaps with that starting line-up it could never be the familiar Manchester United who turned up on the biggest night of their lives. Maybe there was a limit, after all, to the resolve and adaptability of this group of players and manager. They had found a way out of so many predicaments, but perhaps, as we watched United fall behind after five minutes and four seconds of the last Champions League final of the 20th century, they had used up all their lives.

   Carsten Jancker, the big striker leading Bayern's attack in the absence of the injured Giovane Elber, had chased down a bouncing ball just outside the area when Ronny Johnsen caught his leg. Johnsen disputed Pierluigi Collina's decision to award a free-kick, but it was hard to protest too much.

Peter Schmeichel has reviewed what happened next many times. As Mario Basler lined up the free-kick, Markus Babbel shoved himself on to the end of United's defensive wall. Nicky Butt followed, trying to barge him away. Schmeichel had wanted a four-man wall but suddenly six players were affecting his view. That, at least, was his excuse.

For his Uefa ProLicence in coaching, the United goalkeeper studied defending against free-kicks and rewound this incident more than any other. He concluded that Bayern had denied him a crucial second by blocking his line of vision. He rationalised the goal and how he came to be wrong-footed. But, for all his explanations, it still looks terrible. Commentating on ITV, Clive Tyldesley assumed Basler's shot must have taken a deflection as the ball sailed past the wall and into the far corner that Schmeichel should have been guarding. We assumed that too, but replays showed otherwise. Schmeichel looked silly and he knew it – though he remains in no rush to take the blame.

An unsettled United team was now even more on edge. Would it have been different if Roy Keane was there to radiate assertiveness under pressure, as he had done against Juventus? In the middle, David Beckham was involved in everything good for United but he was playing from deep, almost like a quarterback, as he tried to pass his team back on the front foot. There were few outlets for him to pick out. United were missing Beckham's running and crossing down the right, where Giggs had to keep cutting inside on to his left foot only to run into traffic. On the left, nerves were clearly inhibiting Jesper Blomqvist, who was looking for the easy ball rather than taking risks to run at Babbel. The selection of the Swede looked mistaken from very early on.

To watch it again, United are not as bad as I remembered – but they were certainly not the adventurous team we were used to. Lacking service, Andy Cole and Dwight Yorke felt peripheral. There was an absence of the usual attacking energy. United had played 12 more matches than Bayern since both teams qualified together from the group stage in December and, looking on, we wondered if they had run out of gas.

In contrast, Jens Jeremies was full of eager vitality in Bayern's midfield while Lothar Matthäus was frequently able to stride beyond the two centre-backs to make an extra man. With an early lead, Bayern were happy to use the roving Basler on the counter-attack or have Jancker chase down long balls, battling Jaap Stam who looked like his long-lost twin.

Alex Ferguson would later accuse Bayern of 'unambitious containment' and a 'barren philosophy', but why should they take unnecessary risks against one of the highest-scoring sides in Europe? A team with ten Germans in the starting XI had their lead and few worries at the back where the only non-German, Samuel Kuffour, the youngest player on the pitch at 22, was excelling in keeping Cole and Yorke subdued. By half-time, many of the United players knew that it simply was not working. In the biggest match of the season, after all they had accomplished to reach this point, the familiar zest had gone.

HALF-TIME

Ferguson felt a need to be upbeat. He told his players that it was all to play for. They just had to be sharper to the tackle and win back the ball quicker. They had to run twice as hard. But, once again, it was emotion rather than any alteration in tactics that would define his address. Sensing that there was nothing to be lost, he decided to reach for those words from Archibald that he had felt, on the eve of the game, might be too loaded with pressure.

Gathering his players, he told them, 'Lads, when you go out there, if you lose you'll have to go up and get your medals. You will be six feet from the European Cup, but you won't be able to touch it. And I want you to think about the fact that you'll have been so close to it and for many of you that will be the closest you will ever get. And you will hate that thought for the rest of your lives.'

It was a hell of a speech, which Ferguson concluded with familiar words to his players, 'Don't you dare come back in here without giving your all.' It was not clear how United were going to force their way back into this game, but they had to be willing to die trying.

SECOND HALF

As Teddy Sheringham went for a pee at half-time, Ferguson had pulled him for a word and told him to be ready to come on after 15 minutes if United had not forced a goal. We could say that presented the striker with a dilemma – to hope United scored, or not? – but Sheringham is honest enough to say it was not a quandary at all. 'I'm thinking I don't want the game to change. I don't want us getting back into this game. I don't want us to score, and I don't want them to score. Every time someone's attacking, I'm thinking, "Please don't score."'

He sees my raised eyebrow. Is that not a selfish attitude?

'You've got to understand the mentality as a professional footballer. I'm not a supporter, I'm a footballer who wants to play football because I can watch for the rest of my life. This might be my last chance – I was 33 at the time – to be involved in something like this. So for Man U supporters, I'll watch and celebrate with you the year after but this year I want to be a part of it.

'So I'm thinking, "Please don't score." And after 15 minutes it's, "Ted, get warmed up, you're going on." Wow. What a place, pristine pitch, I hadn't played or been there before. A special place, just awesome, like a gladiator's arena, the Colosseum, beautiful. If ever there's a place where the final should be played, that's it for me, the Nou Camp. So, I get the chance to go on, but things still weren't great.'

The game had been screaming out for United to make a change right from the start of the second half. For ITV viewers at home, Ron Atkinson talked about the need to have Giggs and Beckham back in natural positions, perhaps by putting Johnsen in midfield. He also mentioned using Sheringham.

Shortly after Basler tried to score from the halfway line in the 64th minute, catching Schmeichel out of his goal but shooting just over the crossbar, Sheringham was introduced for Blomqvist. There was no surprise that it was the Swede coming off. He knew from his restless preparations that he had never been in the best state to contribute. When he reflects on the night, his mind goes back to a chance in the 55th minute when Giggs hit an inswinging cross from the right and he could not quite apply the finish, sending the ball over the crossbar. 'I can't really reach it, but I should have done,' he says ruefully.

Sheringham's introduction meant a change of shape for United. The midfield became a diamond, with Yorke at the tip of it to link midfield and attack. Giggs was now back in a role on the left, while Beckham shuffled to the right with Butt at the base. It was a more attacking deployment which required a lot of Beckham, in particular, to help out Butt in central midfield while also creating width on the right. But, with 67 minutes elapsed, it marked the first time that United looked something like their usual selves.

According to Gary Neville, 'The second that David came to the right-hand side was the second we believed we had a chance to score a goal and do something. It was the first time that the game came back to some normality for us; the movements, patterns, crosses, precision of the passes into the strikers. For me the game only began when he came in front of me because the partnership I had with him for about five years was telepathic. He was our best player in the final but it was only when we had more of the familiar patterns and combinations that we all started to play.'

United perked up but, in taking more risks, they were bound to leave more space for Bayern, who responded to United's substitution by bringing on Mehmet Scholl for Zickler. It was a clever move which allowed the deft Scholl to exploit the gaps in front of the United defence where Butt was now a sole sentry. The game was more even, but Bayern carried the greater goal threat. In the 73rd minute, Schmeichel saved from Effenberg, who had been unexpectedly quiet, tipping a shot on the counter-attack over the crossbar.

United's search for the goal was allowing Bayern space, and in the 79th minute Basler went on a swaggering run from deep inside his own half, evading a sliding tackle from Beckham out near the right touchline and galloping 50 yards, twisting Johnsen inside out on the edge of United's area. He slipped the ball to Scholl who was heading towards the right of the box but chipped back the other way. As the ball sailed over Schmeichel's head, his heart sank because he knew it was in and the game was over. There is a photograph which captures Scholl wheeling around and already celebrating his decisive goal.

With the strange calm of someone resigned to their fate, Schmeichel turned around to watch the ball fly into the net, only to see it rebound back off the post straight into his arms. Convention would call it a scare for United, but what is striking is the lack of fright; the businesslike way that Schmeichel immediately sets about moving United upfield.

According to the goalkeeper, there was almost a sense of liberation in surviving a chance like that – nothing to lose and all the more reason to go into what he calls 'risk mode'. As he put it in his autobiography, *One*, 'You stop caring about formation and tactical convention. You do not worry what it looks like; you ignore the chance the opposition might score again and embarrass you. You shut out negatives; every pass, movement, action is a positive one. You put strikers on, you throw defenders forward. Sometimes goalkeepers too. There is nothing you won't put on the line.'

Bayern's chances, like that shot against the woodwork, were the price to pay for taking risks. And United had no choice than to keep gambling.

With ten minutes left, Lothar Matthäus signalled that his work was done. At 38, it was understandable that he was tiring. He had played as much in midfield as sweeping behind the defence and Thorsten Fink's fresh legs could see out the remainder of the game.

The most transformative change of the night would come soon after, with 80 minutes and 41 seconds on the clock, when Ole Gunnar Solskjær replaced Cole, who had struggled to make any impression. The service had been lacking and, as Cole admitted, he had become increasingly tense. The change was striker for striker but it was removing an inhibited player for one who brought fresh belief. As ever Solskjær arrived with purpose and an expectation that he would at least enjoy a chance, or three. His first touch less than 30 seconds after coming on was a glancing header from a Neville cross that forced a decent flying save from Oliver Kahn. It was the first serious save the Bayern goalkeeper had made.

'Oh, what a story that would've been!' Clive Tyldesley said on ITV commentary.

United were pressing but still it was Bayern who created the best opportunity. In the 84th minute from a corner, the ball bounced around the penalty area and Jancker pulled off an over-head kick from close range which smacked back off the crossbar. Bayern might have scored four times between the 73rd and 84th minute. By now, George Best had seen enough. Gary Lineker was sitting just behind the United legend and saw him walk out, heading to the bar. Why stay around to watch the Germans celebrate? He had lost the faith.

His successors, trying to emulate the heroics of 1968, had not. Not quite yet. As Best departed, the game was bubbling up into a contest almost for the first time. Bayern had fended off United without any dramas for 86 minutes but suddenly came a rush of action; four chances in 90 seconds. A backheel from Solskjær to Sheringham who could not apply enough power in his shot to properly trouble Kahn; Yorke heading Beckham's cross too far in front of Sheringham; Yorke miskicking horribly after a low cross from Gary Neville; Solskjær directing a header goalward which Kahn saved.

It was a late rally but too little, too late as Beckham's impatient foul on Effenberg allowed Bayern to waste more seconds. As the clock ticked down, Basler was replaced by Hasan Salihamidžić and came to the sidelines motioning to Bayern fans to cheer. He had good reason to believe that he had scored the only goal, the winning goal, in the Champions League final.

As he took his place on the bench, Bayern staff were gathering victory T-shirts and caps for the players to wear in the post-match celebrations. It seemed to the world that this was over.

Even Alex Ferguson was running out of defiance. Down beneath us, he stood practising how to be a good loser. He told himself to accept the defeat with dignity and acknowledge that it was just not United's year.

86

102 seconds

As the clock ticks beyond 89 minutes, Lennart Johansson, the Uefa president, rises up from his seat in the VIP section. He has to make it down to pitchside for the trophy presentation. 'I'm sorry,' he says to Bobby Charlton on his way past.

The ball is deep in United territory. As Denis Irwin plays a long ball forward towards the strikers, Clive Tyldesley on television reflects the sense that time has run out for Manchester United. 'We are in the last of the 90 minutes. What we need now is for the fourth official to hold up a board with about 20 on it . . .'

From our seats, time is even more pressing. With orders from our offices to send the copy for the first editions before the final whistle, one colleague has already filed his 1,000 words about a sad conclusion for Peter Schmeichel as the great goalkeeper's last game for United ends in defeat. Another borrows the famous quote that Lotthar Matthäus had revived on the eve of the final that football is a simple game: 22 men run around and then the Germans win. Matthäus is sitting smugly in the Bayern dugout, his job done, waiting to claim his prize.

I have written about David Beckham and how, after a year when he has overcome so much venom to play the season of his life, he has exhausted his supplies of defiance. Try as he might, and he has fought tenaciously in midfield, he cannot conjure one last game-changing cross or heroic free-kick.

And then, as the clock ticks towards 90 minutes, Markus

Babbel overhits a loose pass back behind Thomas Linke. The defender is pressured by Solskjær into conceding a throw-in high up on United's left wing.

90:03

As the fourth official holds up a board showing three added minutes, Gary Neville sprints across the field from right-back, telling Giggs to leave the throw-in to him. Neville is exhausted, the only outfield player to have been on the pitch for every minute of United's last ten games of the season, but something compels him to keep going.

When we spoke for *Red*, he explained, 'I've wondered a few times since, "Why did I do that? What was I doing running all that way?" And it's simple, really: it's what I'd been taught to do since I was a kid at United. You keep playing, you keep trying, you keep sprinting until the death.' His run is not just the response to one desperate situation but the instincts born of a lifetime at this club, serving under this manager. It is a small thing and yet integral to United's spirit. Keep running. Keep striving.

Neville's throw is headed away out of the penalty area towards Beckham, who still has energy to beat Scholl to the loose ball and drive past his marker. He plays a neat lay-off to release Neville who is still stuck out as an auxiliary left-winger, for perhaps the first time in his life. Countless hours practising on his weaker foot as a kid, kicking a ball against the wall at the Cliff, feel invaluable as, betraying a furious concentration not to miscue, Neville's first-time low cross clips a Bayern defender and is put behind by the stretching Effenberg.

'And that's my contribution to the greatest comeback in history,' Neville laughs.

United have a corner. And then Peter Schmeichel runs upfield.

90:23

'Can Manchester United score? They always score,' Tyldesley says.

Schmeichel is very proud of 11 goals scored in his career, one fewer than Gary Neville and Jamie Carragher combined. But this charge forward is unsanctioned. 'What the hell is he doing?' Ferguson asks Steve McClaren as the big goalkeeper gallops into the Bayern penalty area.

As Beckham prepares to take the corner, he is guided by years aiming for Schmeichel at the Cliff. As he told me, 'When I used to warm up Peter, he would absolutely bollock me for hitting the first man, not putting it into an area that was right for him. He was so harsh on us but that's what sets you up when you are playing in moments like this in the European Cup final. You're losing 1-0 and you don't want to mess up what might be the only opportunity we've got to score a goal. You don't want to hit the first man. You don't want to over-hit it. Once I saw Peter coming up I knew that I just had to put it in an area and let them fight for it, let him get his head on it, cause the confusion. That's why the first corner is more of a chip.'

90:35

Schmeichel's presence is enough to cause confusion. Three Bayern players are drawn towards him. 'Peter Schmeichel is forward ... Beckham, in towards Schmeichel, it's come for Dwight Yorke ... cleared ... Giggs with the shot ...' Tyldesley's voice rises with excitement as he describes the penalty-box scramble.

The corner skims off Linke's head towards the back post where an unmarked Yorke struggles to head it back into the six-yard box. Fink has a chance to clear but miskicks only as far as Giggs on the edge of the area. 'It's pure panic,' Schmeichel says. 'If the player [clearing] takes a quarter of a second more, half a second longer, composes himself, he kicks it into touch and the game is over. But the panic was there.'

Giggs is on his right foot. His first-time mishit is spinning past the post but bounces to Sheringham. He swivels and catches the ball on the turn, glancing it off his shin. 'A scuff off my sock,' he says. His touch, helping the ball into the bottom corner from six yards, concludes the three most significant mis-hits in football history.

Goal?! Oliver Kahn appeals in vain for offside. Sheringham looks across to the linesman before running off to celebrate in front of the United fans, where Beckham leaps on to his back. 'I've never experienced anything like that feeling in my life,' Sheringham says of looking up at the vast bank of United fans, red flares lit, who are now leaping around with giddy abandon.

'Name on the trophy! Teddy Sheringham, with 30 seconds of added time played, has equalised for Manchester United! They are still in the European Cup!' Tyldesley proclaims, as we all look on with amazement.

In the press box, the burst of adrenalin – A goal! A story! – is first about the sporting drama but, a nanosecond later, also the urgent job at hand. Hearts pumping, we try to work out what this means. Our words, about United's defeat, are already flying back home. What now? It is going to be a scramble to correct all that copy, but at least there is going to be extra time to check in with the office and gather a few thoughts.

As we try to compose ourselves, and fresh words, Schmeichel makes it back to his penalty area and starts taking deep breaths to prepare for a whole new contest to start. Beckham feels like crying with emotion. Butt tries to ready himself, shaking his legs potentially for another 30 minutes of graft. Solskjær is delighted that the game has been extended into extra time so that he can properly feel like he has played in a Champions League final rather than just ten losing minutes at the end.

After the initial surge of relief and jubilation on the bench, McClaren interrupts the celebrations to implore Ferguson to restructure the team, thinking they need to revert to 4-4-2. He is thinking about extra time, when Golden Goal applies. 'What are we going to do? Do you want to go back to 4-4-2 and get some semblance of reality about this?' he asks.

'Steve, this game isn't finished,' Ferguson replies. He can smell it. Perhaps we all should have done. We are deep into 'Fergie Time'.

91:34

The game resumes. Bayern pump the ball forward but Jaap Stam is there to win the header and United regain possession. Irwin knocks the ball downfield to Solskjær, who is full of running. Kuffour has tracked him wide. As the clock reaches 92 minutes, Solskjær is happy to play the ball off the defender for a corner. It has taken United less than 30 seconds to win another set-piece. There is an urgency about everything United do; weariness in their opponents.

92:05

'They must be playing defensive. Schmeichel's not coming up for this one,' Ron Atkinson chuckles on ITV. Beckham runs across to take the corner, forcing stewards to move so that he has room for his run-up. This time he decides to put more pace on a ball to the near post. 'Whip this one in and let Teddy get his head on it,' he says.

Sheringham, now feeling 10-feet tall, thinks he is going to score again as the ball arrives just where he wants it, but he has jumped a fraction early. He knows the best he can do is flick it on into the six-yard box. Bayern make only half-hearted attempts to stop him. 'I thought if I head it for goal it's going to go over the bar. In that split second all I can do is head it into an area and hope someone is there,' Sheringham says.

Stam is at the far post thinking the ball is about to fall to him. Fortunately, it is Solskjær who intervenes rather than the big defender. Kuffour has been holding on to Solskjær's shirt as the ball comes in but he releases it, and is stuck on the wrong side of the striker. Solskjær sticks out his right leg. It is a startling finish; not so much a shot as an instinctive diversion of the ball into the roof of the net.

It could so easily fly over the crossbar or catch a man on the post, but Solskjær has put the ball in the one place, straight up, where it has the best chance. It is not a finish he has ever practised. How could you? 'Instinct took over,' he says. 'If you try that again, you guide the ball over or wide. It's lucky but you earn your luck at times.'

Solskjær, who has not played a minute in the quarter- and semi-finals, initially wonders if he is offside. He need not worry. He has just scored the single most significant goal in the history of Manchester United.

92:17

'And Solskjær has won it!' Tyldesley exclaims, as Phil Neville leads a charge of United substitutes off the bench, sprinting across the Nou Camp turf to pile on top of Solskjær and the rest of the team.

'I don't believe it, but it's happened!' Alan Green screams on BBC Radio.

It is the most amazing thing I have seen in sport. I want to exult in the moment yet that goal has plunged us into a nightmare. Now there will be no extra time. The deadline is, well, several minutes ago. The piece I have filed on the biggest night of my career makes no sense; a report of a game that United have lost. And now they have won it in the most dramatic circumstances imaginable (not that any of us could have imagined this).

I grab the landline phone to speak to the desk. In the bedlam inside the Nou Camp they cannot hear anything I say, or vice versa. I try to scream at them. 'I NEED TO CHANGE THE COPY!!!' Nothing comes back. I try frantically typing some words into the computer and sending them down the phone line but the deafening noise has scrambled not just our minds but the technology. Covering sport can be the best job in the world but, at this moment, I feel sick.

We look down to the pitch and try to take in all we can while screaming down phone lines. The TV producers will cut to a shot behind the United goal just in time to catch Schmeichel pulling off a remarkably athletic cartwheel. They will show Bayern fans looking shocked, dumbfounded. Some are crying. In the United end, there is delirium.

My most vivid memory is of staring down at the Bayern players lying prone on the pitch, as if they have been struck down by lightning. Kuffour moves, but only to writhe on the ground as though suddenly preyed on by a Dementor. Pierluigi Collina, the referee, tries to lift the defender, imploring him to stand up for what few seconds remain. He rolls over, despairing, weeping and pounding the ground with his fist as if trying to beat sense into a world that does not make sense any more.

'Manchester United have reached the promised land!' Tyldesley says. 'The two substitutes have scored the two goals in stoppage time and nobody will ever win a European Cup more dramatically than this!'

93:22

There have been 102 seconds on the match clock between Sheringham's equaliser and Solskjær's winner. The ball has only been in play for around 30 of those. There are even fewer left.

The Bayern players eventually take to their feet for the final to resume. They trudge towards the centre circle like the remnants of a vanquished army in shambolic retreat. The ball is in play for no more than 12 seconds; enough time for Effenberg to hoof it forward, and Stam to challenge for a defensive header, and the ball to fall for Butt to volley clear to the halfway line.

The shrill blast from Collina's whistle signals that the game is over. Johansson emerges from the lift and walks to the side of the pitch. 'What the hell has happened?' he asks. 'The winners are crying and the losers are dancing.'

Has football ever generated such extremes of emotion? For Bayern it is not a tragedy but it sure as hell feels like one. For United players the sensation is far beyond winning a game, or a trophy or even a Treble. It feels almost supernatural. Most collapse onto the pitch. Whether that was exhaustion, exhilaration or disbelief, they could not tell you. They are overwhelmed; shocked by their own deeds.

Gary Neville talks of 'an out-of-body experience' after Solskjær scored, lying on his back and crying. 'I am not religious, I don't go to church but I'm looking up thinking "what's just happened?!" It's mind-blowing.' When he finally catches up with Solskjær, all he can think to say is, 'You've no idea what you've just done.' No one in a United shirt can conceive of the magnitude of all they have accomplished.

It is surreal. Emotions bubble up from deep within. Giggs falls on his front and weeps on a football field for the only time in his career. Somehow Beckham keeps running, all the way down the other end to the United fans. As players embrace and leap on top of each other, Cole celebrates and then takes himself off to sit alone, reminiscing about how far he has come, thinking about family, recalling the slights and the sacrifices that drove him on. He thinks of all those times he had been written off. And now, here he is, in the Nou Camp, as part of the most successful English team in history.

How to make sense of this story? As the players jump into each other's arms, no one does it more beautifully than my colleague Oliver Holt, who writes in *The Times* of the 'lust for glory' that has propelled this team to victory. In less time than it took for Sheringham and Solskjær to score those goals, his fingers rattle the words into his machine, 'A thousand flashbulbs recorded the moment. When the final whistle went, they lit up the Noú Camp as though it was noonday in the Barcelona sun and froze the Manchester United players with their arms in the air. It was the instant they passed into legend.'

We all try to capture these moments amid the frenzy. The drama is what we will always remember, more even than the remarkable achievement of winning the Treble. The matter of trophies feels secondary to a comeback that has almost defied belief. Wherever this team stands among the greats, no side has ever produced such drama.

'My whole approach to life could be boiled down to 101 [*sic*] seconds of injury time,' the United manager will conclude some years later – when all of us have caught our breath.

87

Football, bloody hell

Millions of words have been spoken and written about one night in Barcelona yet, all these years later, still none more succinct, evocative or unimprovable than the three which came spontaneously out of the mouth of Alex Ferguson just a couple of minutes after the final whistle.

As we struggled up in the press box to do justice to the sporting miracle we had seen, racking brains and bashing away at keyboards searching for the *mots justes*, Ferguson captured all the emotion and drama perfectly in just three words.

There will be those who claim that 'O Jogo Bonito' – 'the beautiful game' – is the ultimate expression of love for football, especially given that it was popularised by Pelé, but I will take a beaming, disbelieving Glaswegian trying to make sense of the greatest night of his life by giving perhaps the finest of all post-match interviews (yes, ever) to exclaim: 'Football, bloody hell.'

Such an expression could only come from a football lover. A romantic. You can call Ferguson many things – and we frequently did – but that phrase revealed, at heart, the kid from the tenements of Glasgow who loved the game for its risk and its daring and what it could reveal about character. He was saluting the game's ability to lift us out of the mundanities of life with great and unpredictable deeds.

'Football, bloody hell.' There is something universal – and

yet still something idiosyncratically Ferguson – about it. The perfect words at the perfect moment.

He had been dragged to appear in front of ITV's Gary Newbon almost straight from the final whistle. Newbon's own voice cracked with emotion and adrenalin as he went to ask the first question. 'Alex Ferguson, they put you through the mill, into injury time, almost lost the cup and you win it – the new European champions, the Treble, the dream come true for you . . .'

Ferguson let out a strangled gasp, took a deep breath and clutched his head as if he still could not quite fathom what had happened. There was a smile on his face which many in the world may never have seen from this furious, driven man. He was in a place of bliss. He wore a boyish look of astonishment. 'I can't believe it, I can't believe it,' he says. 'Football, bloody hell.'

He paused and quickly found the message he wanted to impart. 'But they never give in – and that's what won it. I'm so proud of them.'

Later he would reflect that the interview felt like a flood of gibberish. 'I didn't mind sounding like an idiot,' he said. 'There was no happier idiot on the planet.' In fact, in less than 30 seconds, he had conjured phrases that will be recalled for as long as anyone seeks to understand Manchester United and Ferguson and all that made them special.

'Never Give In' became the title of a documentary about his life. But 'Football, bloody hell' – well, that speaks not just for Ferguson, or for his greatest night, but for all that draws billions of us back to this endlessly captivating game which can enrage us and inspire us; make us hope and dream and despair; fills us with excitement and wonder; and will never cease to enthral for as long as people kick a ball around a pitch.

88

When the facts are unbelievable

'I am not a religious person at all but sometimes you do look back and have that feeling that it was meant to be. A sense of fate. And so it is written.'

Written, and said. When Clive Tyldesley proclaimed 'name on the trophy' on ITV in the seconds after Teddy Sheringham had equalised, it was commentary at its finest. In four words, he had captured for a vast audience back home a sense of unstoppable forces shaping history. It was a gamble – the score was only 1-1, after all – but Tyldesley went with his instincts, his gut feeling, and was rewarded for taking a risk, which was fitting of the occasion. He had done so after a pause, an expert pause, which added to the gravity.

Name on the trophy. There are millions of United fans for whom this night is still recalled by the words that Tyldesley and Ron Atkinson, his co-commentator, said that evening. It proved the pinnacle for the man off the telly.

Tyldesley produces condensed versions of his match notes from the biggest games he has covered to go on office walls, and the 1999 version from the Nou Camp is by far his most popular. The original pages were bought by Alex Ferguson at a charity auction. The list of facts and stats were useful for commentary but, as Tyldesley says, the challenge was in capturing the great tumult of emotions. He had prepared one line, and was delighted to be able to use it.

'Manchester United have reached the Promised Land,' he said once Solskjær had scored. It was crisp and true.

From his seat high up in the Gods at the Nou Camp, Marcel Reif looked beneath to the scenes of devastation among the Bayern Munich players. He knew tens of millions of viewers on RTL were waiting for him to make sense of what felt to many like a tragedy. In his own state of disbelief, he spoke from the heart. 'I know we are expected to analyse and explain what happened,' Reif said to that vast audience at home. 'I'm not able to, and I don't want to. Why not just be sad?'

And then he turned off his microphone and let the pictures do all the talking.

Reif remembers the line like he was commentating last night, not more than two decades ago. 'There are not many times I look back and I think I said it perfectly, but that is one,' he explains. 'There was nothing to analyse. Maybe the next day you could talk about how you defend corners but not at that moment. That would be too cheap. You have to call on emotion rather than fact when the facts are unbelievable.'

Reif, 72, has commentated on thousands of matches. There has never been one like the Nou Camp in 1999. 'Maybe you could say when Chelsea beat Bayern Munich in their own living room in the Champions League final [in 2012]. But that was not emotional like this because that was lost. This game was already won.'

He reflects on an astonishing night with a lingering sense of disbelief: 'Sometimes commentating is knowing when to shut up. Sometimes there is nothing to be said.'

89

The celebrations that never stop

One of the great privileges of being in the Nou Camp that night came after the final whistle, watching the celebrations that continued long after the game was over; a communion between fans and players that had been 31 years in the making. All that yearning, and craving; all those years when the summit seemed impossibly distant; the more recent times when Manchester United teams had been so close they could almost touch the prize only to falter and slide back to the bottom.

United fans had been dreaming of this moment, some for a lifetime, and they were going to make the most of it. ITV went off for the news but they could have cleared the schedules for hours with the scenes of delirium.

As the United players went over to the fans with their medals and the trophy, club anthems were sung with a gusto not heard before, or since. Flares were lit, tears shed, and memories made for life. There were predictable renditions of 'We Are The Champions' and, out of nowhere, a huge communal singalong to 'Sit Down', the catchy anthem by Manchester band James. But perhaps the most spine-tingling moments came from pin-drop silence. The United fans behind the goal where history was made went quiet as each of their heroes took a turn to grab the trophy and then let out a mighty roar as, one by one, they held it aloft.

Peter Schmeichel was up first, his last act as a United player to lift the cup that had been the club's magnificent obsession.

He passed the trophy on to Teddy Sheringham, who had not felt much love from the United fans. Suddenly tens of thousands were bellowing his name. 'Oh, Teddy, Teddy, he went to Man Utd and won the lot . . .' Sheringham joined in the singing. The FA Cup final had been rewarding but this was something else; lifelong adoration guaranteed by one goal off his sock.

On to David Beckham, who had come through so much in this year of vilification, meeting the hatred with the most out-standing football of his life. He had been United's best player in the final, scrapping right until the end and delivering those two corners. The fans had thrown a protective arm around him after the World Cup and now they let out a roar of appreciation.

Nicky Butt came forward and gave a waggle of his hips, a rare bit of showiness from a player who had stepped up whenever required and never complained when he was omitted. His mate Ryan Giggs was still laughing at that little shimmy as he took the trophy; the wing genius who had come through injuries to score such crucial goals against Juventus and Arsenal to keep the Treble alive.

It was time for the quiet men to step forward. Denis Irwin kissed the trophy and the crowd cheered this 33-year-old paragon of consistency. Then Ronny Johnsen mockingly strained to lift it, and managed to do so without injuring himself. United were at their best with this speedy defender in the team alongside Jaap Stam, who had grown in stature with every month of the season to justify his fee as the world's most expensive defender. Stam had given a new authority to a defence in which Gary Neville had made an unequalled 28 consecutive starts from January to the climax, through all the tests, and never played better as Beckham's accomplice.

Dwight Yorke came forward. Of course he could not perform his trophy moment without a jig and a pirouette. Then it was the turn of Ole Gunnar Solskjær, who had scored the goal that they would be talking about as long as there is a football club called Manchester United.

As Andy Cole took the cup, the crowd burst into his song – 'he gets the ball, scores a goal . . .' – and suddenly this man of shy reserve was laughing and dancing as tens of thousands roared him on and he skipped around.

Roy Keane and Paul Scholes had initially hung back from the celebrations but the two of them were eventually persuaded to walk through a guard of honour. The rest of their teammates formed an arch, and Keane and Scholes ducked through it before collecting the trophy and lifting it high together. It was a beautiful moment and brought one of the loudest cheers of the night. Heartfelt appreciation, and some consolation, for these two players who had suffered on the sidelines.

Eventually, they returned to the dressing room where Keane covered his teammates in champagne and Yorke danced, inevitably, and Beckham posed for photos with the trophy, inevitably, and Albert Morgan, the kitman, was thrown in the team bath, inevitably. The celebrations were only just starting.

It was long after midnight when they reached the banqueting hall at the plush Arts Hotel, on Barcelona's seafront. Hundreds of close friends and family were waiting to celebrate with them. The Champions League trophy was passed around to be held, touched and kissed like a precious new-born baby. A delirious Alex Ferguson, walking along a corridor of the hotel, whisked a woman off her feet for a celebratory waltz. It is as if they were all floating on joy.

There were presentations to be done. Some were formal, as Martin Edwards handed out remaining medals to the staff like Steve McClaren and Dave Fevre, the physio, but others were private moments. Albert the kitman had been wearing Peter Schmeichel's Rolex to keep it safe during games. Schmeichel took the watch off his wrist and handed it over as a fare-well present.

With the trophy placed in the middle of the dance floor, they swayed into the early hours to the disco. When the DJ stopped, Foo Foo Lammar, the Manchester drag queen (real name Frank), went up on stage to perform an impromptu show. By now there were a few who had drunk too much. James Edwards, son of the chairman, said something untoward and Giggs's mum Lynne told him to watch his tongue. When Edwards junior was rude a second time, Giggs leapt in with his fists. He was so drunk that he did more damage to a chair as the two men rolled around on the floor. Butt was on hand to separate them.

As dawn broke, hotel staff implored the players to wrap up the party so that they could start to set the tables for breakfast. Gary Neville wandered out through the half-light along the seafront of Barcelona, reflecting on all that happened, wanting the night to never end. It was the first sleepless night of his life.

No prizes for guessing who was making the most of the evening. With a cigar seemingly fixed in his mouth, given to him by Schmeichel, Yorke led the dancing and drinking. Around 4 a.m., as some of the couples started heading to bed, Yorke was in no mood to stop. He grabbed Jordi Cruyff, who had grown up in the city where his father was an icon, and demanded to be taken out. After a couple of bars they were running out of options until they came across a 'gentlemen's club'. A Champions League medal in his pocket and beautiful women walking around less than fully dressed, Yorke was in heaven.

As the sun came up and the clock ticked towards departure time for the team bus, Yorke invited the most beautiful woman back to the hotel. As the rest of the United staff were coming down for breakfast and loading the gear to depart to the airport, Yorke was escorting his scantily clad companion through the lobby. He cannot recall sharing a word, or knowing her name, but he thinks that they had sex three times. He was so drunk he fell off the bed.

Seeing the time, Yorke threw on his suit, grabbed his medal, said a quick 'muchas gracias' and dashed down to the bus. He was the last man on, still with that cigar in his mouth and a bigger smile than ever.

As Yorke was enjoying himself, we gathered at the Arts Hotel to talk to Ferguson. He sat outside on a first-floor terrace with a dozen or so British journalists. His voice was a little hoarse but he had the contentment, the completion of a man who had solved the mysteries of life. Ferguson's work was never done but, for once, he could afford to pause and to savour all that he and his players had achieved. He was still claiming, as he had done on the eve of the final, that defeat would not have crushed him, but he knew just how close he had come to facing those questions – would United ever win it? Was he condemned always to fall short?

'I was not going to let it obsess me,' he told us. 'The European Cup was always going to be the thing you strive for, but even last night I was relaxed about it. I was accepting that we were going to lose. I was not going to get myself twisted inside about it because I have got a life to live. Now, though, I do feel a sense of fulfilment that I did not feel before.'

He knew the manner of the victory could not have been more perfect. A comfortable 3-0 win would have been deeply satisfying but there was something so right about the comeback and the drama, and all it said about his team. The way they had fought back from the dead had confirmed to the world that this team had a special quality, a personality that went beyond even the feat of the Treble.

'I hope that 20 years from now, when they talk about the

chief characteristic of this particular team, they will always be remembered for their last-minute goals, for never giving in. The 1968 side were men of their time and now my team cannot be ignored. They are men of their time now. I mean, two goals in injury time, who would have thought it? Maybe we were meant to win it. Maybe there was an element of destiny. With Matt's birthday and Bayern Munich all in there, I kept hoping there was a meaning to it. You could tell Matt was looking down on me.'

Ferguson is a hard man but there was romance and senti-mentality as he talked about the sense of fate, of destiny. This kinship with Busby was not affected or contrived. In winning the European Cup, a great manager from the shipyards of Glasgow had emerged from the shadow of a mighty predecessor raised in the coalfields little more than ten miles down the road in Lanarkshire.

Busby still had an office at Old Trafford when Ferguson joined the club. Pipe smoke would waft along the corridors to indicate that the great man was present. He had seen the return to glory before he died in January 1994. He knew that Ferguson was determined to build a United team with the same ethos that the public must be entertained by football of youth, expression and adventure. The game was there to be won, not treated as an exercise in waiting for the other side to make a mistake.

'I was prepared to risk and if you risk in a game of football you deserve to succeed,' Ferguson had told us straight after the final. There are many ways to win a football game but who could dis-pute the sentiment that this was a team that had earned any lucky breaks, and last-gasp goals, through its unrelenting commitment to attack?

To be sitting there with Ferguson counted as another privilege. We were not just witness to sporting greatness but had an ink-ling of how it must have been to listen to the wisdom of Busby after Best and Charlton had helped him to the European Cup

31 years earlier. That had been the club's crowning glory – and now there was another European triumph befitting this famous institution. Busby had come back from near-death in Munich and the shattering of his brilliant Babes to build beloved champions of Europe. Now Ferguson could stand proud alongside him on the back of another sporting miracle.

As we made our way out of the Arts Hotel to fill the souvenir supplements that would celebrate this triumph, Roy Keane walked past looking worse for wear and in one of his dark moods. His eyes were black. Perhaps he was simply hungover, but it looked like he was having a difficult time, and still coming to terms with missing out. It must have hurt to see such remarkable scenes and feel so cut-off.

One United player I spoke to felt strongly that the captain should have been invited up to lift the trophy along with Peter Schmeichel and Ferguson, even if he would almost certainly have refused. Keane declined when Ken Ramsden, a club official, invited him to lead the players off the plane with the trophy when it landed back in Manchester. That job fell to Schmeichel, and the players were saluted from the moment they disembarked, with cheers from airport workers and baggage handlers. Any exhaustion from a sleepless night evaporated as the players saw the first fans at the airport clamouring for a look. It was a glimpse of Beatlemania.

Fans lined the roads even as the open-top bus came in from the airport. Estimates varied from several hundred thousand to as high as 750,000 people on the streets – who knows how anyone gauges these things? – as the bus arrived in Manchester with the players and staff showing off their three trophies. The turn into Deansgate revealed an ocean of people. People clambered up lampposts and hung off scaffolding. Ferguson recalled seeing a building site with people perched on steel beams.

Teddy Sheringham is not given to gushing emotion, but he described the view as overwhelming. 'It was an intensely moving experience,' he said. Andy Cole concurred that it was one of the most memorable experiences of his life. A delighted Dwight Yorke saw a woman whip off her top and swing a bra around her head. He would notice these things.

Gary Neville says that if he had to take one moment from these 11 magical days – 'the best 11 days you can imagine' – it would be turning into Deansgate and seeing the vast sea of faces. 'That was the moment when Manchester became my heaven.' There was one man in particular that stuck in his mind. He was screaming himself hoarse, veins popping out of his neck. To Neville, he looked like a man enjoying the best moment of his life. There were countless thousands just like him.

The euphoria was about football but there was also intense civic pride. After all those years of seeing Liverpool not just as domestic champions but repeatedly kings of Europe, Manchester now had the sporting glory to go with its global renown as a cultural, musical capital. Was there anywhere cooler on earth?

There were 17,000 raucous fans inside the MEN Arena at the end of the bus route. Ferguson led the players inside holding the European Cup; Schmeichel behind with the Premier League trophy; Keane holding the FA Cup. They climbed the stairs on to a platform in the middle of the venue and put the silverware on parade. It was not an elaborate event – a few words of thanks from Ferguson, Keane and Schmeichel and lots of waving – but no one minded. Just to be there, to share in the moment, to sing hymns of praise was enough. The players stood and acknowledged the fans and then Yorke picked up the European Cup, jigging along with Cole as they made their way out.

By now the rest of the players were ready to go home and savour the experience with their families, but Yorke was still not done. He went to the Reform Club in Manchester and was there until 2 a.m. Staggering out, he wondered how he was going to make it home when a police officer saw him. And so Yorke was given a lift in the back of a riot van with that cigar still in his mouth. He still has the cigar in his trophy cabinet along with his medals.

A shower, some sleep and then he was off to the Rectory in Wilmslow where he was soon dancing on the table and ordering B52s by the dozen for anyone and everyone. He seemed determined to prove what Ferguson would say of that moment when the ball flew into the roof of the net in Barcelona: 'The celebrations begun by that goal will never really stop.'

90

Arise, Sir Alex

The celebrations were in full swing inside the Nou Camp when Alastair Campbell, a guest of Alex Ferguson, suddenly remembered an urgent mission. Richard Wilson, the cabinet secretary, had told Campbell that if United won the Champions League, they would rush Ferguson into the honours list with a knighthood. But officials would need to know within 24 hours if he would accept. Campbell saw Cathy Ferguson sitting by the United directors and vaulted over a railing, ignored a protesting steward and asked if she thought her husband would want to be elevated to Sir Alex. 'Don't you think he's won enough already?' she replied, a grounding force even as the rest of the world put Ferguson on a pedestal.

Undeterred, Campbell left a message on Ferguson's phone. The United manager called back and asked to be allowed to sleep on it. He wanted to contemplate what his parents would say, especially his socialist father, but any reservations Ferguson may have harboured were soon brushed aside by his sons. He rang Campbell the following day to say he would be honoured. The knighthood was the most notable of awards showered on Ferguson over the coming months – Freedom of Glasgow and Freedom of Manchester among them – now that he had, beyond any argument, joined the pantheon of the great football managers.

A couple of weeks after the Champions League final, Ferguson's name was confirmed in the Queen's birthday honours list and he

joined the roll of footballing knights which had expanded significantly in the '90s, with Sir Tom Finney, Sir Geoff Hurst, Sir
Bobby Charlton, and an honorary knighthood for Pelé all in that
decade. This trend was another sign of the mainstream boom for
football and how the game, after years of snobbery and contempt
from politicians and beyond, had been embraced by all classes.

New Labour could not wait to elevate Ferguson, but then he
was a vocal backer of Tony Blair and, in 1998, was revealed to be
among the donors who gave more than £5,000 to the Labour
Party. The former shop steward for the shipyard apprentices in
Glasgow had come a long way.

91

Where were you?

Legend has it that one Manchester United fan entered London's Blackwall Tunnel at 1-0 down and emerged when they were 2-1 up. He cannot have been as stunned – or regretful – as those who walked out of the Nou Camp before the finale, moaning about Alex Ferguson's selections and complaining about how the Germans always win. They caught the Metro ahead of the crowds, but also missed perhaps the most thrilling moment of their lives.

If you want to hear about the ecstasy that sport can deliver, the deep fulfilment, just find a United fan who was in Barcelona on 26 May 1999. Alex Ferguson's comment about never-ending celebrations was right. Ole Gunnar Solskjær has been greeted almost every day of his life by United fans, mostly middle-aged or elderly men, wanting to tell him where they were, who they were with, what they were wearing, and how they celebrated when he put the ball in the Germans' net.

As Solksjaer says, 'They come up and say, "That was the best night of my life – but don't tell the wife."' Every player from the '99 team hears it to this day. 'I haven't stopped meeting people wanting to take me back there,' Andy Cole says. 'They'll say, "That night in Barcelona changed my life, forever."'

Just to mention to people that I was writing this book would draw a stream of vivid, wonderful memories from those lucky enough to be in the Nou Camp, or watching at home or in a pub or bar. Interviewing billionaire Sir Jim Ratcliffe, a United fan who was inside the stadium, he was instantly off on a story about one of the unforgettable days of his life. 'I've never kissed so many men as those moments after Solskjær scored,' he laughed. 'Three minutes you never forget in your lifetime, taken from this miserable place to this high that you can't describe.' Priceless, even for a man of his wealth.

A friend, Stuart, was 16 and had a GCSE exam scheduled the following morning after the game but could not miss the chance to go to Barcelona with his dad to support his beloved United. He was meant to arrive back on a plane in the early hours in time for his exam, but the flight was delayed. His dad had to ring up the school to ask for permission for him to arrive late, on no sleep, to sit the paper. Did he pass? 'Who cares?' he laughed.

When I spoke to Sheringham, he worked out that it had been more than 8,000 days since he scored that equaliser. 'And I reckon on average I've spoken about it once a day ever since. That's a lot of times to have the same conversation, but I love it. I love people coming up to me now saying, "I was in South Africa with a load of Germans, and I was the only English person there and it was amazing," or "I was in Zimbabwe and found this little television and managed to find the game." So many people give me these stories. They say, "You must have heard it a million times," but I'll say, "No, no, tell me, tell me so I can relive it with you." I love to hear about that night. It's one of those moments when people know exactly where they were.'

Of course, there was the other side of the story, too. I met Annette, a German film producer and passionate Bayern fan, who was straight off in her own world of reminiscence when I mentioned I was writing about one night in Barcelona. She told me how, after 89 minutes, she nipped away from the television at home in Munich to go to the toilet and put on her shoes to be ready to dash out as soon as the game was over. This was going to be the party of all parties after 23 years waiting for her club to be European champions.

'I threw on a jacket and got a bottle of Prosecco from the refrigerator,' she says, ready to join the hordes on Leopoldstraße. Then she heard a sharp scream from her boyfriend in the TV room. 'He couldn't utter a sound. I hadn't been in the room for exactly 120 seconds and during that time the dream had turned into a nightmare.'

How would she describe the feeling? 'It was like bad sex,' she said. 'Very bad sex!'

Her cousin, Sven, was a truck driver and Bayern fan who drove to Barcelona and picked up four tickets from touts for 500 marks [around £160] each, which was ten times the regular price. 'It was the first and last time I saw my friends cry,' he said. 'When I think about it today, my eyes get watery. Afterwards we went to my truck and drank a lot. I have no more memories after that. All I know is that it wasn't until two days later that I felt able to drive back to Germany.'

There are countless stories and memories that illustrate the universal power of sport. Fans who flew to random points in Europe because it was the only flight available and then had to hitch-hike to Catalonia. Those who came with tickets or, in many cases, without given that more than 55,000 United fans were estimated to have travelled despite an allocation of 38,000.

Many still have the ticket stubs – real or forgeries – that they keep like precious relics. They show that it was just £12 to sit up in the Gods, in the nosebleed section, and £26 in lower tiers behind the goals. Hundreds are thought to have blagged their way in with fake tickets. Everyone remembers where they were.

*

Back in England, the TV audience peaked at 18.8 million at 9.30pm, equivalent to one in four of the population, just as the game reached its unforgettable finale. That was less than the 23 million who watched England's defeat to Argentina a year earlier, but remarkable for a club game.

Even ABUs had tuned in – and for all the United-hatred, it must have been hard not to be swept along by the drama. Perhaps some vindication of what Ferguson had said in the build-up, 'There'll still be the odd one who will jump off Tower Bridge if we win, but I think the majority are swinging towards us.' There would be no winning over many ABUs, but the nature of victory, and the Treble, ensured that United had picked up countless more followers.

English football had a European champion once more, for the first time since the Heysel catastrophe and the subsequent five-year ban on English clubs. United's triumph was a boost for the wider game, even if Liverpool and Arsenal supporters would not care to acknowledge it. Every club would benefit. United were driving the Premier League boom and the next three-year TV deal with BSkyB, starting in 2001, would break the billion-pound barrier for the first time with a leap of almost 90 per cent income per match for top-flight clubs. United were, by far, the biggest draw in town.

United's success propelled a whole new fascination and fan-base, not just in England but across the world. The globalisation of United and the Premier League would soar on the back of this glory. But it was close to home that this story began.

My late father-in-law, Roy, a United fan and season-ticket holder since the '50s who could extol the many virtues of Duncan Edwards from watching that great and tragic figure play, was among the lucky hordes in the Nou Camp. You only had to mention that night to him to set him off reminiscing about where he sat and how the drama unfolded and the celebrations. We would say that he could never remember the dates of his own children's birthdays, and it was true, but 26 May 1999, well, who could possibly forget it? He certainly never did. It was one of the happiest days of his life.

92

Lou

On the radio gantry as the final minutes of the Champions League final played out, Lou Macari was next to Alan Parry to offer his expert advice for Talk Radio. As Teddy Sheringham scored, this Manchester United legend of the '70s and '80s had to shout to make himself heard above the din. 'What a goal!' he bellowed. 'They're going to win it now, Alan. They are going to win this Cup final, I'm certain of that.' He could sense it to his bones.

'There is no sport in the world like it,' Parry told the listeners as United moved up for another corner.

'There is no team in the world like it,' Macari responded. 'This Manchester United team, they are never beaten.'

And then, as David Beckham's corner was flicked on by Sheringham and Ole Gunnar Solskjær stuck out a leg, Macari uttered a cry that gives us both goosebumps as we listen back to the tape more than 20 years later. 'YESSSSS!!!' Macari screams. It is an outpouring of much more than celebration. It is a sound that comes from deep within.

Sitting next to Macari, you can see in his face that he is taken back to that moment. 'For 30 seconds,' he says, 'I forgot about my son.'

Anyone with United, or sport, in their blood has their own personal take of what that moment in 1999 meant to them. For

Macari, there was something profound in the power of football to lift a person out of the deepest lows of life. It was the most wonderful distraction, however briefly. For those giddy seconds, Macari was swept along in the drama of that comeback and the simple joy of football. He could think about something other than Jonathan.

Less than a month before the final, on 28 April, Macari's youngest son had killed himself at the age of 19 in the Trentham area of Stoke. Released by Nottingham Forest the previous year, Jonathan had struggled to find a purpose. In the shock of the suicide, Macari says everything 'more or less went blank' for a while. He sat at home with his wife and two other sons in trauma and disbelief.

As he explains, 'There's nothing to say. It's numbing. You ask yourself what could you have done? Where could you have been? Why didn't you do something? Only when you go through something like that do you understand the hell of it.'

Macari was not sure he could resume his radio punditry, certainly not so soon. He really was not sure about going out to Barcelona, but his other two sons insisted. 'My other lads were there too. They said I should go and do my work. It wasn't easy.' Macari says that he cried when he got off the plane in Barcelona. He was not sure he wanted to be there. He was worried that Jonathan would be disappointed in him. 'Just the fact I've been to a football match ... Everything in the build–up to the game, you could ask me and I wouldn't know. Or the events after it, the celebrations, because you lock yourself away.'

Sitting there for much of the game was painful, with Macari doing his best in fraught circumstances. And then came that late drama and he could hardly fail to be swept along. 'For those two, three minutes you've got away from the tragedy you've gone through. You're thinking about something else. People say you think about it day-in day-out, but you don't, you can't. You'd crack up, and that obviously must happen to a lot of people who experience a similar thing. Their life is torture.'

We listened to that recording in the homeless shelter in Stoke which has been Macari's work and passion since 2016. He had watched the local TV news one night and heard about worsening homelessness in a region where, twice in the '90s, he was the manager of Stoke City. Local politicians were bickering over the scale of the problem so Macari decided to do something about it. 'I just thought, "What have I ever done like this in my life?"'

He set up the homeless shelter which, when I visit, has 43 pods in a warehouse and Macari busy in the office looking after those whom society has forgotten. It is an extraordinary place. Macari is a remarkable man. He scored 97 goals for United, performed great deeds, but this shelter is far beyond anything he accomplished kicking a ball around – though Macari, as much as anyone, also appreciates the power of football to lift the soul.

'I've mentioned it to Ole,' he says. 'Scoring the goal, being the hero, how it gave me a bit of relief. I told him that was my memory of '99, because everyday things take it away from that incident.'

On match days, Macari works as an ambassador at Old Trafford – mostly in the Treble Suite. 'I enjoy keeping involved at the club,' he says. 'It all helps you cope.'

93

No time for losers

To see German faces bereft in defeat was discombobulating. This was the '90s when, much like every other decade, we cursed Teutonic ability to get the job done. To witness distraught German players and tens of thousands of crestfallen fans felt like a shocking overturning of the natural order of things. 'Die Mutter aller Niederlagen' was the headline the following morning in *Süddeutsche Zeitung*. The Mother of all Defeats needed to be explained, though many in Munich wondered if anyone ever could.

The questions haunted them. How did we lose it? How could we lose it?

'I still feel that pain. I still think, "What went wrong?" I still think about it,' Samuel Kuffour said when I spoke to him 20 years later, down a telephone line from Accra, Ghana. Kuffour explained that he had still not fully recovered. He had never been able to bring himself to watch those three minutes again, and never would.

Kuffour is not a man lacking perspective. He knows that it was only football. He also understands real tragedy. In 2003, he had just returned to Germany from the family base in Ghana when he took a call to say that his 15-month-old daughter, Godiva, had drowned in the swimming pool. He looked deep within his religious faith to make sense of his trauma. But if what unfolded in Barcelona was a win that changed lives, and filled hearts with happiness, defeat was going to have a colossal impact, too. Bayern's players reeled from the blow that Kuffour, more than any player, had embodied as he pounded the ground with his fist.

Recriminations centred around the withdrawal of Lothar Matthäus after 80 minutes. German football had revolved around Matthäus for a long time. 'Whenever it gets serious he pisses off,' Mehmet Scholl said with disdain to journalists as he made his way to the team bus in the Nou Camp. It was a dig with a deeper meaning, also referring to the 1990 World Cup final when Matthäus had not felt comfortable taking the late penalty that Andreas Brehme converted for victory. Scholl was fined for his barb, but the debate would not go away. Matthäus was insistent that he was exhausted and, at 38, entitled to be. He said that coming off was anticipated by Ottmar Hitzfeld, the coach.

Stefan Effenberg was unpersuaded. When he published a provocative autobiography in 2003, one chapter was entitled 'What Lothar Matthäus knows about football'. The page was left blank. He revisited Matthäus's substitution with scorn. 'If you're the libero, how can you go off? I'd have needed a broken leg to do that.'

At Bayern's post-match banquet in the Barcelo Sants hotel, a band had been booked for a festive party. Dressed in bow-ties, suddenly the musicians felt out of place and unsure what to play. A funeral dirge? Some players, including Kuffour, took themselves off to their rooms. Carsten Jancker had wept uncontrollably on the field and felt physically sick when he flicked on the television and saw the highlights on repeat. Effenberg sat with him until the early hours, going round and round trying to work out how they had lost a game they had won.

By 3 a.m. some players had eventually drunk enough to cast off their misery. Mario Basler and Matthäus ended up dancing on tables to Britney Spears' 'Hit Me Baby One More Time'. But defeat hit Oliver Kahn particularly hard. 'I wish I could have cried,' he told *11 Freunde* magazine. 'Through crying I could have worked through the feeling of losing. Instead it was a mental and physical collapse.' He reckons that he suffered a form of depression for more than a year.

The agony did not end in the Nou Camp because Bayern still had to play the German cup final on 12 June in Berlin. They lost on penalties to Werder Bremen. Matthäus missed the crucial spot-kick.

---

* By the time that he went to breakfast the following morning, Effenberg had turned his anger into a furious determination to come back and win the trophy. 'I want revenge!' he told his teammates. Still led by Hitzfeld, most of these players would beat Valencia in the 2001 Champions League final in the San Siro, winning on penalties. Kahn was among them. 'If we hadn't won in Milan, Oli would have to play until 50 to forget Barcelona,' Alexander Zickler said.

By then, Matthäus was winding down his career in the MLS in America. A world and European champion, a Ballon d'Or winner and FIFA world player of the year, he is one of the most decorated footballers in history. But he never did win the Champions League.

94

Comebacks

Can anything in sport beat a comeback? Sport gives us a wonderful variety of uplifting triumphs and glories, but a comeback offers a whole different depth of drama, and character. It shows us a different side to our sporting heroes – very often a more appealing, human one like the return of Tiger Woods, after all his personal nightmares, to win the 2019 Masters – because it depends not just on talent but on extraordinary will. On belief.

'The lunacy of optimism,' Matthew Syed called it in *The Times* when he wrote about why the greatest comebacks – Botham's Ashes, the miracle of Istanbul, the miracle of Medinah and the Nou Camp among the most astonishing of my lifetime – are not just gripping sport but a powerful and beautiful metaphor for life.

In our love of the comeback, he rightly reckoned, is an understanding that there is nothing more human than the struggle. And nothing more admirable than overcoming adversity. Logic says that most football teams trailing when the clock reaches 90 minutes have no chance of winning, just as most painters who set out to produce a masterpiece will fail. But it is in our nature – when at our best – to keep striving. Comebacks represent the best of the human spirit in refusing to accept our limitations. They combine not just defiance and resilience, but also optimism and hope.

'Sport is beautiful because it articulates this truth more powerfully than any other arena,' as Syed put it. 'That is why epic comebacks amaze and confound us. They show us what is possible when people refuse to give up, when they hope beyond hope.'

United were the greatest comeback exponents of modern football, perhaps of all time. This team retrieved a losing cause 17 times in 1998-99, including defining triumphs against Liverpool in the FA Cup, to overcome Juventus and Bayern in the Champions League, to clinch the league title against Spurs.

Looking at notable champions of the period, and how many times they fought back from a losing position to avoid defeat in their best seasons, 17 is an extraordinary tally. Arsenal's Double-winners of 1997-98 did it six times, José Mourinho's first champions at Chelsea in 2004-05 seven times and Manchester City under Pep Guardiola in 2020-21 eight times. Arsenal's Invincibles pulled off 13 recoveries to draw or win and keep their run going, but none threatened 17, except these United players the following season when they fought back 16 times to save themselves.

You could say, obviously, that to make a comeback you have to fall behind in the first place and that many of these other champions avoided that predicament through asserting superior control of matches. And it might be true. But was that not also part of the thrilling nature of this United side that they engaged so keenly in open contests? They were willing to take risks. It was in their character to be extraordinarily bold.

Comebacks are the very best of sport. And this Manchester United side were as famous for them as any in history.

95

Redemption

David Beckham took the trophy out onto the pitch in the Nou Camp. His life was starting to be lived out in photographs, and he wanted a memento. He posed for some shots for his personal album and then, holding the cup by one of the big ears, headed back to the bus to join his teammates. Suddenly, he bumped into Sandra and Ted, his mum and dad, in the stadium car park. It was a chance encounter, and a highly emotional one.

Without a word, Beckham rested the cup down on the ground and embraced his father. A year on from St Etienne, and that almost childlike need for comfort as he sobbed in the wake of his red card, this time both men shed tears of joy. Beckham's parents knew better than anybody all that he had endured over the past year. 'It had happened to them, too, in a way,' Beckham reflected. 'That's how it is with your children.'

A season that began with his effigy swinging grotesquely from scaffolding had concluded in triumph, and in sweet redemption. But, talking to Beckham, it was interesting to hear how it had changed him, too.

Beckham is a father of four now. He calls, punctual to the minute, just after he has dropped off his youngest child, daughter Harper Seven, at a play-date. He is heading home to watch TV in his man-cave where there is a photograph on the wall that reminds him exactly why 1998–99 was such a defining year of his life. But it is not the image anyone might expect.

Framed in his home is a photograph from the away trip to West Ham United in August – United's first away game in the Premier League when Beckham discovered the brutal reality of life as a national scapegoat. That afternoon was the first true test of public scorn following his dismissal at the World Cup. However much the malevolence was expected, the scale of it still came as a shock.

The photo shows thousands of grown men screaming obscenities; faces distorted with violent rage. They lift middle fingers and make wanker gestures. Many of them are wearing T-shirts specially made for the occasion proclaiming: 'You've Let Your Country Down, You've Let Yourself Down, You've Let Us Down, You Are Not Forgiven'.

The first time Beckham went over to take a corner, it took strength of will to drown out all the abuse. All these angry men screaming what they would like to do to him, and to his famous wife. 'Such a negative image,' Beckham says of that photo. But he wanted it framed on his wall as a reminder of all he came through. Of his own resilience. Even now, Beckham is startled by how much vitriol he endured, and overcame.

'From the moment going to West Ham and they said, "When you get off the coach, you'll be met by two police,"' he says. 'I'd never had anything like that. The fact that people had gone to so much trouble to have T-shirts made and the hatred in the ground. Especially as an East End boy to get that from somewhere where I'd kind of grown up. I'd had stick before but it was a different kind of hatred that day. I didn't know it could get that bad.'

It was, he says, a sign of things to come for months and years ahead. Death threats sent to the club and to his home. Reporters hanging around not just at his parents' house and his sisters but his grandparents. 'They are elderly people being doorstepped,' he says. 'Messages, letters, hand-delivered when

I'm out, during the night. I was mostly living on my own back then in Manchester. If you didn't have a thick skin, then you're going to grow one.'

Alex Ferguson said that it had changed Beckham and made him less fun-loving. More private, 'with inner reaches that few can penetrate'. Beckham understands what his manager meant; confirms it, even. 'You become colder as a person,' he explains, saying that one outcome of all that abuse was to build a protective shield around himself. He already was stubborn by nature and it made him even more single-minded. And, if there could be an upside, even more determined to play his best football. The best of his career?

'Maybe,' he says. 'It challenged me. When I get something in my mind to do something, nothing can change it. So the stubbornness has always been there but there was a coldness that came with what happened. Not just that season but for the next three or four years.' The coldness that you might find in steel.

Some close to him thought he could be driven out of English football. Beckham says that he never allowed that to become an option in his mind. That was not how they had been brought up at United. 'It was instilled in me at an early age that when things are tough, put your head down and get on with it.'

He talks of Eric Harrison and Nobby Stiles, those tough mentors of the youth team. Decent men but not interested in bellyaching. He had come through the hard schooling from Robson, his hero, and Cantona, Ince, Hughes and Schmeichel. 'They made us tough,' he says. 'And there was all the support I had from the manager, the players and the fans and, of course, my family.'

Beckham stuck at it and through his performances in helping to shape the glorious Treble campaign, he had won over many critics who thought he represented everything excessive about modern professional football. There were plenty of them. It was startling to go back and be reminded of just how much intellectual snobbery there was towards Beckham, particularly at that time. 'The football talent of a Titan, but the mental complexity of a tomato,' Joe Joseph wrote in *The Times*. 'Speech was his second language,' Julie Burchill wrote in a profile – and she admired him.

Burchill made the point that we do not expect our intellectuals to be great footballers, so why do we expect our footballers to be intellectuals, which seemed a very good point, but fascination, popularity and vitriol still came hand-in-hand for the footballer and his famous fiancée. Such is life for a modern celebrity in the face of fickle public opinion, but Posh and Becks invited attention and comment on a rare scale.

That a woman humorously called 'Posh' and an ordinary lad from Essex had become Britain's First Couple seemed too much for some to bear. Burchill thought it was the harsh light their success shone on everyone else's failings that provoked such envy. Seeing the Beckhams with all their opulent success and wealth, 'we are forced to face our own busted dreams, and it hurts'.

The Beckhams were also challenging age-old views; David with his feminine side, sarong and metrosexuality; a partnership of equals of income and profile, and joint interviews in *Vogue*; before long, Victoria joking that her husband tried on her knickers. Beckham had his silver Ferrari Maranello, a first autobiography published before he was 23, and an income drawing as much money off the pitch as on it from his deals with Adidas, Brylcreem and Pepsi.

'Living in the bubble of modern celebrity, Becks and Posh aren't always easy to love, and are sometimes exposed to ridicule by their own childish hubris,' Richard Williams wrote in a profile in the *Independent* as the season came to a close. But he also concluded that Beckham's contribution to United's triple crown had been as important as any player: 'Over the course of the whole season he has responded by turning himself into the very opposite of his image, which is that of a pampered, petulant playboy.'

Beckham had faced so much scorn and overcome it with talent and control. He was not the most articulate sportsman but, with a football at his feet, he had more than said enough. He had carried himself with a resolve and dignity that would, before long, see him made captain of his country.

In the book, *Managing My Life*, that Ferguson had been writing all season, he said that no one should ever underestimate Beckham. But many had done, in the belittling of his voice or deriding the highlights in his hair, the choice of partner and the idea that he was all style over substance. Could he not enjoy fame and glamour while also demonstrating that he was one of the finest footballers around? Not indefinitely on Ferguson's watch but there was no denying all that Beckham had proved this season when so many willed him to fail.

'When the chips are down on the football field, you can bet your life that David Beckham won't be found wanting,' Ferguson concluded. This year of comebacks had been typified by Beckham's personal triumph over the hatred.

On that wall at home is another souvenir which reminds Beckham of his admirable growth through the season. Two shirts hang side by side in a frame from the reunion with Diego Simeone in the quarter-final first leg against Inter Milan. 'My United shirt from the first half and his shirt from the second half that I swapped,' he says. 'To have set up two goals in that game and played as well as I did, especially after everything that had been going on with Simeone. I've still got the picture of me and him shaking hands before the Old Trafford game. The atmosphere was unbelievable. And the following night Brooklyn was born.'

Like that photo from Upton Park, those jerseys marked the journey that Beckham had travelled from the depths of St Etienne to the pinnacle of the Nou Camp. A season which might have broken him but instead revealed depths of his talent, and fighting spirit. 'I've watched those last three minutes in Barcelona over and over again. The emotion doesn't change and in fact it grows. I think that's what happens when you get older. You get more emotional about things. It gets more emotional every time.'

Ask what stands out, he says it is the sight of him hearing the final whistle and breaking into a sprint of celebration; not sure where he was running, or why he was running there, but propelled by a rush of bliss. 'I can't understand the energy I had when the final whistle went because it had been such a long, hard season. So many moments when we were taking games to the last second, the last minute, and that in itself is hard enough physically. You would think after the season we'd had, and I'd had, you would just fall onto the floor and burst into tears. But that run, it's just pure joy.'

The joy of a man standing at the top of his professional world; of a new father; of a man about to be married. 'Yes,' Beckham laughs. 'It was quite a year.'

96

A royal wedding

The wedding of Prince Edward and Sophie Rhys-Jones took place on 19 June 1999. A couple of weeks later, the world gawped at the real royal ceremony of the year as David Beckham and Victoria Adams ascended to thrones in Luttrellstown Castle near Dublin.

It was not a low-key occasion. Fluttering above the battlements was a flag adorned with a crown crest and the gilded letters VBD, for Victoria, Brooklyn, David. The bride wore a tiara. The happy couple finished the evening in matching purple outfits that Prince might have regarded as rather outré. Still, if anyone was going to sit on a throne, at least it should be a couple who had done something with their lives rather than on the back of birthright alone.

When BBC's *Celebrity: A 21st-Century Story* was screened in 2021, the programme opened with the Beckhams, from their engagement in January 1998 to the offer of £1 million from *OK!* magazine for the exclusive wedding photographs. It seemed an exorbitant figure, yet the sale of around 1.7 million copies of the magazine more than justified the outlay. Unprecedented sales recouped more than £12 million.

People feasted on the pictures from what looked like Robin Hood's forest hangout, as the couple were married with bride and groom both dressed in white from head to toe. Beckham looks back on the change of outfits to regal purple and wonders if it might all have been just a little over the top.

The premise of the BBC series was that anyone could become famous in the new millennium. Reality TV would soon take off; *Big Brother* in 2000, *Pop Idol* in 2001. Ordinary people would be able to become celebrities; your cat, too, via this new social media thing which was in its infancy and would start from 2003 with MySpace. But if the early 21st century marked the point where fame for fame's sake became a popular ambition and if Beckham represented part of the trend – 'David was the only player I managed who chose to be famous,' Alex Ferguson said – then it paid to achieve something remarkable first. You had to work damn hard for Beckham's level of renown.

As if to prove the point, the happy couple's honeymoon to the south of France lasted only five days. Ferguson wanted Beckham and the rest of his players back for pre-season training. After all, they had a Treble to defend.

97

Trebles

On the morning of 17 April 2021, Manchester City were set fair for an unprecedented Quadruple. All looked good for Pep Guardiola's extravagantly talented squad to become the most successful side in the history of English football. City had the greatest coach in the game, stellar players packed into the most expensive squad ever assembled (at a cost of more than £800 million) plus seemingly unstoppable form and irrepressible confidence. Everything that a team should need to become trophy-winners, record-breakers, history-makers.

And then they stumbled. First, they lost the FA Cup semi-final at Wembley by a single goal to Chelsea. Then City were unexpectedly beaten in the Champions League final in Porto by the same opponents, who had finished 19 points below them in the Premier League. Combining European and domestic glory had again proved beyond them. It has proved beyond many great teams.

A year after City's attempt at a clean sweep, Liverpool had their own wonderful chance of four trophies in 2021–22. With both domestic cups already secured, Jürgen Klopp's vaunted 'Quad squad' chased history into the final week of the campaign. It looked like they might pull off something extraordinary with just 15 minutes of the Premier League season remaining, only to see City snatch away the title with a sensational recovery (three goals in five minutes from 0-2 down against Aston Villa). Then Real

Madrid beat Liverpool in the Champions League final. Suddenly two cups felt like falling short.

And still Manchester United's achievement in 1998-99 stands alone across all the decades of English football. Still that Treble – of the Premier League, FA Cup and Champions League (don't accept any lesser, cheaper alternatives) – remains gloriously unique.

The uniqueness is surprising. Every metric suggests that a Treble is more likely now than ever. From the start of the European Cup in 1955 for the next four decades, only Celtic (1967), Ajax (1972) and PSV Eindhoven (1988) had pulled off that feat. It had proved beyond every club in the continent's strongest leagues of Spain, Italy, England, France and Germany. That changed in an age when a handful of Super Clubs started dominating as never before. There were four Trebles between 2009 and 2015, from Barcelona (2009, 2015), Inter Milan (2010) and Bayern Munich (2013), who added another in 2020. If Paris St Germain had beaten Bayern in that 2020 European Cup final, they would have become the first French club to pull off the Treble. Wealth gaps were growing, riches and players concentrated in clubs with unprecedented spending power who were able to stockpile superstars. Historic feats were becoming the norm.

We saw the first domestic Treble by an English club (City in 2019) and the first 100-point seasons in England, Spain and Italy, and unprecedented runs of domestic domination by Juventus, Bayern and PSG. Perhaps United's accomplishment in 1999 was a forerunner of this trend – though by no estimation could anyone say they had it easy.

In the FA Cup United played a top-flight team in all but one round and, in Liverpool, Chelsea and Arsenal, faced three of the country's top sides. In the Premier League, they had to clinch the title on the final day, holding off defending Double-winners in Arsenal. Chelsea, in third, lost only three games all season.

United's tally of 79 points seems low by recent standards but not for that period at the end of the 20th century, reflecting more competitive leagues of the time.

No team had previously faced 13 games in Europe, and United did not lose one of them. They had to face Bayern three times, overcome a group of death featuring Barcelona, and beat two of Italy's strongest sides. They did so without any need for extra time or penalties.

United went 33 games without defeat in all competitions which remains an unprecedented run to conclude a season and, of English top-flight teams, has only been bettered by Nottingham Forest from March to December 1978 (39 matches) and the United side of 1993-94 (34 unbeaten). Arsenal's Invincibles have their own special claim to fame, but their 49-match run was scattered with defeats in domestic cups and in Europe.

The Liverpool side of 1976-77 was close to winning the Treble – taking the title, European Cup and almost the FA Cup, left to curse Jimmy Greenhoff's winner for Manchester United in the Wembley final. The 1983-84 vintage under Joe Fagan took the title, European Cup and League Cup but that was *a* Treble rather than *the* Treble.

We could go on, but these ways to measure United's unique success feel almost too prosaic. The records do not begin to capture the full glory of all that United achieved, and the manner in which it was done.

Another English team will win the Treble one day. But they cannot possibly win it like this.

98

The weight of history

One miracle in a lifetime was all that anyone could reasonably expect. But in desperation and naivety, Manchester United turned to Ole Gunnar Solskjær in December 2018 like people go to Lourdes imagining that it will bring a cure.

The club was still reeling from the post-Ferguson convulsions. No Premier League, certainly no Champions League, and not even a discernible strategy since Alex Ferguson had retired in 2013. The Glazers had tried David Moyes (Scottish work ethic), Louis van Gaal (continental wisdom) and José Mourinho (success by any means) without coming close to summoning the strength, never mind the domination, of old.

Running out of ideas, they turned to the man who had delivered the most celebrated goal, perhaps the single greatest moment, in United's entire history. Hadn't Solskjær played under Ferguson for more than a decade? Hadn't he studied the work of the greatest manager of them all? Ole had clinched the Treble. Perhaps it did not matter that he had never coached a leading club, or that he only had eight hapless months at Cardiff City and a couple of titles in the Norwegian league on his managerial CV.

If ever there was a sign that this grand institution had lost its way – trapped by former glories – it was in appointing the hero of the Nou Camp. Solskjær even took the United players to train at the Cliff one day as if running out on that grass and breathing in the Salford air might magically transform them into champions. Predictably, it turned out that restoring United to greatness was not like some family recipe, or secret sauce, that could be handed down from one generation to another. Ferguson's genius for man-management could not be learnt, or inherited, or copied.

On 21 November 2021, after a humiliating 4-1 loss at Watford, Solskjær was sacked. Increasingly grey and wan on the sidelines, he did well to last that long. A decent man, he appeared on United's media channel to talk about his regrets that he had not restored the club's pre-eminence. He dabbed tears from his eyes. Football cannot have made him this emotional since, well, 1999.

Who, after Busby and Ferguson, can make United great once more? It never could be Solskjær. He refused even to park his car in Ferguson's old space at the training ground out of respect, and awe. 'It's still the gaffer's place,' he was reported to have told colleagues. You had to feel a little sorry for him, dropped in out of his depth. As he struggled with the magnitude of the job, we could also see the torments of his former teammates working as pundits. They were forced to contort themselves to protect a friendship – a deep bond – in their appearances on TV.

In other circumstances, Roy Keane would shred a struggling United manager, but how could he do that to a man like Solskjær he genuinely cared for? There is no more clear-sighted pundit than Gary Neville, but he readily acknowledged that sentiment and loyalty triumphed over the hard realities of United's woes. He refused to call for the club to sack the man who changed next to him in the dressing room for all those years.

Paul Scholes could be as blunt about United's tactical failings as he was in some of those tackles of old, but he was never going to make his criticism personal when he had shared such unforgettable times with Solskjær. Even in the dying days of the regime, Peter Schmeichel told me that Solskjær had restored 'the heart and soul of United'. No one could bring themselves to say he had failed. They were bound by the ties of 1999, and the historic Treble.

On the terraces, the supporters must have felt like their loyalties were being exploited as they, too, were caught between demanding better, much better, from United and staying true to the man who put the ball in the Germans' net and gave them one of the best days of their lives.

The loathed Glazers had appointed the Norwegian because they thought he would appease the fans, at least for a while. He would make a connection to a glorious past. He would make everyone feel better. Having Solskjær in charge would remind everyone of when this club was not just a money-making corporation but a thrilling, revered team creating heroes, legends, as it won the game's biggest prizes.

It would remind everyone that Manchester United will never be just another football club. From Busby's visionary greatness to the tragic slaughter of the gifted Babes in Munich; from the attacking verve of the Holy Trinity of Law, Charlton and Best to the renaissance brought about by Ferguson and the mercurial strut of Cantona; to the spirit of the Treble winners never knowing when they were beaten – as Hugh McIlvanney once noted, it all adds up to the sense of a national institution with a spiritual dimension. The United story captures not just the attention of millions of football fans but the hearts and souls. Trophies count, but so does character, tragedy, romance and adventure.

Solskjær returning was meant to remind everyone of how great this club could be and, somehow, to summon back the spirit of the Treble, which remains the most compelling campaign I have covered in sport shaped by characters who fascinate me to this day. Instead, a misconceived appointment ended up showing everyone how far United were from former glories and from the most celebrated accomplishment of all.

Once, they had flown to the moon. But looking up at the sky above Old Trafford as I went to finish this book, that destination had never seemed so far away . . .

99

What happened next...

Peter Schmeichel

If it was impulsive to leave Manchester United in 1999, at least the big goalkeeper departed for Sporting Lisbon, and more sunshine, on an unmatchable high. Returning to English football for spells at Aston Villa and Manchester City before retirement in 2003 caused some tangled loyalties, for Schmeichel and United supporters, though he now serves as a club ambassador while also supporting his son, Kaspar, who has become an impressive goalkeeper for Leicester City and Denmark.

Gary Neville

Retired as a one-club man in 2011 after 602 appearances for United, and 85 caps for England, though 'retirement' is the wrong word where Neville is concerned. The busiest man in Britain has established a property empire, the Class of '92 brand including a university and Salford City in the Football League, while also becoming one of the country's most outspoken and high-profile pundits. He was assistant to Roy Hodgson with England and endured a short, ill-judged managerial stint in

Valencia. Befitting a man with opinions on everything, he has not ruled out the possibility of standing for political office.

Jaap Stam

Alex Ferguson admits that selling the Dutch defender abruptly in August 2001, believing that he was losing his pace due to injuries, was one of his biggest mistakes. Stam had won the title in each of his three seasons at United. He moved to Lazio and then AC Milan, where he played in another Champions League final; on the receiving end of Liverpool's stunning comeback in Istanbul in 2005. Stam says that he is as likely to remember the pain of that defeat as the glory of the Nou Camp. When we spoke, he had recently been fired as head coach of FC Cincinnati in the MLS and moved back to the Netherlands.

Ronny Johnsen

For a player prone to injuries, it is remarkable that the Norwegian continued playing until he was 39, including at Aston Villa and Newcastle United, though with limited opportunities. Indeed, after the Champions League final, his next appearance for United was not until April 2000 on the day another league title was secured. Including the three climactic games to secure the Treble, Johnsen can claim to have a won four trophies with four consecutive matches. He is a pundit and coach in Norway.

Denis Irwin

After 12 seasons at United and 529 appearances, Irwin joined Wolverhampton Wanderers on a free transfer in 2002, aged 36, to move into the second tier. His two years in the Midlands included promotion to the Premier League, and a return to Old Trafford when he was given a wonderful ovation, but it could never match the buzz of United. An occasional pundit in England and Ireland, Irwin enjoys a low-key life in Cheshire.

David Beckham

Where to start? With the tempestuous departure for Real Madrid in 2003 after Ferguson had decided that fame had become too distracting? The 115 appearances for England, including 59 as captain? The game-changing move to LA Galaxy in 2007 thinking his international career was over (it wasn't)? Helping to clinch the 2012 Olympics for London? The creation of a Beckham brand which continues to perform extremely lucratively, albeit controversially as an ambassador for the 2022 Qatar World Cup? Beckham has barely been out of the news, certainly not the gossip columns, for a day since 1998. That is how he seems to like it.

Roy Keane

The explosiveness of his exit from United in November 2005 shocked even those who had witnessed the Irishman's irascibility close up for many years. His rant at Carlos Queiroz, Ferguson's assistant, in the manager's office burnt so many bridges that there was no coming back. Keane went on to Celtic, where he spent six months before announcing his retirement. He enjoyed success as manager of Sunderland, and worked as assistant coach for the Republic of Ireland at Euro 2016, but is best known these days as a characteristically fiery pundit.

Paul Scholes

The midfielder had to wait another nine years to grace a Champions League final, enjoying victory over Chelsea in Moscow. It was shortly after another final, in 2011 and defeat to Barcelona at Wembley, that Scholes announced that he was retiring, aged 36, to join the coaching staff. Six months later, when Ferguson was short in midfield, Scholes was tempted back and played for another 18 months to reach 713 appearances, and 155 goals for United, including ten Premier League titles, three FA Cups and two Champions Leagues. He managed his local club Oldham Athletic for a handful of games in League Two in 2019 and works as a pundit, with a knack for withering analysis.

Ryan Giggs

With 13 titles, as well as four FA Cups, three League Cup wins and two Champions League triumphs by the time he retired in 2014, aged 40, after a record 963 appearances for United, Giggs is one of the most decorated footballers of all time. Becoming player-coach under David Moyes, he was interim manager for four games when the Scot was sacked and then worked for Louis van Gaal, but broke his long ties with the club, stretching back over almost 30 years, when he was overlooked for the manager's job in 2016 and José Mourinho was appointed. Giggs became manager of Wales in 2016 but stepped away late in 2020 pending a court case and resigned in June 2022.

Dwight Yorke

The striker claims that he asked for a sabbatical post-Treble to go off and enjoy himself. It sounds like Yorke, as does his manager's point-blank refusal. While he stayed for three more seasons before moving to Blackburn Rovers, Yorke never quite recaptured the heights of that glorious campaign. When we spoke, he was living in Dubai and playing a lot of golf, working as a United ambassador, often in the Far East, and growing frustrated at a lack of coaching opportunities. In a rare flash of anger, he talked of racism in the game holding him back but, in May 2022, finally had his chance when appointed head coach of Macarthur FC in the Australian A-League.

Andy Cole

After incessant chatter about replacements coming in for him at United, the end was finally clear when Ruud van Nistelrooy joined in 2001 as a highly effective lone striker. Cole joined Blackburn Rovers later that year and within a few months scored the winning goal – pleasingly for him against Glenn Hoddle's Spurs, featuring Teddy Sheringham – in the League Cup final. A peripatetic period concluded at Nottingham Forest, in the city of his birth, in 2008. After kidney failure in 2015, from a virus thought to have been picked up on a trip to Vietnam as a United ambassador, Cole underwent a kidney transplant. When we spoke, he was isolating in lockdown during the Covid-19 pandemic due to a weakened immune system. He has worked as a finishing coach at several clubs.

Nicky Butt

His patience as a deputy midfielder finally ran out in 2004. He could accept being left out for Keane and Scholes but not for Kleberson and Eric Djemba-Djemba. Butt joined Bobby Robson's Newcastle United only for the manager to be sacked within months. Returning to United as a coach for the reserves, he became head of the academy, working with players such as Marcus Rashford and Mason Greenwood, and then head of first-team development, but resigned in 2021 as the club embarked on yet another muddled reshuffle of backroom staff.

Teddy Sheringham

Sheringham won three consecutive titles before the arrivals of Van Nistelrooy and Juan Sebastián Verón prompted a return to Spurs in 2001. It is notable how many of this United squad played deep into their 30s, and Sheringham was 42 when he made his final professional appearance, for Colchester United. He had made more than 700 league appearances. He managed Stevenage in League Two but was sacked after less than a year and told me, shortly before heading off to hone his golf game, that he was not going to return to coaching. He still lives in Camp Nou, in Essex, with a young family.

Ole Gunnar Solskjær

The man who put the ball in the Germans' net has repeatedly had to deny that the slide to celebrate that famous goal was the cause of the knee problems that dogged him at United. He tweaked a ligament but not seriously and played a significant role in the next few seasons, including on the right flank when Ferguson was in the process of ousting Beckham. It was from August 2003 when Solskjær started to suffer with severe cartilage problems, though not until 2007 that he accepted the condition was career-ending. He stayed on as a coach before taking over at Molde in Norway. An unexpected choice as interim manager of United following the sacking of José Mourinho in December 2018, he lasted almost three years, reaching a Europa League final, before a tearful exit with his team seventh in the league.

Jesper Blomqvist

The Swede walked off at the Nou Camp hoping that he could build on an inconsistent first season at United. He never played for the club again. Blomqvist was only 25 but developed knee problems which required surgery and ruled him out for the next two years. He had a short time at Everton from 2001, and then Charlton Athletic, but was never the same player and finished in the lower leagues in Sweden, where he lives near Stockholm developing his culinary career.

Phil Neville

Like Butt, Neville could accept being in and out of the team in the glory years but grew increasingly frustrated when he could not stay in a side faltering with Quinton Fortune and David Bellion. In 2005, he moved to Everton under David Moyes and made his league debut against United, and brother Gary. He retired in 2013 and joined Moyes' coaching staff at United, before going on to coach at Valencia. Neville led the England women's team to the semi-final of the 2019 World

Cup and is manager at Inter Miami, the MLS club part-owned by Beckham.

Henning Berg

A knee ligament injury sustained in the first leg of the semi-final against Juventus was the Norwegian's last appearance of the season. He regained his place the following year, when Johnsen was a long-term casualty, before rejoining Blackburn Rovers in 2000. In 2012, he lasted just 57 days as manager at Ewood Park. His most recent coaching job was at AC Omonia in Cyprus.

David May

After returning from injury in April 1999 just in time for the run-in, May managed to make himself appear integral to the Treble by dominating the photographs on the dais in the Nou Camp. The defender left for Burnley in 2003 after nine years at Old Trafford. He is a presenter on the club's official UTD Podcast.

Wes Brown

With 21 appearances, including starts against Barcelona and Bayern Munich in the Champions League group stage, this was a breakthrough season for the versatile teenage defender who stayed at United until 2011, starting at right-back in the 2008 Champions League final.

Raimond van der Gouw

Making 60 appearances over six seasons as an understudy goal-keeper was always going to be a test of patience for the Dutch goalkeeper: and not always an easy one, especially as Mark Bosnich struggled as Schmeichel's erratic successor. He worked as goalkeeping coach at Sunderland under Keane and most recently at PSV Eindhoven.

Jordi Cruyff

Sent on loan to Celta Vigo in January 1999 after 11 appearances in the Treble season, the winger missed out on the drama. Cruyff stayed for one more campaign at United before moving to Alaves, in La Liga. Last seen acting as technical director at Barcelona, where his father is an icon.

Sir Alex Ferguson

In the summer of 2001, Ferguson announced that he would retire at the end of the season. He not only changed his mind but stayed until 2013, by which time he had amassed an astonishing haul of 25 major trophies; 13 league titles, five FA Cups, four League Cups, two European Cups and the Cup Winners' Cup (plus a FIFA Club World Cup) in his 27 years since moving down from Aberdeen. In 2011, the north stand at Old Trafford was named in his honour. Ferguson suffered a brain haemorrhage in May 2018 and later revealed that he had been given a 20 per cent chance of recovery. Typically, he defied those odds and remains a director on the football board and a club ambassador.

Brian Kidd

His sacking at Blackburn Rovers in November 1999 marked the last time Kidd tried management. Perhaps he always was best suited as a No.2; a role he subsequently filled under David O'Leary at Leeds United, Neil Warnock at Sheffield United, Sven-Göran Eriksson with England (until he developed prostate cancer) and in various roles at Manchester City for more than a decade until retirement in 2021. Kidd said in 2011 that he bore no lingering grudge towards Ferguson, the man he still called 'the boss'.

Steve McClaren

Sensing that he was unlikely to be given the chance to succeed Ferguson at Old Trafford, McClaren embarked on a management career at Middlesbrough in the summer of 2001. His stature was enhanced by winning the League Cup and reaching the Uefa Cup final but the England job, after Luiz Felipe Scolari rejected the chance, proved a leap too far despite extensive experience as Eriksson's assistant. Amid a downpour at Wembley and defeat to Croatia, the national team failed to qualify for Euro 2008. McClaren went to Holland to rebuild his reputation and, remarkably, won the Eredivisie title with FC Twente. His assistant was Erik Ten Hag, the man given the task of restoring United to former glories from the start of the 2022–23 season. McClaren also returned to Old Trafford in a coaching capacity, but to a very different United from the one he found in 1999.

ACKNOWLEDGEMENTS

I only had to dip into my memory to access much of this story. But a book like this requires input, and inspiration, from many people, and I want to thank all of those who generously gave their time, insights and encouragement to make it possible.

Reliving this epic season was, I hope, a pleasure for former Manchester United players but I am still incredibly grateful to David Beckham, Dwight Yorke, Andy Cole, Jesper Blomqvist, Nicky Butt, Teddy Sheringham, Denis Irwin, Paul Scholes, Peter Schmeichel, Phil Neville, Gary Neville and Jaap Stam for their input. There was so much to savour in their reminiscences. It was fascinating to recall the drama but also to hear how their reflections have shifted with time – and how they have too.

Others who helped me go back to that remarkable era included Alex Notman, Martin Edwards, Steve McClaren, Tony Adams, Olly Foster, Des Cahill, Greg Dyke, Alastair Campbell, Lou Macari, David Elleray, Dave Fevre, Piers Morgan, Owen Eastwood, Ramm Mylvaganam, Annette Baumeister, Sir Jim Ratcliffe, Marcel Reif and Clive Tyldesley. Sincere thanks to all.

This book would never have happened without the wise prompting of Keith Blackmore. Keith noted how many times, whenever we reflected on happy years working together, the stories invariably come back to this period, this team and these characters. It was also his recommendation of Craig Brown's masterful *One Two Three Four* biography of the Beatles which gave me the idea for the format of 99 snapshots. That is in no way to invite comparisons – certainly not with Brown's enviable wit and style – but it was a moment of clarity in how to bring different perspectives to the story. Keith and David Chappell have been wonderful friends and mentors over many decades.

Huge thanks to Tim Hallissey, James Restall and Paul McCarthy for reading a draft manuscript and for coming back with so many helpful suggestions – and particularly to Richard Whitehead who not only improved the text with good ideas but also saved me from numerous errors as the eagle-eyed copyeditor. I was delighted when Bill Edgar not only agreed to check the stats but to provide a typically definitive section at the end of the book.

Thanks to Charly Classen, Charlie Brooks and Diana Law for their help in setting up interviews. To Les Snowdon, head of sport, and all at *The Times* as I approach 25 years at the paper, it remains a blast and a privilege to work for one of the world's most prestigious titles among so many talented colleagues.

Ian Marshall and Ian Chapman at Simon & Schuster commissioned *1999* and I hope that, as ardent fans of Manchester United, the end result gives them some succour in challenging times for their club. I appreciate their backing, and my thanks to Fran Jessop for carrying the manuscript over the finish line. David Luxton pulled the deal together and encouraged me to believe that I did have another book in me when I had sworn I would never embark on this consuming process ever again.

My wife Helen might not have been thrilled at the prospect of another book project were it not for the fact that, as the United fan in the family, the subject matter at least brought back many happy memories. Thanks, as ever, for her unwavering support as well as practical help going through all the tapes of interviews. I will never be able to properly express my gratitude to Helen, Joe and Fin for all they give me every day of my life.

Finally, I raise a glass to all those who were on the journey in 1998-99; travelling across Europe, sharing planes and trains, press boxes and late-night bars after matches. As I mention in the prologue, my first-edition piece from the Nou Camp truly was a mess, but to read back the cuttings was to see how brilliantly so many colleagues coped in the maelstrom of drama and deadlines and panic.

Other than the perils of late twentieth-century technology, reflecting on that era made me deeply nostalgic. I am thoroughly unapologetic about declaring that they were the good old days – indeed, some of the very best of days. It was truly a joy to be following this extraordinary team through so many epic contests alongside great friends including Oliver Holt, Marc Aspland, Matt Lawton, Paul Hayward, Lee Clayton, Paul McCarthy and many more.

If some of that sense of thrill and wonderment has come through in my writing then I feel incredibly lucky to be able to share it. We are often told as sports writers that we have one of the best jobs in the world and, in 1999 perhaps more than any other year, who could possibly dispute it?

Matt Dickinson, May 2022

BIBLIOGRAPHY

Tony Adams. *Sober – Football, My Story, My Life* (Simon & Schuster, 2017)

Patrick Barclay. *Football – Bloody Hell! The Biography of Alex Ferguson* (Yellow Jersey Press, 2010)

David Beckham. *My World* (Hodder & Stoughton, 2000)

David Beckham. *My Side* (CollinsWillow, 2003)

Dennis Bergkamp. *Stillness and Speed: My Story* (Simon & Schuster, 2013)

Tony Blair. *A Journey* (Arrow Books, 2011)

Mihir Bose. *Manchester Unlimited: The Money, Egos and Infighting Behind the World's Richest Football Club* (Orion, 1999)

Tom Bower. *Broken Dreams: Vanity, Greed and the Souring of British Football* (Simon & Schuster, 2003)

Adam Brown and Andy Walsh. *Not For Sale: Manchester United, Murdoch and the Defeat of BSkyB* (Mainstream, 1999)

Julie Burchill. *Burchill on Beckham* (Yellow Jersey Press, 2001)

Alastair Campbell. *The Blair Years* (Arrow, 2008)

Andy Cole. *The Autobiography* (2000, Andre Deutsch)

Andrew Cole. *Fast Forward: The Autobiography* (Hodder & Stoughton, 2020)

David Conn. *The Football Business: Fair Game in the '90s?* (Mainstream, 1998)

Michael Crick. *The Boss: The Many Sides of Alex Ferguson* (Simon & Schuster, 2002)

Eamon Dunphy. *A Strange Kind of Glory* (Aurum Press, 2007)

Greg Dyke. *Inside Story* (Harper Perennial, 2010)

Martin Edwards. *Red Glory: Manchester United and Me* (Michael O'Mara, 2017)

David Elleray, *The Man In the Middle* (Time Warner, 2004)

Alex Ferguson. *Managing My Life* (Hodder & Stoughton, 1999)

Alex Ferguson. *The Unique Treble* (Hodder & Stoughton, 2000)

Alex Ferguson. *My Autobiography* (Hodder & Stoughton, 2013)

Alex Ferguson with Michael Moritz. *Leading* (Hodder & Stoughton, 2015)

Ryan Giggs. *Giggs: The Autobiography* (Michael Joseph, 2005)

Daniel Harris. *The Promised Land: Manchester United's Historic Treble* (Arena, 2013)

Glenn Hoddle. *My 1998 World Cup Story* (Andre Deutsch, 1998)

Oliver Holt. *If You're Second You Are Nothing: Ferguson and Shankly* (Macmillan, 2006)

Jamie Jackson. *The Red Apprentice: Ole Gunnar Solskjær: The Making of Manchester United's Great Hope* (Simon & Schuster, 2020)

Roy Keane. *Keane: The Autobiography* (Penguin, 2002)

Ned Kelly. *Manchester United: The Untold Story* (Michael O'Mara, 2003)

Stephen F. Kelly. *Red Voices* (Headline, 2000)

Andy Mitten. *Glory Glory! Man Utd in the '90s: The Players' Stories* (Vision Sports Publishing, 2009)

Piers Morgan. *The Insider: The Private Diaries of a Scandalous Decade* (Ebury Press, 2005)

Gary Neville. *Red* (Bantam Press, 2011)

Gary and Phil Neville. *For Club and Country* (Manchester United Books, 1998)

Paul Scholes. *My Story* (Simon & Schuster, 2011)

Peter Schmeichel. *The Autobiography* (Virgin, 1999)

Peter Schmeichel. *One: My Autobiography* (Hodder & Stoughton, 2021)

Phil Shaw. *The Book of Football Quotations* (Ebury Press, 2008)

Teddy Sheringham. *Teddy: My Autobiography* (Warner Books, 1999)

Jaap Stam. *Head to Head* (CollinsWillow, 2001)

Daniel Taylor. *This Is the One. Sir Alex Ferguson: The Uncut Story of a Football Genius* (Aurum, 2007)

Clive Tyldesley. *'Not for me, Clive': Stories from the Voice of Football* (Headline, 2021)

Jim White. *Manchester United: The Biography* (Hachette, 2008)

Jim White. *A Matter of Life and Death. A History of Football in Death. A History of Football in 100 Quotations* (Head of Zeus, 2014)

Jim White. *Premier League: A History in 10 Matches* (Head of Zeus, 2014)

100 Quotations (Head of Zeus, 2014)

Dwight Yorke. *Born To Score* (Macmillan, 2009)

Manchester United Opus (Opus, 2006)

Magazines:
FourFourTwo
New Statesman
OK!
United We Stand
The UTD Podcast
talkSPORT – Football, Bloody Hell! How United won the Treble

Documentaries:
Sir Alex Ferguson: Never Give In (2021)
The Treble: Official Season Review (1999)
The Last Dance (2020)

STATISTICS

The ultimate comeback

The Champions League final against Bayern Munich was the only occasion since the Second World World in which Manchester United won a match (without extra time) despite having trailed going into stoppage time.

90 mins	Man Utd 0, Bayern 1
91 mins	Man Utd 1 (Sheringham), Bayern 1
93 mins	Man Utd 2 (Solskjær), Bayern 1

Invincible after Christmas

The 3-2 home loss to Middlesbrough on 19 December proved to be United's last defeat of the season in any competition. Their subsequent undefeated sequence is without equal.

Longest unbeaten runs (all competitions) up to end of season by a top-flight club

Man Utd, 1998-99	33 games
Preston, 1888-89	27
Tottenham, 1966-67	24

On the straight and narrow

United's generally comfortable wins gave way to a series of tense, narrow victories in the home straight on their path to history.

Man Utd average victory margin in Treble competitions

19 wins up to February 6	2.65 goals
15 wins after February 6	1.4 goals

Leaving it late

United famously came from behind to clinch the title against Tottenham Hotspur and also to win the Champions League final against Bayern Munich. In fact, falling behind only to finish strongly was a trait of theirs in the second half of the season.

Times scored first goal of match, 19 Dec onwards

United 18	opponents 12

Times scored last goal of match, 19 Dec onwards

United 26	opponents 4

Flying away

United's three highest scores of the season all came away from home.

21 Oct, Champions League	Brondby 2, Man Utd 6
16 Jan, Premier League	Leicester City 2, Man Utd 6
6 Feb, Premier League	Nottingham Forest 1, Man Utd 8

Solskjær helps United cut down Forest

By beating Nottingham Forest 8-1 at the City Ground, United scored the most goals by an away team in a top-division match since Boxing Day 1963, when Blackburn Rovers defeated West Ham United 8-2 at Upton Park.

Ole Gunnar Solskjær became – and remains – the only substitute ever to have scored four times in a top-flight game.

At the time Solskjær was only the second substitute to have recorded a hat-trick in the top division; Frank McAvennie had done so for West Ham, also against Forest, in May 1992.

Of the seven substitutes now who have hit a top-flight hat-trick, Solskjær made the latest entrance: he arrived in the 71st minute at the City Ground.

Rule of three

United lost five games in all competitions during the season – and conceded exactly three goals each time.

Defeats in 1998–99 season

9 Aug, Charity Shield	Arsenal 3, Man Utd 0
20 Sept, Premier League	Arsenal 3, Man Utd 0
21 Nov, Premier League	Sheffield Wednesday 3, Man Utd 1
2 Dec, League Cup	Tottenham 3, Man Utd 1
19 Dec, Premier League	Man Utd 2, Middlesbrough 3

Busy at the business end

Four players were on the pitch throughout the three matches that completed each leg of the Treble – against Tottenham Hotspur

(Premier League), Newcastle United (FA Cup) and Bayern Munich (Champions League).

Played every minute of the trophy-clinching last three games:
Peter Schmeichel
Gary Neville
Ronny Johnsen
David Beckham

Three different paths to glory

United's Treble is acknowledged as *the* Treble, consisting of the League, the main domestic cup and the leading European trophy. But three other trebles have been recorded by English clubs.

Other (lesser) trebles achieved by English clubs

Liverpool, 1983-84	League, League Cup, European Cup
Liverpool, 2000-01	FA Cup, League Cup, Uefa Cup
Manchester City, 2018-19	League, FA Cup, League Cup

Every second counts: the most dramatic moments of the Treble season

Man Utd 2, Liverpool 1 (FA Cup 4th round)

2 min, 25 sec	Michael Owen heads Liverpool in front from Vegard Heggem's cross
88 min, 3 sec	Dwight Yorke makes it 1-1 after Andy Cole heads a David Beckham free kick back across goal
91 min, 8 sec	Ole Gunnar Solskjær drives home the winner after team mate Paul Scholes controls a long ball forward by Jaap Stam
93 min, 55 sec	Match ends

Man Utd 2, Arsenal 1 (FA Cup semi-final replay)

16 min, 43 sec	David Beckham gives United the lead from 25 yards
68 min, 20 sec	Dennis Bergkamp makes it 1-1 with another long-range shot
73 min, 16 sec	United's Roy Keane is sent off: he receives a second booking for tripping Marc Overmars
91 min, 15 sec	Arsenal are awarded a penalty after Phil Neville trips Ray Parlour
91 min, 55 sec	Peter Schmeichel saves Dennis Bergkamp's spot kick
93 min, 22 sec	Normal time ends
108 min, 10 sec (extra time)	Ryan Giggs puts United 2-1 up after a 60-yard run

Man Utd 2, Newcastle 0 (FA Cup final)

8 min, 31 sec	Teddy Sheringham comes on as a United substitute for the injured Roy Keane
10 min, 6 sec	Sheringham scores United's opening goal from a Paul Scholes pass
52 min, 37 sec	Scholes makes it 2-0 after a Sheringham lay-off

Man Utd 2, Bayern Munich 1 (Champions League final)

5 min, 7 sec	Bayern's Mario Basler opens the scoring from a free kick
90 min, 35 sec	Teddy Sheringham equalises for United after Ryan Giggs scuffs a shot
92 min, 17 sec	Ole Gunnar Solskjær volleys the winner from a Sheringham flick
93 min, 22 sec	Bayern kick off
93 min, 35 sec	Match ends

Appearances in starting XI in Treble competitions (games as substitute in brackets, English unless stated)

Peter Schmeichel (Danish)	55: (34 Premier League, 8 FA Cup, 13 Champions League)	United career: 1991-99
Gary Neville	53: (34 Premier League, 7 FA Cup, 12 Champions League)	United career: 1992-2011
Roy Keane (Irish)	52 (+2 sub): (33+2 Premier League, 7 FA Cup, 12 Champions League)	United career: 1993-2005
David Beckham	52 (+1): (33+1 Premier League, 7 FA Cup, 12 Champions League)	United career: 1992-2003
Jaap Stam (Dutch)	49 (+1): (30 Premier League, 6+1 FA Cup, 13 Champions League)	United career: 1998-2001
Dwight Yorke (Trinidad and Tobago)	48 (+3): (32 Premier League, 5+3 FA Cup, 11 Champions League)	United career: 1998-2002
Denis Irwin (Irish)	44 (+3): (26+3 Premier League, 6 FA Cup, 12 Champions League)	United career: 1990-2002
Andy Cole	42 (+7): (26+6 Premier League, 6+1 FA Cup, 10 Champions League)	United career: 1995-2001
Paul Scholes	37 (+12): (24+7 Premier League, 3+3 FA Cup, 10+2 Champions League)	United career: 1994-2013
Ryan Giggs (Welsh)	34 (+5): (20+4 Premier League, 5+1 FA Cup, 9 Champions League)	United career: 1991-2014
Nicky Butt	31 (+13): (22+9 Premier League, 5 FA Cup, 4+4 Champions League)	United career: 1992-2004

Jesper Blomqvist (Swedish)	29 (+8): (20+5 Premier League, 3+2 FA Cup, 6+1 Champions League)	United career: 1998-99
Ronny Johnsen (Norwegian)	28 (+7): (19+3 Premier League, 3+2 FA Cup, 6+2 Champions League)	United career: 1996-2002
Phil Neville	27 (+14): (19+9 Premier League, 4+3 FA Cup, 4+2 Champions League)	United career: 1995-2005
Henning Berg (Norwegian)	18 (+7): (10+6 Premier League, 5 FA Cup, 3+1 Champions League)	United career: 1997-2000
Wes Brown	16 (+4): (11+3 Premier League, 2 FA Cup, 3+1 Champions League)	United career: 1998-2011
Ole Gunnar Solskjær (Norwegian)	14 (+19): (9+10 Premier League, 4+4 FA Cup, 1+5 Champions League)	United career: 1996-2007
Teddy Sheringham	10 (+15): (7+10 Premier League, 1+3 FA Cup, 2+2 Champions League)	United career: 1997-2001
David May	5 (+2): (4+2 Premier League, 1 FA Cup)	United career: 1994-2002
Raimond van der Gouw (Dutch)	4 (+1): (4+1 Premier League)	United career: 1996-2002
John Curtis	1 (+3): (1+3 Premier League)	United career: 1997-99
Jordi Cruyff (Dutch)	0 (+8): (0+5 Premier League, 0+3 Champions League)	United career: 1996-2000
Jonathan Greening	0 (+4): (0+3 Premier League, 0+1 FA Cup)	United career: 1998-2001
Mark Wilson	0 (+1): (0+1 Champions League)	United career: 1998-2000

Played for another club that season

Dwight Yorke	1 app for Aston Villa v Everton in August before moving to United
Jordi Cruyff	10 apps for Spanish team Celta Vigo after joining them on loan in January

Manager

Sir Alex Ferguson

Seasons in charge before Treble campaign	12 (appointed Nov 1986)
Seasons in charge after it	14 (retired May 2013)

Games . . .

By colour

Red shirts	46 games (30 Premier League, 9 Champions League, 7 FA Cup)
White shirts	11 games (6 Premier League, 1 FA Cup, 4 Champions League)
Black shirts	2 games (2 Premier League)

By location

Home	29 games
Away	26 games
Neutral	4 games (2 Villa Park, 1 Wembley, 1 Nou Camp)

By stadium

Old Trafford	29 games
Villa Park	3
Stamford Bridge	2
Nou Camp	2
23 grounds	1

By day

Saturday	22
Sunday	14
Monday	0
Tuesday	1
Wednesday	21
Thursday	1
Friday	0

By referee (most common)

David Elleray	6
Graham Barber	5
Paul Durkin	4
Peter Jones	4
Gary Willard	4
Graham Poll	3
Mike Reed	3
Mike Riley	3

Goals

Dwight Yorke	29 (18 Premier League, 3 FA Cup, 8 Champions League)
Andy Cole	24 (17 Premier League, 2 FA Cup, 5 Champions League)
Ole Gunnar Solskjær	15 (12 Premier League, 1 FA Cup, 2 Champions League)
Paul Scholes	11 (6 Premier League, 1 FA Cup, 4 Champions League)
Ryan Giggs	10 (3 Premier League, 2 FA Cup, 5 Champions League)
David Beckham	9 (6 Premier League, 1 FA Cup, 2 Champions League)
Roy Keane	5 (2 Premier League, 3 Champions League)
Teddy Sheringham	4 (2 Premier League, 1 FA Cup, 1 Champions League)
Denis Irwin	3, all pens (2 Premier League, 1 FA Cup)
Ronny Johnsen	3 (3 Premier League)
Nicky Butt	2 (2 Premier League)
Jordi Cruyff	2 (2 Premier League)
Jesper Blomqvist	1 (1 Premier League)
Gary Neville	1 (1 Premier League)
Phil Neville	1 (1 Champions League)
Jaap Stam	1 (1 Premier League)
Own goals	2 (2 Premier League)

Assists

David Beckham	22 (14 Premier League, 8 Champions League)
Dwight Yorke	20 (12 Premier League, 8 Champions League)
Paul Scholes	12 (9 Premier League, 2 FA Cup, 1 Champions League)
Andy Cole	11 (5 Premier League, 4 FA Cup, 2 Champions League)
Teddy Sheringham	6 (3 Premier League, 2 FA Cup, 1 Champions League)
Jesper Blomqvist	5 (3 Premier League, 2 Champions League)
Ryan Giggs	5 (2 Premier League, 1 FA Cup, 2 Champions League)
Nicky Butt	4 (4 Premier League)
Denis Irwin	3 (2 Premier League, 1 Champions League)
Gary Neville	3 (3 Premier League)
Phil Neville	3 (2 Premier League, 1 Champions League)
Henning Berg	2 (2 Premier League)
Ole Gunnar Solskjær	2 (1 Premier League, 1 FA Cup)
Jordi Cruyff	1 (1 Premier League)
Jaap Stam	1 (1 Premier League)

Combinations

Of the team's 123 goals, 100 featured an assist by a United player. Dwight Yorke was involved in 47 of those 100 teammate combinations, whether assisting or scoring.

Combined for most goals (assist/goal, either way round)

Yorke/Cole	15
Yorke/Beckham	9
Yorke/Scholes	7
Yorke/Solskjær	4
Scholes/Cole	3
Scholes/Solskjær	3
Scholes/Sheringham	3
Sheringham/Solskjær	3
Giggs/Cole	3
Beckham/Giggs	3

Most common assist-goal

Beckham assist, Yorke goal	9
Yorke assist, Cole goal	8
Cole assist, Yorke goal	7
Yorke assist, Solskjær goal	4
Scholes assist, Yorke goal	4
Yorke assist, Scholes goal	3
Giggs assist, Cole goal	3
Beckham assist, Giggs goal	3
Scholes assist, Cole goal	3
Scholes assist, Solskjær goal	3

Goals . . .

By location

Home	65
Away	52

By half

First half	51
Second half	71
Extra time	1

By source

Penalties	3 (all Irwin: 2 to his right, 1 to his left)
Corners	7 (6 by Beckham, including both goals in Champions League final)
Direct free kicks	5 (all Beckham: 4 to his left, 1 to his right)
Other free kicks	6
Throw-in	1
All others	101

By method

Right foot	74 (Cole 21, Yorke 14, Solskjær 10, Beckham 9, Scholes 4, Irwin 3, Keane 3, Johnsen 2, Sheringham 2, Butt 1, Giggs 1, G Neville 1, P Neville 1, Stam 1, Watson 1 og)
Left foot	24 (Scholes 7, Giggs 6, Yorke 4, Solskjær 3, Cruyff 2, Cole 1, Keane 1)
Header	25 (Yorke 11, Giggs 3, Cole 2, Sheringham 2, Solskjær 2, Blomqvist 1, Butt 1, Johnsen 1, Keane 1, Short 1 og)

By location of score

In goal area	31 (including both in the Champions League final)
Elsewhere in penalty area	77
Outside penalty area	15

By number of touches taken by scorer, including shot

1 touch	89
2 touches	21
3 touches	7
4 touches	2
5 touches	1 (Scholes v Blackburn)
6 touches	2 (Beckham v Wimbledon; Scholes v Brondby)
12 touches	1 (Giggs v Arsenal)

By direction of shot (as attacker looks)

To left of goalkeeper	49
To right of goalkeeper	63
Over goalkeeper Through goalkeeper's legs	1

By area of build-up (from United's perspective)*

Left	29
Centre	59
Right	35

*For the three penalties scored, the area of the build-up to the concession of the penalty is counted.

Crosses (excluding corners) that led to goals

Beckham	18
Blomqvist	4
Cole	4
Irwin	3
Scholes	3
Giggs	2
G Neville	2
P Neville	2
Solskjær	2
Berg	1
Brown	1
Butt	1
Total	43

By substitutes

Solskjær	8
Sheringham	3
Cruyff	2
Scholes	2
Cole	1
Giggs	1
Keane	1
Total	18

League finishing positions of United's six FA Cup victims

Arsenal	Prem, 2nd
Chelsea	Prem, 3rd
Liverpool	Prem, 7th
Middlesbrough	Prem, 9th
Newcastle	Prem, 13th
Fulham	Third tier, 1st

1998–99 trophies in context

League title	United's 12th Current total: 20
FA Cup	United's 10th Current total: 12
European Cup/Champions League	United's 2nd Current total: 3

How they fared before and after

1997-98

League	2nd
FA Cup	5th round
Champions League	quarter-finals

1999-2000

League	1st
FA Cup	did not enter (clashed with Club World Cup)
Champions League	quarter-finals

Most games for United in one season

2008-09	66
2016-17	64
1993-94	63
1998-99	**63**
2002-03	63

The Treble Matches

12 Aug, Champions League 2nd qualifying round, 1st leg (United wore red shirts): Man Utd 2 (Giggs 16, Cole 81), Lodz 0. Att: 50,906

15 Aug, Premier League (red): Man Utd 2 (Sheringham 79, Beckham 90+4), Leicester 2 (Heskey 7, Cottee 76). Att: 55,052

22 Aug, PL (white): West Ham 0, Man Utd 0. Att: 25,912

26 Aug, CL 2nd qualifying round, 2nd leg (white): Lodz 0, Man Utd 0. Att: 8,000

9 Sept, PL (red): Man Utd 4 (Solskjær 38, 63; Yorke 45, 48), Charlton 1 (Kinsella 32). Att: 55,147

12 Sept, PL (red): Man Utd 2 (Yorke 21, Johnsen 48), Coventry 0. Att: 55,193

16 Sept, CL group match (white): Man Utd 3 (Giggs 17, Scholes 24, Beckham 64), Barcelona 3 (Anderson 47, Giovanni pen 60, Luis Enrique pen 71). Sent off: Butt, Man Utd, 70 min. Att: 53,601

20 Sept, PL (black): Arsenal 3 (Adams 13, Anelka 34, Ljungberg 84), Man Utd 0. Sent off: Butt, Man Utd, 51 min. Att: 38,142

24 Sept, PL (red): Man Utd 2 (Irwin pen 18, Scholes 79), Liverpool 0. Att: 55,181

30 Sept, CL group match (white): Bayern Munich 2 (Elber 11, 90), Man Utd 2 (Yorke 29, Scholes 48). Att: 53,000

PREMIER LEAGUE TABLE, end of September

		P	Pts
1	Aston Villa	7	17
2	Derby	7	12
3	Wimbledon	7	12
4	West Ham	7	12
5	Newcastle	7	11
6	**Man Utd**	**6**	**11**
7	Leeds	7	11
8	Liverpool	6	11
9	Chelsea	6	11

3 Oct, PL (black): Southampton 0, Man Utd 3 (Yorke 11, Cole 59, Cruyff 74). Att: 15,251

17 Oct, PL (red): Man Utd 5 (Cole 19, 88, Giggs 45, Beckham 48, Yorke 54), Wimbledon 1 (Euell 39). Att: 55.265

21 Oct, CL group match (red): Brondby 2 (Daugaard 35, Sand 90+3), Man Utd 6 (Giggs 2, 21, Cole 27, Keane 55, Yorke 60, Solskjær 63). Att: 40,530

24 Oct, PL (red): Derby 1 (Burton 74), Man Utd 1 (Cruyff 86). Att: 30,867

31 Oct, PL (red): Everton 1 (Ferguson 30), Man Utd 4 (Yorke 14, Short og 23, Cole 59, Blomqvist 64). Att: 40,087

PREMIER LEAGUE TABLE, end of October

		P	Pts
1	Aston Villa	10	22
2	**Man Utd**	**10**	**21**
3	Arsenal	11	20
4	Liverpool	11	16
5	Middlesbrough	10	16
6	Chelsea	9	16
7	Leicester	11	16
8	West Ham	11	16

4 Nov, CL group match (red): Man Utd 5 (Beckham 7, Cole 13, P Neville 16, Yorke 28, Scholes 62). Brondby 0. Att: 53,250

8 Nov, PL (red): Man Utd 0, Newcastle 0. Att: 55,174

14 Nov, PL (red): Man Utd 3 (Scholes 32, 58, Yorke 44), Blackburn 2 (Marcolin 65, Blake 74). Sent off: Sherwood, Blackburn, 48 min. Att: 55,198

21 Nov, PL (red): Sheff Wed 3 (Alexandersson 14, 73, Jonk 55), Man Utd 1 (Cole 29). Att: 39,475

25 Nov, CL group match (white): Barcelona 3 (Anderson 1, Rivaldo, 56, 72), Man Utd 3 (Yorke 25, 68, Cole 53). Att: 67,648

29 Nov, PL (red): Man Utd 3 (Solskjær 45, Keane 46, Butt 77), Leeds 2 (Hasselbaink 29, Kewell 52). Att: 55,172

PREMIER LEAGUE TABLE, end of November

		P	Pts
1	Aston Villa	14	29
2	**Man Utd**	**14**	**28**
3	West Ham	15	26
4	Arsenal	15	25
5	Chelsea	13	24
6	Leeds	15	23
7	Middlesbrough	15	23
8	Liverpool	15	22

5 Dec, PL (white): Aston Villa 1 (Joachim 55), Man Utd 1 (Scholes 47). Att: 39,241

9 Dec, CL group match (red): Man Utd 1 (Keane 43), Bayern Munich 1 (Salihamidžić 56). Att: 54,434

CHAMPIONS LEAGUE GROUP D FINAL TABLE

		P	W	D	L	F	A	Pts
1	Bayern Munich	6	3	2	1	9	6	11
2	**Man Utd**	**6**	**2**	**4**	**0**	**20**	**11**	**10**
3	Barcelona	6	2	2	2	11	9	8
4	Brondby	6	1	0	5	4	18	3

*Man Utd qualified for quarter-finals as one of the two best runners-up in the six groups.

12 Dec, PL (red): Tottenham 2 (Campbell 70, 90+1), Man Utd 2 (Solskjær 11, 18). Sent off: G Neville, Man Utd, 39 min). Att: 36,058

16 Dec, PL (red): Man Utd 1 (Cole 45), Chelsea 1 (Zola 83). Att: 55,159

19 Dec, PL (red): Man Utd 2 (Butt 62, Scholes 70), Middlesbrough 3 (Ricard 23, Gordon 31, Deane 59). Att: 55,152

26 Dec, PL (red): Man Utd 3 (Johnsen 28, 59, Giggs 62), Nottingham Forest 0. Att: 55,216

29 Dec, PL (red): Chelsea 0, Man Utd 0. Att: 34,741

PREMIER LEAGUE TABLE, end of December

		P	Pts
1	Aston Villa	20	39
2	Chelsea	20	37
3	**Man Utd**	**20**	**35**
4	Arsenal	20	35
5	Leeds	20	33
6	West Ham	20	32
7	Liverpool	20	31
8	Middlesbrough	20	30

3 Jan, FA Cup 3rd round (red): Man Utd 3 (Cole 68, Irwin pen 82, Giggs 90+3), Middlesbrough 1 (Townsend 52). Att: 52,232

10 Jan, PL (red): Man Utd 4 (Yorke 10, Cole 39, 68, Solskjær 80), West Ham 1 (Lampard 89). Att: 55,180

16 Jan, PL (red): Leicester 2 (Zagorakis 35, Walsh 73), Man Utd 6 (Yorke 10, 63, 84, Cole 49, 61, Stam 89). Att: 22,091

24 Jan, FA Cup 4th round (red): Man Utd 2 (Yorke 89, Solskjær 90+2), Liverpool 1 (Owen 3). Att: 54,591

31 Jan, PL (white): Charlton 0, Man Utd 1 (Yorke 89). Att: 20,043

PREMIER LEAGUE TABLE, end of January

		P	Pts
1	**Man Utd**	**23**	**44**
2	Chelsea	23	43
3	Aston Villa	23	43
4	Arsenal	23	42
5	Leeds	23	36
6	Liverpool	23	35
7	Wimbledon	23	35
8	Derby	23	34

3 Feb, PL (red): Man Utd 1 (Yorke 65), Derby 0. Att: 55,174

6 Feb, PL (white): Nottingham Forest 1 (Rogers 6), Man Utd 8 (Yorke 2, 66, Cole 7, 49, Solskjær 80, 87, 90+1, 90+4). Att: 30,025

14 Feb, FA Cup 5th round (red): Man Utd 1 (Cole 20), Fulham 0. Att: 54,798

17 Feb, PL (red): Man Utd 1 (Cole 60), Arsenal 1 (Anelka 48). Att: 55,171

20 Feb, PL (red): Coventry 0, Man Utd 1 (Giggs 78). Att: 22,594

27 Feb, PL (red): Man Utd 2 (Keane 79, Yorke 83), Southampton 1 (Le Tissier 90+1). Att: 55,316

PREMIER LEAGUE TABLE, end of February

		P	Pts
1	**Man Utd**	**28**	**57**
2	Chelsea	27	53
3	Arsenal	27	50
4	Aston Villa	27	44
5	Leeds	26	42
6	West Ham	27	40
7	Liverpool	27	39
8	Derby	27	38

3 Mar, CL quarter-final, 1st leg (red): Man Utd 2 (Yorke 6, 45), Inter Milan 0. Att: 54,430

7 Mar, FA Cup 6th round (red): Man Utd 0, Chelsea 0. Sent off: Di Matteo, Chelsea, 45 min. Sent off: Scholes, Man Utd, 86 min. Att: 54,587

10 Mar, FA Cup 6th round replay (red): Chelsea 0, Man Utd 2 (Yorke 4, 59). Att: 33,075

13 Mar, PL (red): Newcastle 1 (Solano 16), Man Utd 2 (Cole 25, 51). Att: 36,776

17 Mar, CL quarter-final, 2nd leg (red): Inter Milan 1 (Ventola 63), Man Utd 1 (Scholes 88). Man Utd win 3-1 on aggregate. Att: 79,528

21 Mar, PL (red): Man Utd 3 (Solskjær 55, G Neville 63, Beckham 67), Everton 1 (Hutchison 80). Att: 55,182

PREMIER LEAGUE TABLE, end of March

		P	Pts
1	**Man Utd**	**30**	**63**
2	Arsenal	30	59
3	Chelsea	29	56
4	Leeds	30	54
5	West Ham	30	46
6	Aston Villa	30	44
7	Liverpool	30	44
8	Derby	30	40

3 Apr, PL (red): Wimbledon 1 (Euell 5), Man Utd 1 (Beckham 44). Att: 26,121

7 Apr, CL semi-final, 1st leg (red): Man Utd 1 (Giggs 90+1), Juventus 1 (Conte 24). Att: 54,487

11 Apr, FA Cup semi-final (Villa Park) (red): Man Utd 0, Arsenal 0. Sent off: Vivas, Arsenal, 95 min. Extra time played. Att: 39,217

14 Apr, FA Cup semi-final replay (Villa Park) (white): Man Utd 2 (Beckham 17, Giggs 109), Arsenal 1 (Bergkamp 69). Sent off: Keane, Man Utd, 74 min. Extra time played. Att: 30,223 (Other semi-final: Newcastle 2, Tottenham 0)

17 Apr, PL (red): Man Utd 3 (Solskjær 35, Sheringham 44, Scholes 62), Sheffield Wednesday 0. Att: 55,270

21 Apr, CL semi-final, 2nd leg (red): Juventus 2 (Inzaghi 6, 10), Man Utd 3 (Keane 24, Yorke 34, Cole 84). Man Utd win 4-3 on aggregate. Att: 64,500

(Other semi-final: Bayern Munich beat Dynamo Kiev 4-3 on aggregate)

25 Apr, PL (red): Leeds 1 (Hasselbaink 32), Man Utd 1 (Cole 56). Att: 40,255

PREMIER LEAGUE TABLE, end of April

		P	Pts
1	Arsenal	34	69
2	**Man Utd**	**33**	**68**
3	Chelsea	34	65
4	Leeds	34	60
5	Aston Villa	35	55
6	West Ham	35	54
7	Middlesbrough	35	50
8	Derby	34	48

1 May, PL (red): Man Utd 2 (Watson og 20, Beckham 46), Aston Villa 1 (Joachim 33). Att: 55,189

5 May, PL, (white): Liverpool 2 (Redknapp pen 69, Ince 89), Man Utd 2 (Yorke 23, Irwin pen 56). Sent off: Irwin, Man Utd, 75 min. Att: 44,702

9 May, PL (white): Middlesbrough 0, Man Utd 1 (Yorke 45). Att: 34,655

12 May, PL (red): Blackburn 0, Man Utd 0. Att: 30,436

(Arsenal's 1-0 defeat away to Leeds United a day earlier allowed United to move a point clear here)

PREMIER LEAGUE TABLE, ahead of final day

		P	Pts
1	**Man Utd**	**37**	**76 (goal diff +42; F78, A36)**
2	Arsenal	37	75 (goal diff +41; F58, A17)
3	Chelsea	37	72
4	Leeds	37	66
5	Aston Villa	37	55
6	West Ham	37	54
7	Derby	37	52
8	Liverpool	37	51

16 May, PL (red): Man Utd 2 (Beckham 42, Cole 47), Tottenham 1 (Ferdinand 24). Att: 55,189. Referee: Graham Poll

Man Utd (4-4-2): Schmeichel – G Neville, May, Johnsen, Irwin – Beckham, Keane, Scholes (sub: Butt, 69min), Giggs (sub: P Neville, 79) – Yorke, Sheringham (sub: Cole, 45)

FINAL PREMIER LEAGUE TABLE

		P	W	D	L	F	A	Pts
1	**Man Utd**	**38**	**22**	**13**	**3**	**80**	**37**	**79**
2	Arsenal	38	22	12	4	59	17	78
3	Chelsea	38	20	15	3	57	30	75
4	Leeds	38	18	13	7	62	34	67
5	West Ham	38	16	9	13	46	53	57
6	Aston Villa	38	15	10	13	51	46	55
7	Liverpool	38	15	9	14	68	49	54
8	Derby	38	13	13	12	40	45	52
9	Middlesbrough	38	12	15	11	48	54	51
10	Leicester	38	12	13	13	40	46	49
11	Tottenham	38	11	14	13	47	50	47
12	Sheff Wed	38	13	7	18	41	42	46
13	Newcastle	38	11	13	14	48	54	46
14	Everton	38	11	10	17	42	47	43
15	Coventry	38	11	9	18	39	51	42
16	Wimbledon	38	10	12	16	40	63	42
17	Southampton	38	11	8	19	37	64	41
18	Charlton	38	8	12	18	41	56	36
19	Blackburn	38	7	14	17	38	52	35
20	N Forest	38	7	9	22	35	69	30

22 May, FA Cup final (Wembley) (red): Man Utd 2 (Sheringham 11, Scholes 53), Newcastle 0. Att: 79,101. Referee: Peter Jones

Man Utd (4-4-2): Schmeichel – G Neville, May, Johnsen, P Neville – Beckham, Keane (sub: Sheringham, 9), Scholes (sub: Stam, 78), Giggs – Cole (sub: Yorke, 60), Solskjær

26 May, CL final (Nou Camp, Barcelona) (red): Man Utd 2 (Sheringham 90+1, Solskjær 90+3), Bayern Munich 1 (Basler 6). Att: 90,000. Referee: Pierluigi Collina

Man Utd (4-4-2): Schmeichel – G Neville, Stam, Johnsen, Irwin – Giggs, Beckham, Butt, Blomqvist (sub: Sheringham, 67) – Yorke, Cole (sub: Solskjær, 81)

Results in other competitions in 1998–99

Charity Shield
9 Aug: Arsenal 3 (Overmars 33, Wreh 56, Anelka 71), Man Utd 0. Att: 67,342

League Cup
28 Oct: 3rd round: Man Utd 2 (Solskjær 106, Nevland 115), Bury 0. Extra time played. Att: 52,495

11 Nov: 4th round: Man Utd 2 (Solskjær 57, 60), Nottingham Forest 1 (Stone 68). Att: 37,237

2 Dec: 5th round: Tottenham 3 (Armstrong 48, 55, Ginola 86), Man Utd 1 (Sheringham 71). Att: 35,702

INDEX